MEN, BEASTS, AND GODS

Books by

GERALD CARSON

The Old Country Store
Cornflake Crusade
The Roguish World of Doctor Brinkley
One for a Man, Two for a Horse
The Social History of Bourbon
The Polite Americans
Men, Beasts, and Gods

MEN, BEASTS, AND GODS

A History of Cruelty and Kindness to Animals

GERALD CARSON

CHARLES SCRIBNER'S SONS

NEW YORK

For all the animal nations, who feel but cannot explain

Preface

This book is about the relationships that have existed between mankind and the lower animals from those prehistoric eras we have to guess about down to the present time. It is also about the ideas that men have articulated to explain their attitudes. The human view of the beast world has been ambivalent, a knife-edge balancing of fear with fascination, affection with exploitation, kindness with cruelty, the whole complicated by theological explanations of the universe and clouded by self-deceit. It is always interesting. But even more interesting would be the animals' point of view. That, unfortunately, is not available to us.

We do, however, know this: animals have been largely at the disposal of *Homo sapiens* since he evolved into a cunning, predatory overlord of the creatures of the earth, the only vertebrate that freely chooses to torture or kill all forms of sentient life and is able to do it. Yet, so versatile is man's range of responses—and we must not overlook this—he is also the only species that feels tenderness, the only animal that weeps.[1] Man alone knows, sometimes, the difference between good and evil. He alone possesses language and so can organize his experience, abstracting from the past what is useful for the future.

Because of his extraordinary gift of imagination and abstract thought, man has looked at animals as gods, slaves, subjects for art, moral examples, a source of food and fiber, and sometimes as companion and friend. All of this has occurred without our ever really understanding the wonderful, mysterious furred and feathered creatures who are, as the entomologist and humanist William Morton Wheeler wrote, "our only companions in an infinite and unsympathetic waste of electrons, planets, nebulae and stars," and a source, therefore, of "perennial joy and consolation."[2]

Thus self-interest adds its decisive weight to the ethical obligation of trusteeship which calls upon us to treat subhuman creatures mercifully. So far as rights are concerned, they have, after all, quite as good a title to this planet as we have, if not a better one. They got here first.

G.C.

Millerton, New York
September 1972

Contents

PART III
NO MORE ROOM IN THE ARK?

MEN, BEASTS, AND GODS

HUMANITY IS POISED MID-WAY BETWEEN GODS
AND BEASTS AND INCLINES NOW TO THE ONE
ORDER, NOW TO THE OTHER; SOME MEN GROW LIKE
TO THE DIVINE, OTHERS TO THE BRUTE, THE
GREATEST NUMBER STAND NEUTRAL . . .

—PLOTINUS (A.D. *c.* 205–270)
Third *Ennead*

PART
I

100,000 Years

of Living Together

1

Men, Beasts, and Gods

In the beginning there was Stone Age man, so far as this account is concerned, and behind him, standing in deep shadow, thousands of generations of hominoid creatures. Today man is still here, remarkably similar to his Cro-Magnon ancestor, with the same-sized brain, the same genetic inheritance, the same emotions and urges, but with more sophisticated instruments for accomplishing his purposes than sticks and stones and reindeer bones.

Cut a man open and one finds that he is a vertebrate mammal strikingly similar in anatomy to the primates with whom he is grouped as a matter of zoological classification.[1] Yet sometime, somewhere, an absolute discontinuity separating men from animals occurred that detached our predecessors from the apes and monkeys and all the other 4,000 species of mammals. Man learned to use his brain to improve his condition. The animal, after millions of years of evolution, still lived largely by its senses. It could connect smoke with fire but not a weapon with the next meal. Only man, the great amateur of the animal kingdom, can do that.

3

Lacking specialized biological equipment for the hunt or for defense—no sharp teeth, no claws, no venom or stinger—man nevertheless became, despite his thin skin, fragile bones, and limited strength, a spectacular biological success.[2] When, some million years ago, our primate ancestor descended from the trees to the grassy plains of Africa, he abandoned out of necessity his diet of fruit. Pushed by hunger, he learned to walk erect, which freed his hands for making and using weapons. This Paleolithic hunter discovered high-protein animal food and how to cook it, learned to attack in groups, and through the use of speech to pass along what he had learned.[3] It was a stunning achievement. These forebears of ours were rough customers, irascible primates still, now become formidable and unique adversaries since they swung a well-sharpened hand ax.[4]

And always there were animals in the environment—mysterious, competing, appealing, or threatening, more perfect than man within the limits of their own marvelous adaptations, yet piteous in their weakness, managing somehow to live with, around, or in spite of, primitive man. Those that lacked the urge to take flight or couldn't adjust became extinct.[5] As the hominoid hunters and food-gatherers entered the stage of agriculture and permanent campsites, some ten thousand years ago, certain animals joined the human economy. How this came about, whether by design or happenstance, is a matter of conjecture. Pet-keeping may have introduced the idea.[6] Certainly taming, a necessary prerequisite to the usefulness of any animal, is man's oldest and most impressive accomplishment in experimental biology.[7]

In the case of the dog, descendant of the wolf, and generally regarded as the first animal to be domesticated, the initiative may have come from the other side: the dog admired the reindeer hunters' refuse heaps. At any rate, social relations developed and man found that he could not, or at least would not, live without the dog. There were clear mutual advantages in the search for food. The dog had the nose, the man the eyes. The dog was faster, the man more cunning. The dog also defended the camp against predators, was an agreeable social companion, helped herd the domestic livestock, and in a pinch could be eaten.[8] Material that is perhaps fossilized dog dung has been found associated with human habitations and dated as being between 35,000 and 60,000 years old.[9]

Agriculture brought grain storage, rodents, and the need for pest control. Enter the cat, first introduced in Neolithic Egypt as a commensal—one who eats at the same table—because of the soaring population of rats and mice in a grain-growing civilization. "It is still a question," writes Weston La Barre, the cultural anthropologist, "whether the cat has any interest whatever in man save as a . . . provider of food." La Barre also points out that it is significant that man has never tamed any animal that was not already a social animal in its feral state.[10] Modern man's only accomplishment in this area has been to refine breeding methods.[11]

Geese may have been the next domestication, interesting companions and good eating. "It cheers me to look at them," says Penelope, wife of Ulysses, of her twenty geese.[12] Pigeons seem to have been tamed in what is now Iraq *circa* 4500 b.c., chickens in India between 3300 and 2500 b.c., the elephant semidomesticated at about the same time. The kings of Old Kingdom Egypt tried to tame hyenas, monkeys, the ibex, the oryx, two forms of gazelle, and the mongoose, and there is extant a tomb picture of an antelope wearing a collar.[13] Beasts of burden followed, the horse, donkey, and water buffalo, and for amusement the fighting cock, bred for a bloody sport, imported into western Europe from Asia and of permanent interest as a gambling device.[14]

The human-animal relationship was both intimate and withdrawn. It is a reasonable guess that for late Stone Age man animals represented attraction, repulsion, and an anxiety associated with matters not revealed. The natural world was vast and unreasonable, filled with terrors and enchantments. There were witches and demons to be exorcised, taboos to be observed, divinities to be propitiated, and natural forces like storm and flood to be deflected or controlled by an appeal for supernatural intervention. Everything in the environment meant something—but what? Men saw guardian spirits in rocks, hills, flowing springs, and sacred groves. It was believed that the gods were capricious and easily angered. Primitive peoples, observing the strength, speed, and elusiveness of animals, concluded that they must be wise and powerful, leagued with the unseen and temperamental deities. Perhaps animals were themselves demigods. Men saw no incongruity between animal worship and animal exploitation. The individual beast could be commonplace, the species divine.[15] And through homeopathic magic, by which like produces like, emerging man thought to acquire the admired traits of animals by eating their flesh: the deer for its swiftness, the dog for its tracking ability, and so on.

The gods were considered to be zoomorphic; that is, they exhibited the characteristics, sometimes the actual forms, of animals, and so various degrees of sanctity were accorded many species.[16] Prudently, our prehistoric ancestors sought to associate themselves with the higher powers through claiming common descent with the venerated animal. Later, within historic times, animals held to be sacred were not eaten even when the food supply was precarious. For example, the followers of Zoroaster in ancient Persia could not imagine eating a dog. The Iranians, Hindus, Libyans, Phoenicians, and Egyptians were prohibited from eating the flesh of the cow, and according to Diodōrus Sicŭlus, a Greek historian who flourished in the latter half of the first century B.C., during a famine the Egyptians preferred to eat each other to violating the taboo against cow beef.[17]

It is interesting to notice that the modern use of animal emblems still carries on the cult of the totem, which is at least as old as Neanderthal man. Bird or beast symbols express the greatness of our state and nation. An important American totemic center has been Detroit, where the automobile industry, in the 1920s, introduced its own menagerie in the form of radiator ornaments. Packard had its pelican, Lincoln its greyhound. Cadillac displayed a heron, and there were several eagles, including one on the Kissel White Eagle Speedster that would flap its wings when the engine overheated.[18] And still today, Detroit automobile manufactures connect their products in the public mind with speed, vitality, and savage power through the use of symbolic names like Barracuda, Mustang, and Impala along with such predators and raptors as lions, tigers, wildcats, falcons, and cougars. In spectator sports, too, we have a bewildering variety of totemistic names—the Buffalo Bisons and Texas Longhorns, the Princeton Tigers and the Cincinnati Bengals—while at Ann Arbor, Michigan, home of the Wolverines, tribal name for the University of Michigan football team, the local police defeated the county sheriffs at football in an arena called the "Pig Bowl." Other instances of a residual totemistic culture that readily come to mind from quite diverse areas of contemporary life are Zamba, Jr., the lion who symbolizes the financial strength of his client, the Dreyfus Fund, and the Black Panthers, who are not to be confused with the Pittsburgh Panthers.[19]

Although ants can prepare for the future, apes use a stick for a tool, and the birds and bees have some means of communication, man alone can make records, and the earliest records extant are pictures of animals, scratched on bone, modeled in clay, and painted or incised on the walls of secret caves. With astonishing anatomic accuracy and aesthetic sensibility, the Paleolithic artists of southwest France and northern Spain wielded their burins and brushes to depict the horse, the menacing bison, the great mammoth and woolly rhinoceros, the leap of the stag and the heavy march of the European bear. There is as yet no satisfactory technique for decoding the meaning of this Stone Age art, but the prevailing opinion among anthropologists about the paintings, made some 30,000 years ago, is that they represent magic and were designed to bring success in the hunt. Thus the caves may be regarded as the first churches and the animal drawings the first religious art, although Professor George Gaylord Simpson, the Harvard paleontologist, does not rule out the possibility that the motive may have been entirely recreational, which would make our cave-dwelling ancestors the first Sunday painters. Human figures, incidentally, are comparatively rare and awkwardly executed in comparison with the technically advanced beast drawings. The animal, clearly, was the focus of interest.[20]

Turning to the Far East, one encounters the Oriental concept of *akimsa*—nonviolence—an attitude toward life difficult for the Western mind to grasp, since it affirms the sacredness of all life, a unity that includes even insect pests. This sense of reverence without limit is reinforced in Chinese, Persian, Arab, and Hindu teachings by the belief that there was little difference between the soul of an animal and of man, and that in successive reincarnations a human soul might enter the body of an animal, or vice versa. From this doctrine arose the practice of vegetarianism. Some 300 million people today formally believe in reincarnation and promise to avoid doing any fatal injury to any living being.[21] This identification of humanity with the totality of sentient life is so paramount among the devout that they will let an injured animal linger and suffer rather than end its misery. The sacred cows may starve, but they do it slowly and peacefully.

The doctrine of the absolute sacredness of all life is carried to a rigorous conclusion by the Jainist monks of India, who sweep insects from their path to avoid crushing them and wear a mask over the mouth to prevent the accidental entry of the tiniest gnat. This teaching is difficult to harmonize with the concept of biological evolution. The evolutionist sees each form of life dying to support another. The woodpecker eats the grub, fish must die to feed the fish hawk, and so on right up to man. But in the Western humane view, killing must be based upon necessity and minimum pain. Buddhism, too, contains compassionate elements, yet it did not prevent the great princes of India from removing surgically the eyes of fine horses in order to replace them with jewels, or the humble Hindu from beating his donkey so long as he didn't kill him.[22]

Among the Egyptians, whom Herodotus called the most religious of men, animals and birds are represented in profusion on the tombs and in the jewelry that has survived. Numerous statues and drawings indicate the regard this ancient people felt for their sacred cats, the *Felis lybica* of North Africa, revered as a symbol of freedom. Some 180,000 mummies of this independent-minded creature have been found near Cairo.[23] There were many other divinities of a higher or lower order among the Egyptians. Among the more important were Anubis, the dog or jackal god, the hawk Horus, the ram Harsaphes, the cow Hathor, Uto the vulture goddess, the crocodile Sobek.[24] The ox—not the literal animal, but its abstract character—was revered as a symbol of patience and usefulness. "It was not the cat or the ox, for example, that the Egyptians worshipped," Montaigne quotes Plutarch as saying, "but that in these animals they worshipped some image of the divine attributes." The bull was an important symbol. It was the winged bulls of the Babylonians and the bull images of Syria that led to the bitter denunciations of the Hebrew prophets, Amos and Hosea, upon the need of the people for a *visible* god.[25]

The kings of Assyria, the Egyptian pharoahs, the Indian maharajas, and Mongol princes combed the known world for exotic animals, especially the cheetah, highly esteemed as hunting companion and symbol of rank. Rare animals had a special usefulness as ceremonial gifts, as reparations, or as bribes. They played a role, therefore, in diplomacy. And they could inspire awe in the lower orders as the people observed their rulers living in luxurious intimacy with the revered animal-gods.[26] Training methods were undoubtedly severe. There was no society for the prevention of cruelty to animals operating in Mesopotamia, the valley of the Nile, or Peking to call to account the trainers who relied upon starvation and the whip.[27]

The ancient Greeks lavished affection upon animals, especially horses, dogs, and birds. Aristotle, while writing and lecturing at Athens, produced the world's first great encyclopedia of zoology, his *History of Animals*, in which he wrote with remarkable insight that animals possessed many of the psychical attributes found in man, the difference being only one of degree. Pythagoras, the philosopher of the sixth century B.C., also taught kindness as a duty toward all subhuman creation and held, like the Buddhists, that human souls passed into animals after death. He opposed meat eating on ethical grounds, since justice does not permit men to injure other species. Plutarch arrived at the idea of mercy by a different route. Kindness, he declared, should be practiced for its own sake, as a part of the good life, and he reproached Cato for abandoning the faithful horse that had carried him safely through the wars when he was consul in Spain. Plutarch himself could not send to the slaughterhouse an ox that had worked for him, and had warm praise for the Athenians, who, after they had completed the Parthenon, directed that the mules and hinnies that had helped to build the great temple should be turned loose and allowed thereafter to graze wherever they wished.[28]

There are compassionate anecdotes about dogs in Plato's writings, while in the seventeenth book of Homer's *Odyssey* occurs one of the most moving episodes of its kind in all literature. There one may read of how Ulysses returned home after twenty years of wandering, disguised as a beggar. At the door, lying on a dunghill, was his dog, Argus, old, neglected, full of fleas, and dying. Argus wagged his tail and dropped his ears in recognition when he heard Ulysses' voice. The faithful animal tried to rise but was too weak to come to his master, while Ulysses turned his head away to hide his tears.[29]

Even the gods, in Greek thought, had animal favorites and

would, in special situations, assume the shapes of their pets. Zeus approached Leda with no good purpose in mind disguised as a swan, and took the form of a bull to kidnap Europa and carry her off to Crete. These and other similar deities, such as Pan, the lustful he-goat, were presented on the Greek stage, sometimes in sequences that included actual coitus between animals and humans.[30]

The moral principle that the beast world was entitled to considerate treatment at the hands of man was reinforced by a widely held belief among the Greeks that any wrong done to an animal would be avenged by the gods or by nature. To each creature, then, great or small, was granted the right to pursue its own concerns, its own physical vivacity and joy in living. It was this humane point of view that moved the poet, Bion, to say: "Boys stone a frog in sport, but the frog dies in earnest."[31] Yet, on the darker side, such evidences of tenderness did not prevent the ancient Greeks from forcing bears to dance, setting dogs on cats, or incorporating the Asiatic cockfight into their culture.[32]

Roman law applicable to animals was harsh. Beasts were private property and regarded as *things* to be used or used up at the owner's complete discretion,[33] a pagan attitude that was incorporated into the Christian conception of the universal scheme of things. During the climactic period of Roman power, patrician families were devoted to their household pets, and for the usual reasons—their beauty, their quaintness and their affectionate ways. The admired animals destroyed vermin, provided sport, and in the vogue word of our own time, provided status. The ruling class maintained private menageries, aviaries, fishponds, and game parks for hunting.[34] Well-placed citizens kept a guard dog in the atrium, and set in the walls of their dwellings a mosaic calling attention to the animal's presence in the words *cave canum*—"beware the dog." A flock of geese was maintained at public expense, since by their giving the alarm the Capitol had been saved from the Gauls in 387 B.C.; and Caesar enhanced his prestige when he went up to the Capitol escorted by forty elephants carrying torches in their trunks to light the way.[35] Surely this must have been one of the most spectacular sights seen in classical times.

Since the Romans believed that the gods were constantly preoccupied with human events, it was of the highest importance to learn their will and to interpret correctly any spectral evidence that came to hand. Here, too, the animal kingdom rendered distinguished service. It was a settled belief that the birds were the bearers of divine messages. What was required, then, were the services of certain wise men, organized as the College of Augurs, who analyzed the omens. This was accomplished by examining the entrails of chickens, a science or art with interesting analogies to the modern practice of composing stock market letters.[36]

The Romans made the discovery that voyeurism and cruelty could be combined in entertainments with enormous mass appeal. The beast contests may have originated in the funeral games. Or possibly they developed from hunting or baiting of native species of the Italian peninsula. It is known that, in the time of Augustus, foxes were turned loose in the Circus Maximus with firebrands tied to their tails. At any rate, the spectacles lost any character of religious rite they may ever have had and became simply licensed cruelty.

By the second century B.C. the whole known world was being scoured for raw material as the games became more bloody and more perverse. Novelties were continually introduced, such as chaining a bear and a bull together for a fight, while human beings were thrown to bulls that had first been tortured with hot irons. Martial, the Roman poet and epigrammatist, mentions an instance of a woman fighting with a lion. Elephants, rhinoceroses, hippopotamuses, leopards, and lions were force-fed intoxicants to drive them into a frenzy. Those who survived the arena battles were shot from the ampitheater seats by archers who had paid for the privilege, an arrangement something like our duck stamps of today. The form of combat that stirred the masses most deeply was between a captured Gaul, a criminal, or a Christian and a wild animal, a procedure that did not violate the ethics of the period because the human being was going to be executed anyway. Sometimes the victim in this blood-spattered carnival was compelled to act out a ghastly parody of classical literature such as the legends of Prometheus, Daedalus, or Orpheus.[37] The limit was reached when Pompey as dictator topped all previous spectacles with a slaughter of African elephants so revolting that for once the plebs had more than enough. As the great, wounded beasts finally pleaded with the crowd for pity by agonized trumpeting, the populace rose up and cursed Pompey for his ruthlessness.[38]

The horror of the Circus Maximus, so baffling to the modern mind, is relieved in one instance by the appealing story of Androcles and the lion—of how, in the time of the emperor Claudius, Androcles, a runaway slave, hid in a cave in the African desert. Here he was suddenly confronted by a lion, which, instead of attacking, presented Androcles with a swollen paw. The slave relieved the beast's distress by removing a thorn. Captured again, Androcles was put in the death enclosure only to be greeted by his lion opponent with every sign of affection. It was, of course, the same lion.

We know what Montaigne meant when he wrote, "Nature herself has, I fear, fastened on man a certain instinct of inhumanity . . . ." Whether cruelty derives from cultural tradition or the genes, a matter of sharp debate today, it knew no limits in the ampitheaters of Rome. So insatiable was the demand for wild beasts, as many as 11,000 dying in Trajan's triumph celebrating his conquest of Dacia, that several species of large beasts that had fighting capabilities, among them the European lion, the aurochs, and the Libyan elephant, were either destroyed or so reduced in numbers that they later became extinct.[39] The bloodbath ended only with the decay of Roman military power. But if the road to pagan Rome was a *via dolorosa* for the animals, the way of the Cross was scarcely less hard, although for entirely different reasons.

2

No Hope of Heaven

Hebraic thought rejected the numerous divinities of Mesopotamia and Egypt. Instead of acknowledging many gods,
with limited powers, the Jews worshiped one and only one
—all powerful, all wise, all seeing, a supergod. The animal deities
were dead, and with them departed the companionable, pagan idea
of men and animals being knit together by their natures and the
cycling of souls from one to the other. Equipped with the one-god
concept, the Semitic peoples dealt at arm's length with the zoological world, affirming the absolute uniqueness of man, made in
God's own image.

Through all historic time, man has oscillated between acknowledging his kinship with the natural world or denying it. The Jews
denied it. The book of Genesis makes this clear when God explains
to Noah about the beasts, ". . . into your hands are they delivered."[1]
From this time on, as Professor Lynn White, Jr., has written, "Man
and nature are two things and man is master."[2] All is for man—
the stars in their courses, the warmth of the sun, the sheep with

their fleeces, the ox whose neck is conveniently shaped to take the yoke, the beast-creatures of the forest to be hunted for recreation, as food, and to train men in warfare, the gracious vine and the olive trees, which are of no concern to the lower animals but designed solely for man's comfort and amenity.[3]

Yet the plight of animals under Judaism was not as harsh as this man-centered theology would suggest. The Jews were not rapacious hunters; Esau and Nimrod never qualified as great folk heroes.[4] There is no record of beast combats among the Hebrews, and the rabbinical writers displayed a neighborly attitude toward the animal kingdom. Maimonides, in fact, postulated some kind of immortality to compensate the animals for their suffering in this world.[5] The zoological overview of the Talmud was even broad enough to include those animals that inconvenienced the human household. "Thou thinkest that flies, fleas, mosquitoes are superfluous, but they have their purpose in creation as means of a final outcome," one passage runs.[6]

According to the Talmud, the laws of the Sabbath may be set aside for the rescue of an animal in danger, and many incidents in the Old Testament emphasize compassion toward the lower creation, such as the episode of Rebekah at the well, chosen to be Isaac's wife because she offered water to Abraham's servant. Part of her test included a scrutiny of her attitude toward animals. She passed when she said, "I will draw *water* for thy camels also . . ."

Bible text-hunters do not find, however, consistent, disinterested concern for animal life. This is especially true of the New Testament, where Saint Paul asked, "Doth God care for oxen?" Allusions that contain humane elements often have in view some other object than the relief of an animal for its own sake, such as the advancement of agricultural efficiency or the protection of a property interest to which the alleviation of pain was incidental. The whole future of the Judaic-Christian attitude toward animal life is foreshadowed in that ominous verse in Genesis beginning, "And the fear of you and the dread of you shall be upon every beast of the earth." Thus it was established that this is man's world and that the gap between *them* and *us* is unbridgeable.

Yet the folk mind did insist upon building bridges through sympathy. The men of Palestine understood sheep. There are some 140 references to sheep in the Bible and about the same number to lambs. The role of the shepherd as guardian is indicated in the metaphor of the Psalmist, "The Lord is my shepherd, I shall not want . . ." The Old Testament farmer was charged not to muzzle the ox while it was threshing out the grain or make his beasts of burden work on the day of rest. Lost animals were to be taken care of whether the owner was known or not. Dogs are mentioned in the Scriptures pejoratively, as scavengers; cats not at all. But King David meditated upon why the fly and spider were created and later was saved by their help. In general, one finds a good many references and inferences that suggest sympathy for sentient creatures.

The animal sacrifice sanctioned by Judaism may seem scarcely neighborly. But the dignity of the animal was recognized, and the slaughter was treated as a tragic necessity. We have here an instance of the distinction that humanitarians still insist upon between the ethics of killing and the ethics of hurting. This difference is absent in Hinduism and Buddhism, which explains why India is no paradise for the sacred cow. Perhaps the most unqualified statement of concern for animal life in the Old Testament is the verse, "A righteous *man* regardeth the life of his beast . . ."[7]

There are few teachings attributed to Christ that enjoin humane treatment of animals upon his followers, and this lack of clear utterance has often distressed the Christian clergy. In one remarkable instance a good but somewhat addled Anglican clergyman was inspired, literally, as he believed, to supply certain animal-regarding passages from the New Testament, which he felt sure had existed but had been lost. One of his "restored" verses began: "And Jesus took a young cat . . ." and introduced in parable style a lesson on the merciful treatment of *Felis domestica.*[8] Thus a well-disposed but eccentric parson tried to remedy the indifference toward animal life that has characterized the nearly 2,000 years of Christian teaching.

With the emergence of Christianity as a world religion, the scheme of redemption isolated man still further from the rest of the natural world. The animals had no equity on earth, no citizenship in Heaven, and on the whole have remained, as Major C. W. Hume, well-known British scientist and humanitarian, has written, "outside the purview of Christian theology."[9]

The doctrinal position of the Roman Catholic Church was summed up in the thirteenth-century commentary of Saint Thomas Aquinas, who adopted Aristotle's conclusion that there is no future life for animals. Following Roman law, Aquinas denied that animals can have rights. Even today French law, adhering to this precedent, punishes cruelty to animals only if it occurs in public so as to scandalize human observers.[10]

Aquinas did recommend kindness, not because of any valid claim that the world of nature had on man, but because the effect of mercy toward the brute creation "is to dispose men to pity and tenderness for one another."[11] The *New Catholic Encyclopedia* (1967) repeats the Thomist analysis, but softens the position a little by observing that man "has duties with regard to animals . . . as he has toward all things intended by God for human benefit," and calls particular attention to the work in the animal welfare field now carried on in the United States by the National Catholic Society for Animal Welfare.[12]

The liturgy of the Church does, in fact, provide for the public blessing of animals that live in symbiosis with man. On the fete day of Saint Anthony, patron and protector of the lower animals, a service called the Benediction of Beasts is held annually at the door of the church of Saint Eusebio in Rome, and every Roman sends his horse, mule or donkey, even monkeys and parrots, to be sprinkled and sanctified. The ceremony is also performed at Pinerolo, Abruzzo, and at other places where the economy is still based upon plow agriculture, and popular engravings of the saint hang in all stables to invoke his protection for the farm animals. At many locations in Spain a similar custom is observed on the same day, January 17, especially in Andalusia. Invocations to the patron saint of animals are also pronounced in certain parts of France. Sheep from La Camargue that spend the summer months on the high plateaus of the Dauphiné are herded together there for the ancient blessing of the flocks in the presence of their shepherds and the tourists. One picturesque festival, called the Blessing of the Mules, is held annually at Amélie-les-Bains-Palalda, a spa near the Spanish frontier. The mules, in festive trappings, are brought through the town by leaders dressed in traditional Catalonian costume, followed by dancers. After the animals receive the blessing at the front of the church, the consecrated bread is distributed to the people.[13]

On one occasion in the middle sixties the reverend father of the abbey at Saint Michel de Frigolet, near Tarascon, went even further and included the town's autos, motorcycles, scooters, and Vespas, which caused one puzzled Protestant to wonder why unpowered bicycles were discriminated against.[14]

In any event the Church, although it regards animals still as things, does arrive, through its own catena of subtle reasoning, at the position that men should treat the lower creatures with consideration since God created them. Yet animal welfare work has lagged in most Catholic countries. For while a merciful Cardinal Manning might have the most cultivated sensibilities concerning beasts, the Neapolitan peasant, having learned from his parish priest that animals are not "moral persons," can go home after Mass and with a clear conscience give his donkey a thorough taste of the switch.[15]

Meanwhile, many persons both inside and outside the Church have suggested another idea, that animals, having no hope of future bliss, merit for that very reason especial consideration while here on earth. It has been said of one of the great princes of the Church, Cardinal Robert Bellermine, who would not disturb the fleas that got their livelihood in his famous beard, that he used to allow the small parasites to bite him, saying, "We shall have heaven to reward us for our sufferings, but these poor creatures have nothing but the enjoyment of this present life."[16]

There was always a gap between theory and practice, between the theological puzzles of the Church fathers and the upwelling affections of human nature in its sunnier moods. The medieval knight loved his falcon, the king his menagerie, the prioress, as Chaucer tells us, her "smale houndes" and

> *She wolde wepe if that she saw a mous*
> *Caught in a trappe, if it were ded or bledde.*

Especially in connection with those social animals most capable of returning human love, the bishops struggled, often in vain, to turn the minds of monks and nuns from their "dogs or birds, both great and small" to the offices of the Church. At Saint Gallen, Switzerland, the monks owned badgers, marmots, and bears. The Ladies of the Trinity at Caen kept larks, while in England, William of Wykeham rebuked the nuns of the religious houses at Romsey,

Wherwell, and Saint Mary's Winchester for risking their souls by
bringing to church their pet birds, rabbits, and hounds.[17] Priests
fond of falconry were even known to take their hawks with them
to Mass and set the hooded raptors on the altar; and in one of his
capitularies Charlemagne found it necessary to forbid abbots and
abbesses to own hunting animals. The problem kept coming back.
At one time the papal legate ordered the zoophiles of Notre Dame
of Paris to renounce harboring animals that were harmful, useless,
or merely diverting and amusing, such as bears, stags, crows, monkeys, *"et autres."* But in defiance of the hierarchy, many men and
women who had taken the vows of the religious life found, as have
other men in all times and places, that "it is good to know the feel
of other life, to wipe away the loneliness of being man."[18]

Sometimes the attachment of the clergy to animals overflowed
normal limits, and there are instances in the Penitentials that set
forth criminal acts, where the confessor fixed the penance to be
undergone by bishops, priests and deacons for acts of sodomy.
Havelock Ellis, for example, mentions one document that includes
this item: " *'Episcopus cum quadrupede fornicans VII annos . . .'"*[19]

The medieval conception of society was rigid and authoritarian,
a place for everything and everything in its place, as determined
by the Church and the state. Life was short, uncertain, disease-
ridden, coarse, and violent. Its drama was largely in the hands of
the Church, with a constant ringing of bells, parading of sacred
relics, and the vision of epidemics, the dance of death, and the Day
of Judgment always vivid before men's eyes. Although the human
population lived in intimacy with beasts, men were strangely in-
curious about them, and the Dark Ages added little to zoological
knowledge. Men looked beyond the natural world, seeing it not as
the immediate reality but as a system of symbols through which
it was possible to learn the purposes of the divine will. The ant was
Brother Ant to such a radical and democrat as Saint Francis of
Assisi, but to the Church an ant was an ant. It was useful, however,
in its symbolic way, for illustrating homilies on industriousness.[20]

So animals appeared as emblems or shadows of the religious
truths on altar frontals, capitals, parapets, chimney pieces, shields
and coats of arms, in the relief carvings of choir stalls, in tapestries
and stained glass windows; while the spandrels of entrance doorways show the lion of Saint Mark, the bull of Saint Luke, and the

eagle of Saint John holding holy books. In this symbolic system the lamb represented Christ; the dove, the Holy Ghost; the pelican, the Lord's Supper; the peacock, immortality; the horrid imaginary monster, the hydra, heresy; while the cock was associated with the tragedy of Jesus.[21]

To choose one example from a multitude of possibilities, above the entrance to the basilica of Saint Androche at Saulieu, in Burgundy, appear the eagle of Saint John and the sculptured bull of Saint Luke, while inside the ancient fabric the corbels of the capitals bring together a whole menagerie of familiar animal forms as illustrations of Christian allegory. Among these astonishing carvings one may see represented a cockfight, including the figures of two handlers, one showing joy, the other chagrin. There are the dancing bears that the populace watched with delight when they went to the market fairs. Balaam appears, mounted on his she-ass, shown at the moment when he was stopped by the angel of Jehovah. In an Annunciation to the Shepherds, one guardian blows his horn while a dog torments two embattled goats. Classical mythology is also represented. The owl of Minerva, Roman goddess of wisdom, looks down solemnly upon the choir and side aisles.[22]

Demons and dragons, too, appeared in the monumental sculpture of the Romanesque period to ward off the Devil and his minions from consecrated buildings. Human emotions keep breaking through the theoretical abstractions. At Laon, chief city of the department of Aisne in France, the magnificent cathedral of the twelfth and thirteenth centuries is decorated with sixteen sculpted figures of oxen, placed at the corners of the towers. These figures, according to one amiable tradition, gratefully commemorate the services rendered by real oxen in drawing heavy stones for the construction of the edifice. In similar fashion, at Florence, in Italy, a bas-relief pays loving homage to a donkey who carried marble and wood for building the Pitti Palace.[23]

In the Middle Ages the owl was feared and detested because of its hoots, shrieks, hissings, and snappings. Owls were also unwelcome because they were believed to be the messengers of death. Cats, especially black ones, were regarded with special abhorrence because of their association in the folk mind with witches. It was held that a favorite device of Satan was to assume the form of an animal, often a dog, and many witches confessed to having had intercourse with the Adversary in the shape of an animal.[24] A pope of the Renaissance, Innocent VIII, ordained that when witches were burned at the stake, their cats were to be burned with them. In fact, as late as the seventeenth century, it was risky for an old woman to have a cat as a pet.[25]

It is with relief that one turns to a more agreeable episode concerning this charming animal. In the *Golden Legend,* a medieval compilation of churchly lore, there is mention of a monk who held a cat in his lap " 'deliciously' contrary to monastic rule."[26] A modern scholar points out that a dog and a cat were often included in a medieval ship's company, because by staying alive on a wreck they preserved the legal rights of the owners of the vessel and its cargo.[27]

Since medieval literature is seldom concerned with direct experience, it reflects but little the actual attitudes of society toward animals. Beasts appear in the illuminated borders of the books of hours as religious symbols: Saint Anthony and his pig, the blind Saint Hervaeus being led by his wolf, which, apparently, served him well as a seeing-eye wolf. The designer of one English tomb was not above indulging in an animal pun: in Wells cathedral two hares crouch at the foot of Bishop Harewell.[28] Familiar birds, quadrupeds, reptiles, and fish appear as illustrations of the eternal Christian verities in collections of prose and verse with the general title of physiologi or bestiaries. These beast fables also dealt with the supposed traits of fancied brutes taken from wonder tales or put-ons gathered by sailors and travelers about zoological marvels they had encountered or heard about on their journeyings.

Secular writers used the animal tale to recommend the prudential virtues or to censure human vanities. The fox plundered like a feudal lord. The donkey brayed like an ignorant priest conducting the liturgy. Chaucer's Chanticleer mistranslated Latin for his unlettered wife in a comic mixture of conceited man and barnyard fowl.

According to the *Physiologus,* the crocodile wept false tears and so symbolized hypocrisy. The phoenix was a bird that set fire to itself in its old age and rose renewed from its own ashes and so "teaches us to believe in the resurrection."[29] The legend of the unicorn flourished hardily from the earliest Christian era to the end of the Renaissance. This deerlike creature had a single, long, sharp horn protruding from its forehead, a symbol of chastity and virility. The spiraled horn may still be seen on the heraldic crest of Great Britain.[30] The werewolf, to cite just one more example of zoological myth, was an ogrelike figure useful until quite recent times for frightening little French children into good behavior. But now, Mr. Laurence Wylie tells us in his delightful account of life in the French village of Rousillon, the role of the *loup-garou* has been taken over by threats about rats, real-life animals that unquestionably do gnaw and bite.[31] A later chapter (Chapter 7) will take up some American contributions to the Western world's menagerie of fantasy animals, such as the side-hill gouger and the squonk.

In medieval hagiography the saints are often represented as having a special tenderness for all living creatures. Many legends dwell upon wonderful happenings and mutual charities that came to pass between holy men and the beasts. When a monk stepped on a lizard, Saint Philip of Neri rebuked him: "What has the poor creature done to you?" Like the Franciscans of the thirteenth century, Saint Philip welcomed all sentient life as having been shaped by God's hand. It was a cardinal point that the lower animals could recognize and respond to holiness. Thus we have the story of Saint Pachomius, in which the anchorite is described as summoning crocodiles to ferry him across a river, much as one would hail a taxicab. When Saint Francis preached to the birds, in the well-known tale, they flapped their wings in spiritual ecstasy. Saint Kentigern of Glasgow "caused a wolf to come and draw the plough in place of the ox that it had killed" and another wolf obligingly carried Saint Froilanus's baggage for him.

The Celtic saints seem to have had especially close relationships with their four-footed friends of the forest. Saint Cainnic, an Irish solitary, was acquainted with a stag that came to him in his retreat and would hold his book on his antlers while the holy man read his codex. Despite what has already been said here of the neglect of cats during the Dark Ages, when four Irish scholars went to sea for the love of God, they took nothing with them, only at the last minute the youngest said, "I think I will take the little cat." It is a temptation to enlarge immoderately upon this pleasant subject, but I shall exercise stern restraint and merely allude to Saint Nannon, who established a flea sanctuary in Connaught and a delightful bear mentioned by the poet, Robert Mannyng, who came to keep a hermit company and made "fayre chere as a bere myght."

These instances of gentleness in beasts, and as one chronicler put it, God's own pity in men, serve as a reminder that the compulsion to impute our own feelings to animals, known as anthropomorphism, is as old as man himself.[32] Anthropomorphism is now quite out of fashion. Yet Professor R. J. Pumphrey, a Fellow of the Royal Society, has written with obvious relish that the conventional biologist of today, when applying, as he must, the method of analogy when comparing the psychology of beasts and men "generally looks as sheepish and embarrassed about it as if his bedroom had been found full of empty whisky bottles."[33]

Since historic records of the upper levels of society are always more abundant than the annals of the poor, it is not surprising that we know more about the animal associations of princes than we do of peasants and villeins. In the ninth century, the emperor Charlemagne was the fortunate owner of a splendid elephant named Aboul Abbas, the gift of the powerful Caliph of Bagdad, Harun al'-Rashid. The great beast's headquarters were at Aachen, but each spring he was marched around to be seen and marveled at, with a camel corps as escort, surely a thrilling sight in the streets of Speyer, Strasbourg, or Augsburg. And it was all for the greatness and glory of Charlemagne.[34]

The Crusades introduced, or reintroduced, exotic animals to Europe. Louis IX of France, Saint Louis, sent a gift elephant to his cousin, King Henry III of England, the first pachyderm seen in that country since prehistoric times.[35] The general statement that the Middle Ages had little curiosity about animals needs to be bent a little bit to allow for this enthusiasm for collecting. Other high personages with a passion for possessing strange and wild animals were Frederick II, emperor of Germany and king of Sicily and Jerusalem; the various popes seated at Avignon during the "Babylonian captivity"; and René I, Good King René of Provence, who maintained not only a pride of lions but doctors and nurses to care for their health. Henry III of France should also be mentioned in this connection. Henry built up an extraordinary private zoo, then changed his mind about it and on January 20, 1583, shot all his animals because he dreamed they were going to eat him.[36]

Animals that lived as intimate companions in noble households include a pet dog of Mary Queen of Scots, which she dressed in a blue velvet suit. Henry II of France had bread baked especially for his dog, and Francis I slept with a tame lion at the foot of his bed. When dwarfs were objects of fashionable amusement, a French duchess had a locksmith make a pair of iron collars, one for the neck of her dwarf girl, Belon, the other for Her Grace's monkey.[37]

On a lower social level, one gathers from piecing together fragmentary information that there was much going and coming of mountebanks, jugglers, and showmen who wandered about Europe exhibiting trained goats, ponies, horses, and bears who danced on their hind legs in the squares of the market towns or beside the clock tower.[38] On holy days in England, bulls and bears were baited for the delight of the villagers, and according to William Fitzstephen's account of life in London in the twelfth century, "the schoole boyes do bring Cockes of the game to their Master, and all the forenoon delight themselves in Cockfighting."[39]

Hunting, hawking, and coursing, in which the hare was pursued until it collapsed or was torn to pieces by hounds, were the exclusive privileges of high personalities. The feudal system threw every protection around the dogs of the aristocracy. For a thousand years peasants could not possess hunting dogs or weapons capable of bringing down big game. But hunger often drove them to poaching and the capture of "inferior" animals with snares. The risks were enormous. Any intrusion by the lower classes upon the aristocratic pastime was punished without pity under the forest laws. In England, from the time of Canute, a freeman who resisted the king's deer wardens lost his freedom. A serf had his right hand chopped off. If caught a second time he was put to death. If he took a deer his eyes were plucked out.[40]

Animal experiments, neglected in the Middle Ages, were revived in the Renaissance and provided the basis for the science of comparative anatomy and a more precise knowledge of the physiology of the nervous system. But until the end of the eighteenth century experimenters had to be cautious in drawing analogies with human neural physiology lest they get into difficulties with the Inquisition over the question of the soul.[41] Anatomical studies tended to blur the sharp distinction the Church made between man and beast, and so undermined the foundations of revealed religion. The fact that some men could wiggle their ears and that all men had a vestigial tail could only lead to dangerous thoughts. Man, one might conclude, from evidence accumulated by dissection, was not a fallen angel but a creature who had worked his way up from the worm and reptile, as the discovery of organic evolution was to demonstrate some centuries later.

The reflection that the lower creatures suffered, although innocent, troubled many consciences. But the official dogma stood firm that brutes had neither personality, "intellective soul" nor future life. Their place in the universe was fixed forever in Genesis 1:28, that they lived and died for the convenience of man. As late as the middle of the last century, Pius IX refused permission for the formation in Rome of a society for the prevention of cruelty to animals on the grounds that it was a theological error to suppose that man had any duty toward animals.[42] To many Catholics with a deep affection for animals, the Church's position omits a large part of human experience and makes Paradise seem a singularly unattractive and lonely place. But if the animals had no hope of redemption, they did nevertheless have responsibilities here on earth, derived from their being under the government of the Creator. Their conduct was judged, of course, by human standards, and the law was applied with severity when correction was needed. The development of this peculiar conception of animals living under law is traced in the chapter that immediately follows.

3

Bugs and Beasts Before the Law

A striking feature of the jurisprudence that evolved in medieval times was the establishment of legal compacts between men and animals. Bugs, birds, small mammals, and the larger domestic quadrupeds were supposed to live according to the law and to be familiar with the statutes. It was a kind of backhanded acknowledgment, perhaps, that animals had a place of some sort in the society of men. A surprising amount of litigation occurred, especially in France, and brought much misery to the unfortunate victims whom the baliffs caught *in flagrante delicto*. One modern investigator, pursuing this aberration of the scholastic mind, has devoted a whole book to the subject. The author compiled 191 instances of beast prosecution, undoubtedly one of the most extraordinary expressions of man-centered thought that one may encounter in all social history.[1]

It requires a considerable act of the imagination for a person living in the culture of the twentieth century to understand the involute thought of the medieval legal mind, and the high seriousness of our ancestors in arraigning cabbageworms, he-goats, and indeed, all animal kind, domestic and wild, in a court of justice where to the solemn tolling of bells they were tried for such crimes as homicide, mayhem, assault, felony, misdemeanors, malicious mischief, or trespass against the human community. One has to start with these premises:

That the biblical account of the Creation and the Fall of Man are literally true.

That the earth and everything on it exists for man's use and enjoyment.

That natural science, in the form of the Ptolemaic astronomy, confirms this, since the earth is the center of the universe.

That the world is the setting for a Miltonic struggle between the forces of good and evil for the salvation or eternal damnation of mankind.

The beasts were caught up in this by no means unequal struggle, in relationships to man that could be on occasion affectionate, symbiotic, or bloody. In this grand spectacle of moral warfare, the priests and the saints and the secular power were ranged against the ranks of demons, wizards, and necromancers who were believed to be able to enter the bodies of the lower animals in order to work mischief through them. The miracle literature of the Church cites numerous instances of devils appearing in the guise of blackbirds, mules, mares and horses, bulls, pigs, dogs, rooks, worms, lions, and tigers. Sometimes animals demonstrated that they knew how to take evasive action. Saint Regulus, bishop of Arles and Senlis, once cast a devil out of the body of a man and the fiend tried to enter an ass. But the sagacious beast made the sign of the Cross on the ground with his forefoot and repelled the invader.[2]

Believers in sorcery and familiar spirits were not confined to the lower levels of society. Several popes; Montesquieu, famous author of *The Spirit of the Laws* (1748) and a member of the French Academy; James I of England—all accepted the reality of wizards and the black arts, while Joseph Glanvill, a man of scientific reputation and a founding Fellow of the Royal Society, wrote a treatise upholding the idea that supernatural powers could be exercised by persons in league with evil spirits.[3] On the positive side, a long list of animals are reported by the homilists as having done men a good turn, especially in feeding hermits who were out of provisions. One of the more striking instances of such acts of animal benevolence was related by the Bollandists in the *Acta Sanctorum* concerning Saint Stephen, third abbott of Cîteaux. Once when the holy man was very ill, a bird brought him a fish. And what is more remarkable, the fish was already cooked.[4]

The right to try, judge, and sentence dumb animals for injuries done to human beings traces back to the law of Moses: "If an ox gore a man or woman that they die; then the ox shall surely be stoned, and his flesh shall not be eaten; but the owner of the ox shall be quit." Papers were served on the offending animals by an officer of the court, who read them in a loud voice at places where the culprits were known to congregate. These documents were filled out with all technical formality including a description of the said animals. Thus, if the proceeding was against rats, the defendants were described as dirty, grayish rodents who lived in holes. After the accused had been cited three times, judgment could be entered against them by default if they remained obdurate.[5]

When the case went to trial, an advocate was appointed for the defense, and the defendants were required to show cause why they should not be summoned. If no satisfactory excuse was forthcoming, they were then ordered to appear. If they failed to do so, they were warned to leave the district, or could be consigned to damnation by the dread curse of the Church. This power was not one to be invoked lightly. Once when Saint Bernard, according to old records, said to a bluebottle fly that was buzzing around his ears, "Be thou excommunicated," all the flies in a whole province fell dead.[6]

If the animals persisted in being obstinate, their contumacy was not attributed to any lack of competence on the part of the court but to the superior power, temporarily, of Satan and his minions. Sometimes vermin were generously forewarned of their peril. In the year 1545 the wine growers of Saint Julien, a commune west of Bordeaux, whose growths still appear on good wine lists, complained to François Bonnivard, Doctor of Laws, of the ravages of a certain coleopterous insect, known today to entomologists as *Rhynchites auratus Scopoli*, an ordinary sort of weevil or snoutbeetle that infests vineyards. First public prayers were said, then the Mass was celebrated on three successive days and the Host borne in solemn procession around the boundaries of the vineyards. The weevils were ably defended. But the verdict went against them. The next step would have been to strike the creatures with the divine anger by means of the Church's great weapon, the malediction. But the arthropods did not wait for the thunderbolt. They decamped. Forty-one years later they returned and a second trial took place. The record filled twenty-nine folio volumes, but the action was finally compromised when the authorities agreed to set aside a plot of ground outside the village for the sole use of the beetles in perpetuity.[7]

Sometimes it was extremely difficult for the civil authorities to determine whether a cloud of noxious insects that attacked the crops had been incited to their evildoing by a fiend or were legitimate scourges sent by God to chastise His erring children. In such instances the Church decided, since it presumably could make nice distinctions based upon the facts of each case, and often the clergy took over with sprinklings of holy water and pronounced anathemas against the maybugs or snails that were troubling the farms and gardens.[8]

The reasoning by which animals could be excommunicated was that all creatures are subject to God. God is the author of canon law. Therefore, animals are subject to its provisions and penalties. In setting the Church's thaumaturgic machinery in motion when the peasants were vexed with worms, slugs, locusts, or whatever, the ecclesiastical powers required first that the people pay up their tithes. The results were sometimes spectacular. In Valence in 1585 a prosecution against caterpillars was argued by both theologians and lay lawyers with such subtlety and exhaustive detail that the proceedings dragged on for months. "Meanwhile," wrote a later historian who lived in a more skeptical age, and was aware of the life cycle of lepidopterous creatures, "Meanwhile the insects died out."[9] Saint Thomas Aquinas, the great interpreter of medieval Christianity, allowed in his vast synthesis, *Suma Theologica*, that curses could be directed against irrational brutes when they were being used by the powers of hell; that is to say, the authorities could take aim at the Devil through the animals he had corrupted. But the beast trials were not charades. For animals that could be seized, they were a cruel reality.

Lifeless objects could also be prosecuted and punished—objects that chanced accidentally to take human life and were therefore subject to formal destruction.[10] The idea was as old as the writings of the pagan poets of antiquity. To the Greeks, if a murderer could not be found, the instrument used was punished, for the avenging spirits of the dead, the Furies, had to be appeased. This conception, touching both inanimate things and sentient beings, had biblical analogies—the cursing of the serpent in Genesis, David's malediction against the mountains of Gilboa, which were deprived of rainfall, and in the New Testament, the curse Christ laid upon the barren fig tree of Bethany. Thus an ancient principle persisted. A French commentator has mentioned an example of the effectiveness of the Church's anathema directed against the vegetable kingdom. A priest of Burgundy excommunicated an orchard because the fruit tempted the children to stay away from Mass. The orchard ceased to bear until the Duchess of Burgundy interposed and caused the curse to be lifted.[11]

According to the archives of the French criminal courts, pigs in particular seem to have suffered severely at the hands of the law, probably because they were numerous, had easy access to homes and huts, and roamed the towns and cities freely as scavengers. Thus it was especially easy for them to get into trouble. Once in court, hogs frequently acted disrespectfully with their gruntings and squealings, and this disorderly conduct told against them. There was a further handicap that swine had to endure. Demons were especially fond of dwelling in them. Many swine were duly convicted of being "possessed" and were executed, especially if their color was black.[12]

When a hog was judicially burned it was not then considered to be roast pork. To eat an animal caught in blood guilt and elevated by reason of capital punishment to the level of man, would have savored of cannibalism. The solemn atmosphere of the proceedings may be inferred from these words, pronounced by the mayor of a French village upon a pig convicted of having caused the death of a child:

> We, in detestation and horror of this crime, and in order to make an example and satisfy justice, have declared, judged, sentenced, pronounced, and appointed that the said pig, being detained as prisoner and confined in the said abbey, shall be,

by the executioners, hung and strangled upon a gibbet. In
witness thereof we have sealed this present with our seal.[13]

Similar trials took place in almost every country of Europe. The
defendants, in addition to the species already mentioned, have
included ants, asses, bloodsuckers, bulls, cockchafers, cocks, cows,
eels, dolphins, goats, moles, serpents, sheep, wolves, worms, all
brought to the bar of justice over a great span of time, extending
from A.D. 824, when moles were prosecuted in the valley of Aosta,
to 1906 when a dog was sentenced to death in Switzerland.[14] In
Switzerland, incidentally, animals could under certain circumstances appear as witnesses. If a house was broken into at night and
the owner killed the intruder, the question arose as to whether or
not his act was justifiable homicide, for he might have enticed the
victim to enter and then murdered him. But the defendant could
establish his innocence by producing a dog, cat, or cockerel that
lived with him and had witnessed the death of the burglar. The
householder was required to declare his innocence under oath in
the presence of the dumb animal. If the beast did not contradict
him, the court held that he had cleared himself. The legal theory
was that Heaven would intervene to bestow the gift of speech
upon the beast rather than allow a murderer to escape.[15]

Condemned animals that were physically in the custody of the
law were killed by a variety of methods. They could be lightly
singed, then strangled; burned at the stake; buried alive; sometimes
tortured before being strung up on a gibbet. Animals were even
put to the rack in order to extort a confession.[16] No confession was
expected, but this act of cruelty made it certain that due form was
being observed. Domestic beasts met the ignominious death of
human criminals, for as intimate members of the human community, they were treated with the same public contempt as felons in
a similar fix. If the wrongdoing occurred on a Friday, that fact
constituted a serious aggravation of the offense.[17]

It must have been a vivid moment, packed with drama and high
excitement, when a vast concourse of people—nobles, men-at-
arms, priests in cassock and cowl, falconers with hooded hawks
upon their wrists, huntsmen with hounds on leash, old men leaning on their staves, hags with their reticules, fine ladies in velvet
and feathers—gathered in the public square of the old Norman

town of Falaise in 1386 to see justice done on the body of an animal. A sow was dressed up in a new suit of man's clothing, mangled about the head and forelegs, and hanged—the penalty for maiming and killing a baby in a similar manner.

The elements of this scene are not entirely a matter of conjecture, for an artist was employed to fresco the moment of punishment on the west wall of the transept of the Church of the Holy Trinity. There it remained for more than 400 years.[18] Even the expense to the state for this execution is known. It was ten sous, ten deniers, and a pair of new gloves for the hangman, who was no common butcher but a public official, a *maître des hautes oeuvres*, or high functionary. The new gloves indicated that he incurred no personal guilt in the discharge of his duty but left the gallows with clean hands.[19]

The countries in which animals have been held accountable to human law include Belgium, Denmark, England, Germany, Italy, Portugal, Spain, Scotland, Turkey, the American colonies, and the United States. The Russians, true to their historic mode of punishment, are known to have sent a billy-goat to Siberia.[20] The beast trial must have been a commonplace in England during the age of Elizabeth I, for Shakespeare includes, in Gratiano's invective against Shylock, this reference to such proceedings:

> *Thy currish spirit*
> *Govern'd a wolf, who, hang'd for human slaughter*
> *Even from the gallows did his fell soul fleet . . .*

Perhaps the most fascinating case of which we have knowledge, in which every legal dodge and dilatory action was employed by an inspired defense, occurred at Autun in Burgundy in 1522. The rats of the ancient canton of Lucenay, near Autun, were accused of having feloniously eaten up and wantonly destroyed the barley harvest and were ordered brought before the bishop's vicar, who exercised jurisdiction in such cases. The vicar appointed Bartholomé Chassenée as counsel to represent the rodents. Chassenée, then a young lawyer, won professional renown by his ingenious defense of the rats and was elevated to the high position of president of the Parlement de Provence, a judicial post corresponding to that of chief justice. Chassenée also subsequently wrote a learned treatise on the application of the law to animals and insect offenders and used the precedent of Autun when he defended the Vaudois—simple, devout Alpine shepherds and farmers who were being harrassed as heretics. The rat case, Chassenée argued in defense of the Vaudois, had established the precedent that "even animals should not be adjudged and sentenced without a hearing."[21]

At Autun, when Chassenée's client rats failed to appear, their attorney attacked the summons as being defective on the ground that it had been too local and individual in character and called for the appearance of some but not all the rats. Many, he insisted, had not heard of the accusation. The curates of every parish, therefore, were given the task of notifying all the rats in their ecclesiastical care. Once again, after due notice, the rats failed to appear. The lawyer then pointed out that the rats were widely scattered and required more time, since great preparations would have to be made for such an extraordinary assemblage. The judge granted the plea.

Again on court day there were no rats on hand. The attorney then assured the court that his clients were most anxious to comply but were entitled to have all the safeguards of justice thrown around them in responding to the summons. Under existing circumstances, they were detained by the fear of certain "evil-disposed cats kept by the plaintiffs." Chassenée demanded that before the rats could obey the writ, the accusers should be required to post bonds guaranteeing the good behavior of their pets. At this point the complainants gave up and the proceedings were adjourned *sine die.*[22]

The difficulties encountered by a simple agricultural people in protecting their property from zoological depredations sometimes tempted them to try the efficacy of the black arts. Humble peasants, finding justice through law slow, uncertain, and expensive, were led to try charms and spells obtained from practitioners of forbidden arts who carried on a contraband traffic in exorcisms. This placed them in competition with the Church. Any poor shepherd, certainly, who resorted to sorcery to keep the wolves away from his flock risked being cursed by bell, book, and candle and dying by stake and faggot. Since men generally believed in the existence of Devil-directed forces, it was the logic of the Church, fully supported by the state, that those who attempted to practice witchcraft should suffer heavily for dabbling in Satanic rites.

There were, of course, skeptics. Even while men still believed that evil spirits could be expelled by whipping a cat, Jean Racine ridiculed the criminal prosecution of beasts in his one venture into comedy, *Les Plaideurs* (1668). In this divertissement the poet of classical French tragedy caricatured the follies of judges and litigants in the time of Louis XIV. A dog is tried for making off with a capon. The defense pleads with high-flown oratory and learned references to Latin maxims and the citation of such authorities as Aristotle and Pausanias. The dog, it develops, has recently become a father. So the litter is brought into court to play upon the judge's sympathies.

"*Venez, pauvres enfants,*" exclaims the L'Intimé for the defense, exhibiting the pups, "*qu'on veut rendre orphelins.*"

Dandin, the judge, is distracted with the racket. And the puppies are not housebroken.

"*Tirez donc,*" shouts Dandin in alarm. "*Quel vacarmes! Ils ont pissé partout.*"

But the L'Intimé insists that the puddles are only the tears of the prospective orphans. Finally Dandin relents, reflecting that he does not want the puppies to go on welfare. The comedy was warmly commended by the man best able to appraise such a work, Molière himself, and upon being performed at Versailles it made the Sun King laugh.

As late as the end of the seventeenth century in French Canada, a plague of doves was anathematized for crop damage, and shortly disappeared, the birds being migratory.[23] Only a few years ago our near-contemporary, William Morton Wheeler, the distinguished entomologist, found that Canadian crop pests were still exorcised by parish priests, "some being most successful in suppressing cutworms while others are more deadly to potato-beetles." The dates of exorcism were set, Wheeler continued, with the assistance of government agricultural bulletins so as to occur just before the pupation of the insects. Sure enough, the pests vanished "with amazing and edifying promptitude immediately after excommunication."[24]

Other North American beast trials include at least two in seventeenth-century New England. Cotton Mather records the execution at New Haven of a "wretch, one Potter by name" for sodomy, the authorities first killing before his eyes the animals which he had abused.[25] John Winthrop, also, wrote in his *History of New England from 1630 to 1649* of "one Hackett, a servant in Salem . . . found in buggery with a cow, upon the Lord's day." Man and beast were executed.[26]

An attempt to prosecute an animal came to light in New York City as late as 1877, when a Celtic lady, Mary Shea, of Bottle Alley, near Mulberry Street, appeared as complainant in Tombs Police Court, calling for retributive justice against an organ-grinder's capuchin monkey, named Jimmy, who had bit her. The judge explained to Mary that he could not commit an animal. She left the courtroom in high indignation, her finger still wrapped in her handkerchief, exclaiming with scorn, "This is a nice country for justice." The monkey, meanwhile, in scarlet coat and velvet cap trimmed with gilt lace, curled his tail around the gas fixture on the magistrate's desk and tried to shake hands with His Honor. The police blotter showed this record: *Name*: Jimmy Dillio. *Occupation*: Monkey. *Disposition*: Discharged.[27]

Today the legal remedy for injuries by animals to human beings or to property consists of a civil action for damages against the owner of the animal. But ancient ideas dissipate slowly and sometimes linger in forms of which later generations are unaware. Folklorists have found traces of a medieval practice—driving away unwanted animals with writs of ejectment—in Scotland, Ireland, France, and the United States. Those Americans who have ever heard casually of such a notion as writing a letter to rats, for example, have undoubtedly disbelieved what they heard on the subject. But it is, in fact, an ancient usage. An episode of this sort came to light during a will contest in Baltimore County, Maryland, in 1888. A necessary element in this form of conjuring was to provide another abode for the unwelcome guests. In the Maryland case, the rats were directed to go up the lane, then "past the stone house," and to "keep on until they came to the large white house on the right, and turn in there . . ." This, they were assured, "was Captain Low's house and they would get plenty to eat there." The feelings of Captain Low about this arrangement are not known.[28]

A Maine countryman also wrote a letter to the rats, rubbed it with grease to make sure his correspondents would be interested, rolled it up, and mailed it by placing it in a rathole. Dated October 31, 1888, the missive was addressed to "Messrs. Rats and Co." and began chattily:

> Having taken quite a deep interest in your welfare in regard to your winter quarters I thought I would drop you a few lines which might be of some considerable benefit to you in the future seeing that you have pitched your winter quarters at the summer residence of —— No. 1 Seaview Street. I wish to inform you that you will be very much disturbed during cold winter months as I am expecting to be at work through all parts of the house, shall take down ceilings, take up floors, and clean out every substance that would serve to make you comfortable, likewise there will be nothing left for you to feed on, as I shall remove every eatable substance; so you had better take up your abode elsewhere.

The writer then helpfully recommends a farm

> where you will find a splendid cellar well filled with vegetations of [all] kinds besides a shed leading to a barn, with a good supply of grain, where you can live snug and happy. Shall do you no harm if you heed to my advice; but if not, shall employ "Rough on Rats."[29]

One cannot but admire the judicious mixture of sweet reasonableness, threat, and terror set forth in this remarkable communication. The suggestion of a neighbor's barn as a suitable alternative for the rats is clearly in the authentic tradition of the canny Yankee.

Today animals appear from time to time in court records as property, as evidence, or because they barked, scratched, or bit, but not as witnesses or defendants. Their risk of being declared criminals has vanished, it is true. But they are no longer treated as people, either.

4

The Animal–Machine Theory

Big Daddy, the dying partiarch who dominates the second act of Tennessee Williams' *Cat on a Hot Tin Roof*, declares at one point, "The human machine is not so different from the animal machine or the fish machine or the bird machine or the reptile machine or the insect machine."

In so speaking, Big Daddy, who is by no means a member of an intellectual elite, demonstrates how powerfully the mechanistic view of men and animals retains its vitality after a run of considerably more than three hundred years.[1]

The background for this durable instance of philosophic materialism is this. Great advances were being made in the knowledge of animal bodies by the anatomists of the sixteenth and seventeenth centuries, despite the opposition to natural science of such thought-leaders as Nicholas de Malebranche, the French metaphysical theorist, who said, "Men are not made to consider gnats," and Cornelius Jansen, bishop of Ypres, who declared, in the same vein, ". . . the secrets of nature . . . are

36

none of our business . . ."[2] This is a point of view that may be traced back to Saint Augustine, who condemned the desire for knowledge as just one of the lusts of the flesh. For a thousand years it had been believed that man was short one rib on one side because God had taken a rib from Adam to create Eve. But no one had thought of counting ribs to check out the accuracy of the Garden of Eden story. Now men were shaking off the quiddities of scholasticism and observing the world about them. Observing—and counting ribs. So they explored and described the structure of moths, flies, fish, frogs, birds, the crocodile and the horse, the ox, sheep, bear, lion, dog and cat, the bat and the monkey.[3] "Here is my library," said René Descartes, the great French mathematician and scientist of the seventeenth century, to an inquirer as he pointed to a quartered calf he was dissecting.[4]

But Descartes was both devout and prudent where Roman Catholic doctrine was concerned. Attempting to formulate exact rules for scientific advances while shielding his religion from the consequences of rational inquiry, the philosopher excluded man from his anatomical experiments. Man could think. "I think, therefore I am," ran Descartes' famous sentence. Man could feel, for feeling was a function of thinking. And man was morally free, possessing an immortal soul that oysters and sponges and all lower creatures lacked. It was, therefore, one thing to dissect the brutes, but quite another to compare their physiology with man's. Such experiments could lead to wicked conclusions contradicting the scriptural account of Creation. This would constitute defiance of the authority in matters of faith of the Council of Trent, which forbade the interpretation of the sacred texts in any way contrary to the opinion of the Church.

If the bodies of men and beasts were strikingly similar, and it was evident that they were, was the animal soul—or, as we should term it now, mind, consciousness, *life*—also made of the same stuff as the human soul? If it was, the Christian apologists would have to concede immortality to mice and water bugs and include them in the grand scheme of future rewards and punishments. That would make the beasts morally equivalent to man, or reduce man to being a species of animal. This was heretical.[5] But if the animal soul dies when the body dies, perhaps the human soul does also, a conclusion not even to be thought of.[6]

The difficulty, known in the history of philosophy as the Mind-Body Problem, was resolved by Descartes by separating the soul and the body completely. Thinking and feeling were attributes of soul. The body, he said, was simply a complex machine. Since animals couldn't speak, it followed that they couldn't think. If they couldn't think, then they couldn't feel. This ingenious chain of reasoning is the origin of the beast-machine doctrine, one of the most dramatic, aberrant and influential events in intellectual history. The animal machine, according to Descartes, was activated by "animal spirits," which were considered to be gases flowing through the nerves and capable of moving the muscles.[7] But all the world's fauna, from the ants to the ape machines, those parodies of humankind, were completely lacking in ideas, freedom of action, knowledge, or feeling. They were like a watch or clock with wheels, springs, gears, and weights, although more wonderful than any inventions of man, because they were the product of the divine engineer, "made by the hand of God." Marvelously contrived though they were, however, the beast-creatures were mere automatons.[8] Thus man was elevated above all the rest of creation, for only he possessed an immortal soul. For him alone the moral choice existed: no cross, no crown. For all the other swarming creatures of the planet there was no equity either in the here or the hereafter.

It was a black day for the animals when Descartes worked out this absolute distinction between man and beast. The philosopher's followers adopted his speculations as ruthless dogma, and proceeded to satisfy their curiosity with torturing and killings while they marveled that mechanical robots could give such a realistic illusion of agony. Denying to animals all subjective experience, the virtuosi of the period nailed their victims to boards by their four paws before demonstrating over and over again that the blood does indeed circulate; and Malebranche, an intellectual heir of Descartes, according to a well-known anecdote, kicked his dog just to hear what he termed the "creaking of the machine."[9]

Anyone could play. A fascinated lay public, enamored of the new science of physiology, found it an exciting pastime to carve up, dismember, gut, and inspect the quivering viscera of the unfortunate creatures they were able to capture. In England, after the Restoration, genial hosts with a dilettante interest in cadavers entertained the Beautiful People of the epoch with a dish of tea and a demonstration of the new air pump, which suffocated countless guinea pigs, rabbits, birds, cats, sheep, and dogs. Robert Boyle, inventor of the pump, was the age's hero. Poisons, mindless blood transfusions, drownings, all had their place among these bizarre interventions. One can only say of them that cruelty had topped out and could go no further than it did during the mania for burning, impaling, or starving in some "pretty experiment," as Samuel Pepys, the diarist, phrased it.[10]

As a result of all the puppies cut apart or drowned in warm milk, it did become overwhelmingly clear that man was physiologically a good deal nearer to the lower creatures and farther from the angels than had formerly been supposed; and many men of good will became acutely uncomfortable when they reflected upon the way mankind was discharging the trusteeship given in the ninth chapter of Genesis, over "every living creature." A correction was due, to rectify that quirk of the human mind which Weston La Barre has described as "the ability to know things that are not so" and which he calls "an extraordinary and unique peculiarity of man among animals. . . ."[11]

The Cartesian hypothesis raised a swarm of objectors. Some thinkers took a closer look at the zoological world and became convinced that the lower animals have their joys and sorrows, that they seek pleasure, avoid pain, and cling valorously to life even as we do, while displaying all of the variations of individual personalty.[12] To the critics of the theory, it seemed plain that all forms of life represented a continual progression from the lower to the higher forms, men and animals sharing a common fate, as it was given in Ecclesiastes: "For that which befalleth the sons of men befalleth beasts . . . as the one dieth, so dieth the other; yea, they have all one breath. . . ."

Another group of opponents kept the argument going because they found an assault upon Descartes' teachings, which reinforced traditional values, a convenient means of discrediting Church and king and censuring the pretensions of men, while John Locke in England pointed out that those who clung to the animal-machine proposition did so ". . . only because their hypothesis requires it."[13]

After a century of controversy, Julien Offray de la Mettrie, French physician and religious skeptic, pushed the mechanistic concept to its ultimate conclusion. In his book *L' homme machine* (1748), La Mettrie followed the argument where it led and concluded that if animals were machines, then so were men. The lively doctor's writings produced a scandal, and the author paid for his audacity in the loss of his post as regimental surgeon and was obliged to flee first from France, later from the Netherlands, to escape the wrath of the theologians. La Mettrie found sanctuary at the court of Frederick II of Prussia, where he was warmly received. He died of indigestion after having overeaten of a game pie. Providence, it was felt in ecclesiastical circles, had vindicated itself handsomely.[14]

Another critic of Descartes, Abbé Pierre Gassendi, French mathematician and philosopher, argued that animals had intelligence similar to man's but not quite as much of it, and Bernard Le Bovier de Fontenelle, skillful popularizer of the principal tendencies of eighteenth-century French thought, attacked the dog-watch-clock analogy by pointing out that when the male dog machine mounted the female dog machine there would soon be "a third little machine." This was something that never happened between two watches.[15] By the time of the Enlightenment, the physiologists had discarded Cartesian mechanics and concluded that animals and men both lived under natural law, and they enlarged their conception of the humane ideal to include the beast world.[16] Some speculative thinkers maintained that the beasts, being able to live zestfully and entirely in the moment, enjoyed substantial advantages over the human situation. Montesquieu, for example, in his *Spirit of Laws*, pointed out that animals took better care of themselves than human beings did and if they did not have our hopes, they also did not share our fears. They were mortal, but they did not have to live with knowing it.[17]

Descartes' dualism, the mind here and the body over there, has never completely died out. But modern biologists see man as being no more special than any other species. Each species, genus, family, and so on is the sum of its evolutionary past. Each solves the problems of existence according to differing positions in the great scheme of life.[18] Darwin established this as a fact after careful observations that the movements of animals are "almost as expressive as those of man."[19]

The analogies by which men have ascribed extraordinary abilities to animals have sometimes been pushed too far, especially by those who have loved their pets not wisely but too well. My own favorite anecdote in this genre has to do with the female cat, Grisette, owned by Madame Antoinette Deshoulières, who with her circle of Parisian friends found it amusing to write letters and poems that they pretended were the compositions of their companion animals. Grisette was greatly admired and courted by both feline and canine friends, who corresponded with her through the secretarial aid, of course, of their human owners. One male cat named Tata on one occasion sent Grisette his compliments, accompanied by expressions of extreme regret that he had been made unworthy of her love by a cruel operation. Grisette reproved him for making a bawdy remark and turned serenely to a learned and Platonic correspondence with a canine friend named Cochon.[20]

The materialistic explanation of man, the attempt to bring him totally within the purview of physics or chemistry, never seems to exhaust itself. "Today," according to the late philosopher and naturalist, Joseph Wood Krutch, "psychology, sociology and even biology tend more and more to think of man as a machine—something which merely obeys laws, responds to conditioning, can be manipulated . . ."[21] The beast-machine idea surfaces again among those who oppose humane treatment of animals on the ground that they cannot feel pain, or that they don't feel pain *very much*. Usually such rationalizations are closely linked with some form of profit, as in the case of the argument that it costs too much to slaughter animals humanely. And echoes of the animal-machine idea occur in a statement made by Pius XII to the effect that when the lower animals are killed in a laboratory or an abattoir, "their cries should not arouse unreasonable compassion any more than do red-hot metals undergoing the blows of the hammer, seeds spoiling underground, branches crackling when they are pruned, grain that is surrendered to the harvester; wheat being ground by the milling machine."[22] All of these groups, commercial, vivisectionist, and ecclesiastical, are quick to raise the cry of sentimentality when any attempt is made to consider the mental or emotional life of subhuman creatures.

It remained for the reformed churches to display a new lenity toward other forms of life than our own and "to find a new expression for emotions which have been repressed by existing conventions. . . ." John Wesley and the Methodists were forward in this matter, following Martin Luther, who had given a gentle and encouraging answer when a little girl, grieving over the death of her dog, inquired of him: "Will there be dogs in the other world?"[23] Pity followed when the popular mind, responding to its own best intuitions, concluded that animals did have feelings after all. The seventeenth century was an excellent time to be a cat, at least in French intellectual circles, and it is pleasant to record that Descartes himself, despite his big theoretical idea, was devoted to a pet, a very fine dog named Monsieur Grat, who carried off with aplomb the dignified role of being a philosopher's dog. Theists continued to grapple with "the animal problem," but poetry came nearer the mark when Alexander Pope made the beast the friend and teacher of man because "All are but parts of one stupendous whole."[24]

A new mood appeared in literature, especially in England, expressed in kinsman phrases saluting the animals as "fellow creatures," "friend," "brother," or "fellow mortal," and many found joy and consolation in this new state of conscience.[25] The attitude may be summed up in the words "rights for animals," the subject of the next chapter.

5

A New Idea:
Rights for Animals

The English have long enjoyed a reputation for exhibiting an exceptional devotion to animals. They are "a nation of pet-keepers," a London magazine has acknowledged.[1] The supporting evidence for this national fondness is totally convincing.

As long ago as the seventeenth century, John Bunyan complained that an Englishman would rather go for a walk with a dog than a Christian. In our own time, animal-loving Britons were horrified when *The Mirror* of London broke the story that the ceremonial horses that perform so splendidly in the Changing of the Guard are sold in old age to a "knacker's yard," a Briticism for slaughterhouse, to be turned into horsemeat. A widow at Halberton shares the wine and wafer with her terrier at Holy Communion, and on Animal Sunday, the Sunday nearest to the Feast of Saint Francis, many worshipers bring their animal friends to share the service. All are reported as seeming to know that they are in a consecrated spot.[2] The annual holiday of swan-upping is still celebrated according to hallowed tradition, when the swans on the

Thames are counted and marked.³ The Earl of Cranbrook exercises bats in his bathroom, and the medical officer of Portsmouth has suggested the installation of artificial lampposts in the city's streets and parks as a dog amenity. Retired colonels write furiously to the newspapers from their clubs about the abuse of pit ponies in the coal mines and the continued tolerance of the leg-hold trap in Scotland. The English humanitarian must wrestle with the vivisection issue and the question of vegetarian dining and maintain his equanimity when accused of being a busybody, a crank, or both.

Statisticians estimate that there are more than 4 million dogs in Great Britain—a small country, remember—and more than 6 million cats and about five million caged birds. Altogether these pet categories equal about half the human population of England. The English read some twenty-eight weekly or monthly journals about animals, and support not only the venerable and still-vigorous Royal Society for the Prevention of Cruelty to Animals, but also the Mammal Society, the League Against Cruel Sports, the Fauna Preservation Society, the National Society for the Abolition of Cruel Sports, the Council for Justice to Animals and Humane Slaughter Association, the Universities Federation for Animal Welfare, the Home Rest for Horses in Hertfordshire, the International Council Against Bullfighting, the Catholic Study Circle for Animal Welfare, the Performing Animals' Defence League, the Royal Society for the Protection of Birds, the Battersea Dogs' Home, the Bird Lovers' League, the Tail Waggers' Club of Great Britain, and to round off this partial list, the Canine Defence League. A French observer, meditating upon the English devotion to animals, has made this somewhat wry remark on the British character: "In the eyes of an Englishman there are only two really civilized races in the world: the English and the animals."⁴

Yet the English, who would be shocked at anyone's molesting the pigeons in Trafalgar Square or the gulls on the Embankment, who knit warm woolen jackets for pets and spend often meager pensions for dog meat, also incite greyhounds to tear hares apart, beat badgers to death with spades, smear the faces of advantaged boys and girls with blood from the tails of massacred foxes in a kind of puberty rite. King George V loved parrots, butchered partridges.⁵ Thinking about animals is strangely compartmentalized: fox hunters are revolted at cruelty to circus animals, bird shooters denounce deer hunters, and loyal members of the RSPCA eat pâté de fois gras.

Nor is English law less illogical. Beat a cat and go to prison. Chase and kill a fox and become, conceivably, Master of the Hunt. These anomalies are not, of course, peculiar to the English, but may be observed in all mankind who love the animals that are large, popular and aesthetically pleasing but bypass difficult questions relating to the treatment of less-appealing forms of sentient life.

When one reflects that decent people have tolerated slavery, adjusted to crucifixion as a routine procedure, and torture as an instrument of justice, that watching the insane at Bedlam was once a popular recreation in London, and attending the public hangings at Tyburn was another, it comes as an anticlimax to learn that cats were hunted down because they were a reminder of the owl, and that every dog reputed to be rabid was persecuted to death.[6] It is difficult to stand aside and observe one's own culture. Blind spots develop because of familiarity and custom. If the sports and pastimes of the English up to, say, 200 years ago reveal an almost unbelievable callousness toward animals, this must be said also: men were treated no better. Boiling in oil was legal until 1547, and there were still over 200 capital offenses on the statute books at the beginning of the nineteenth century.

For hundreds of years, on Shrove Tuesday, a day of merrymaking just before Lent, both city and country folk enjoyed the pastoral diversion of "throwing at cocks"—i.e., hurling sticks and clubs at a rooster, tied down so only its head was visible. If its legs were broken, it was mounted again on improvised splints so the sport could continue, and sometimes the game was played with cats.[7] At Beverley, in Yorkshire, during a market fair, a shepherd essayed to eat a live tomcat for the edification of the crowd, succeeded, and pronounced himself "neither sick nor sorry."[8] At the beginning of the eighteenth century, seeing the town in London meant a visit to Westminster Abbey and an inspection of the zoo at the Tower of London. The regular admission was three pence, but visitors could save the entrance fee by bringing a live dog, cat, or other pet and pushing it between the bars to feed the royal lions.[9]

The great national sport of the yeomanry for centuries, and of the squirearchy, too, was the baiting and worrying of chained, defenseless bulls and bears by English bulldogs, a breed especially developed for that purpose. Queen Elizabeth I complimented foreign ambassadors with such "merry disports,"[10] and Shakespeare recognized the popularity of the bear gardens when he had Slender say, in *The Merry Wives of Windsor*:

> *Why do your dogs bark so? be there bears i'*
> *the town?*

John Gay also refers to the parade that traditionally preceded a baiting:

> *Led by the Nostril walks the muzzled bear.*

A medieval folk belief survived in a law stipulating that every bull must be baited before being butchered because tormenting the beef animal was supposed to improve the quality of the meat."[11] An American scholar who has studied the manuscript records of the borough of Suffolk in East Anglia found that the butchers of Sudbury had been indicted for selling meat that "hadn't been chased enough by the dogs . . ."[12]

A variant was called "bull running." This amusement, a festive event for over seven hundred years, was carried out in a holiday atmosphere, as an annual feature of life in the lusty town of Stamford, Lincolnshire. In this sport a great concourse of townspeople harried a frantic bullock while mastiffs tore off pieces of its flesh. Only energetic action in the nineteenth century by the Royal Society for the Prevention of Cruelty to Animals, the Home Secretary, a troop of the Fourteenth Dragoons, and a dozen constables brought from London finally put an end to the riotous scenes.[13]

The teasing and torturing of bears and bulls was defended on the grounds that it was a vigorous and manly sport, that it accustomed a martial people to bloodshed and prepared them to fight the French. One finds here a crude but interesting instance of the survival of sympathetic magic in the notion that the spectators at animal fights would acquire the courage and tenacity of the bulldog, often sketched by modern cartoonists as a totem of the British character.

During the period of the Commonwealth and the Protectorate, the Puritans ordered bear baiting to be put down from time to time, not, according to Macaulay's celebrated gibe, because it gave the bears pain, but because it gave the spectators pleasure. The orders had little effect, according to the researches of that formidable historical detective, Professor J. Leslie Hotson. He quotes one enthusiastic report of a charming spot called the Paris Garden, which offered the fragrance of shrubs and flowers, music, and "the shouting of men, the barking of dogs, the growling of the bears, and the bellowing of the bulls, mixed in a wild but natural harmony," all of which John Taylor, "the Water Poet," delineated in his *Bull, Beare and Horse* as "honest sport, and lawful merriment."[14]

The bear gardens of England were permanently closed in 1835. Yet in this same year cat skinners, who whipped off a cat's "jacket" and sold the skins for imitation fur, leaving the animals in the street, often still alive, could only be punished for violation of the Paving Act, which prohibited creating a nuisance in the street.[15] And cockfighting, a recreation dating from at least the time of the Roman occupation, continued to be popular with all levels of society. The squirrels twirling treadmill cages outside shops to attract trade, the dogs required to turn a spit, the annual game of clubbing a ram to death by the young gentlemen of Eton College, the whipping of pigs to make their flesh more tender—these, too, were the commonplaces of a coarse age. Performing animals were conditioned to do bizarre tricks by methods best not inquired about: the learned pig, the dog that mimicked a drunken man, the horse that could pick up gloves on command, count by pawing, or, as Gervase Markham, author of books on country pursuits, wrote, "piss when you would have him."[16]

The closing decades of the eighteenth century brought a changing social outlook. A friendlier, more personal and charitable disposition toward animals appeared, not so much a movement as a state of mind, personal rather than philosophic, emotional rather than intellectualized. Evangelical religion played a significant part. So did the new literature of sensibility, which climaxed in Laurence Sterne's character, Uncle Toby, a man of such heart and kindly feelings that when a fly tormented him at dinner he caught

it and, "Go, says he, lifting up the sash . . . why should I hurt thee?
—This world surely is wide enough to hold both thee and me."[17]

The animal kingdom benefited also from a reform in manners
and from the spreading doctrine of the rights of man, which was
so striking a feature of the Enlightenment and was well rooted in
England and the American colonies before the Revolution of 1789.
For all these reasons together, a new kindliness toward beasts was
evident in the attitudes and social arrangements of men. "Nature"
became a sort of code word of the epoch and "Nature's great chain
of being" its magic phrase, much as "evolution" summed up the
thought of the next century; and Goethe cleared away ambiguities
in saying, "Every animal is an end in itself."[18] Humanitarianism
represented a decisive turning away from the harsh doctrines of
Roman jurisprudence and the indifference of theological angelism,
which set man off from the rest of the biological world as a kind
of god-in-training. The new empathy toward animals paralleled
other indications of a quickened public conscience, such as the
growing agitation over the slavery question, prison reform, child
welfare, and better care for the old, the sick, the orphan, and the
insane. Not so much speculative as empiric, these forms of social
action were congenial to the Anglo-Saxon temperament. The position regarding animals that emerged was that any creature that can
anticipate and experience pain possesses rights so far as the human-animal relationship is concerned.[19]

This new way of looking at the zoological world was inspired in
great part by English men of letters. Jeremy Bentham, economist
and writer on jurisprudence, saw the treatment of animals as the
next issue after slavery and advocated legal measures for the protection of animals.[20] For the Lake poets, the novelists of sensibility, the
utilitarian school of writers—yes, and the eccentrics who always
flock to any new rallying point—the animal cause was not a matter
of abstract theory but a deeply emotional commitment.

One Scottish divine called kindness to animals "the charity of a
universe,"[21] and Robert Burns regretted the exclusion of animals
from the eighteenth-century "social compact" theory of society:

> *I'm truly sorry man's dominion*
> *Has broken nature's social union.*

The new perspective appears in William Cowper, who loved his hares so tenderly and wrote of his old cat, Puss, "I knew at least one hare that had a friend." Burns saluted a mouse as "fellow-mortal" and James Thomson, pacing in his lodgings on a wet Sunday, reflected with agitation upon the captive birds and wild animals in the Regent's Park Zoo, exclaiming "How they must suffer!" Other voices—those of Coleridge, Pope, Shenstone, and Wordsworth—were raised in protest against the spectacle of animal misery, and Dr. Samuel Johnson excoriated the fox hunters who harried a small, inedible British beast with horses, hounds, and spades. On the personal side, the fondness of both Dr. Johnson and Bentham for their cats provides a genial footnote to literary history.[22]

But the shift in temper was slow and hesitant, as with all great turning movements in human thought. When, for example, a vicar of the Church of England ventured in 1772 to preach a sermon censuring the abuse of animals, taking as his text the verse in Proverbs, "A righteous man regardeth the life of his beast . . ." his parishioners received the message with "almost universal disgust" and could only conclude that their priest had either turned Methodist or gone mad.[23]

Yet it was England that took the lead for animal justice, and moved the subject from theorizing about "the animal question" to the field of political action. In 1809 the Scottish Lord Thomas Erskine, then lord chancellor, presented a bill to prevent malicious and wanton cruelty to a quite restricted list of domestic animals, the horse, ox, sheep, and pig. Though the proposal was narrow in scope, the dome of the rotunda of the House of Lords rang with wails and caterwauls, mewings and cock crowings. But the bill passed, and then failed by a narrow margin in the House of Commons.[24] It was going to be painfully difficult to recognize formally the rights-of-animals concept and to punish aggression against the beasts without trespassing upon the rights of private property. John Lawrence, an authority on the horse, wrote of an occasion when he saw a man beating his horse "until the blood spun from its nostrils." When Lawrence remonstrated, the driver replied, "God damn my eyes, Jack, you are talking as if the horse was a Christian."[25]

The middle classes were responsive to the idea of animal rights because of their attachment to the reformed churches and because they were unaccustomed to the blood-stained episodes of the hunting field. But men reached the compassionate view by various routes. And some of the humanitarians were fierce indeed in pushing their gentle aims.[26]

Lord Erskine was a natural spokesman for the animal cause, for it is still remembered that he took his dog with him to legal consultations, owned a goose and two leeches, and once published a sprightly pamphlet on the agricultural services of rooks.[27] Erskine later joined in another and more successful effort in behalf of his animal clients. The measure, introduced in Parliament as "An Act to Prevent the Cruel and Improper Treatment of Cattle," became known generally as the "Martin Act" or "the animals' Magna Carta." It was introduced in the House of Commons by Colonel Richard Martin. When the bill was deposited at the clerk's desk, the House was filled with the sound of wailing cats. Martin was an influential Protestant Irish member for County Galway who lived in his own castle and enjoyed the personal friendship of George IV. The king nicknamed him "Humanity Dick" because of his devotion to the cause of animal welfare. Martin's bill, like the previous one, was narrowly drawn, to fragmentize the opposition. It applied only to the larger domestic animals, excluding all wild creatures as well as dogs, cats, and birds. The legislation was later interpreted by the courts not to include the bull. But it passed, accompanied by jeers, jokes, hisses, and cries of "Hare! Hare!" Martin's act received the royal assent on July 22, 1822, entering history as 3 Geo.IV, cap.71.[28]

The Martin Act made cruelty, which was not indictable under common law, an offense per se. Before this enactment, barbarity had to include malice toward the owner of the animal, not the beast itself.[29] Martin made many subsequent efforts to enlarge the law's application, but all were defeated by clever parliamentary tactics on the part of those opposed Yet honor enough remains for the man who established it as a legal principle that animals have certain minimal rights,[30] and other men came forward to carry on. Amendments were successfully added in 1835, 1849, 1854, and after, drawn so as to include wildlife and mental suffering.

All previous acts were consolidated in 1911 under the Protection of Animals Act.[31] Although now regarded as outdated, it still remains the principal British statute concerned with cruelty to animals. Loopholes exist. Notable omissions are offenses against foxes and other animals pursued by the aristocracy as a field sport. (The subject of hunting, as the term is used in England, is discussed in Chapter 6.)

Many attractive anecdotes survive regarding Dick Martin, and the combination in his personality of urbanity and quick wit, of devotion to his task, of his legal skill and staying power. He was the very pattern of the Irish gentleman. The fact that Colonel Martin was as formidable as a duelist as he was in repartee undoubtedly served him well when he rose to plead for the recognition of animal rights. But the idea of an abstract and inherent justice for animals continued to arouse resistance and incredulity in many minds. The magistrates of England enforced the new act with professional torpor, and the demand for action from the community in general developed slowly. The social atmosphere is suggested in a comic song sung at the time in the music halls. The mood is set in the first pair of couplets:

> *If I had a donkey wot wouldn't go,*
> *D'ye think I'd wallop him? No, no, no!*
> *But gentle means I'd try, d'ye see,*
> *Because I hate all cruelty.*[32]

Martin himself, according to contemporary accounts, went to the notorious horse market at Smithfield to collect evidence against cruelists.[33] He was constantly accused of being hopelessly sentimental, and this is a good place to spell out the distinction between humane feelings and sentimentality. Humaneness is concerned with the miseries or abuse of sentient creatures, for it is based upon an attitude of reverence for life. Sentimentality is self-regarding, concerned not with the feelings of animals but with one's own reactions to the animals, usually those beasts which are useful or popular. It represents a shallow discrimination. It is sentimental, for example, to confuse killing and hurting.[34]

Sentimentality is the always-present peril of humanitarian literature, as when dogs are represented as being devoted to the social betterment of rabbits, or in James Thomson's tribute to a cat "with

velvet tongue ne'er stained by mouse's blood," thus making the
Felidae, in gross contradiction of their true natures, good
humanitarians, too. Kindness to animals had, at any rate, become
in the early nineteenth century an acceptable moral precept, supported by an optimistic faith in the natural benevolence of man
and the utilitarian argument that the new principle would lead to
justice in human society and so be of advantage to man.[35] This
hope has been repeated by many voices over a long span of time,
although it was rejected with scorn by the animal-loving German
philosopher, Schopenhauer, who wrote, "So we are to have pity on
animals simply for practise. . . ."[36]

France was not far behind England in animal protection legislation. In 1845 Jacques-Phillipe Delmas de Grammont, general and
statesman, acting with other highly placed persons, founded the
Société Protectrice des Animaux and in 1850 pushed through an
act similar to the English statute, known as the Loi Grammont.
Thus both France and England gave an early and positive response
to the position summarized by Bentham when he wrote of the
beasts exploited by men: "The question is not, Can they reason?
nor Can they *talk?* but Can they *suffer?*"[37]

6

The Beginning
of Animal Protection

T wo years after the passage of the Martin Act, there being no
adequate machinery for enforcement, the Society for the
Prevention of Cruelty to Animals came into being, a private
organization with a mandate to work in the schools, circulate
tracts, employ inspectors, prosecute offenders, and announce convictions.[1] It enjoys the distinction of being the oldest animal protection society in existence. Something of the sort had been
attempted earlier in Liverpool, but the effort had faltered and
disappeared from view. In 1824, then, a small group of persons of
good will toward animals, under the leadership of the Reverend
Arthur Broome and including "Humanity Dick" Martin, of
course, and among others William Wilberforce, the philanthropist
who had worked successfully for the abolition of slavery in the
British Empire, gathered at Old Slaughter's Coffee-House in Saint
Martin's Lane, famous then as a resort of painters and sculptors.
Out of this assembly came the SPCA, the first organized effort to
make the new animal defense law effective and to work for its

53

improvement when experience indicated that changes were needed. Thus modestly was introduced a concept which "has now become a great and essential movement of modern civilization."[2]

The first years were difficult. At one time the Honorable Secretary of the SPCA, the Reverend Broome, was thrown into debtor's prison because the society could not meet its obligations, which the most recent historian of the RSPCA describes as "a most unfortunate position for a clergyman of the Church of England."[3] The society fought on many fronts with slender resources. It set out to ameliorate nauseous conditions at the Smithfield cattle market; to punish cat skinners and the abuse of dogs as draft animals; to outlaw the fighting dogpits, alleviate the misery of cab, cart, and van horses, and encourage the magistrates to do their duty.[4]

Fortune smiled in 1835 when the Duchess of Kent and the then Princess Victoria allowed their names to be added to the list of lady patronesses. In 1840, after Victoria had become queen, she commanded the society to add the prefix "royal" to its name, and she herself, when the RSPCA wished to establish a Queen's Medal, carefully sketched a cat into the group of animals shown on the proposed design. This association with the royal family has continued ever since and given the Royal Society great leverage.[5]

Branches were soon added, and similar associations quickly appeared in Ireland, Germany, Austria, Belgium, Holland, and considerably later, in the United States. In 1884 the RSPCA assisted in the formation of a parallel organization for the protection of defenseless children.[6] In this area the United States was in the lead, for the New York Society for the Prevention of Cruelty to Children had gotten under way a decade before this, also as an offshoot of animal humanitarianism.

The constables or inspectors of the RSPCA wore green uniforms and badges, carried truncheons, but were otherwise unarmed. In their carrying out of the society's aims they were attacked and roughed up on many occasions. The policy of the society was to enforce the law, gain a little in improved legislation when possible, and keep pressing for more.[7] This has been the pragmatic way, both in England and America, to advance the humane cause.

The activities of the RSPCA have varied according to changing circumstances, the social milieu, and new technology, such as the virtual elimination of the workhorse by the internal combustion engine. Humanitarian activities have a high visibility, which the RSPCA has recognized in its publications, its work with the younger generation, and in sponsoring such appealing affairs as the colorful Sands Parade of donkeys and ponies on the beaches of Somerset in August, and the traditional London Cart Horse Parade. This event goes back to 1885, when it was initiated by the Baroness Angela Burdett Coutts, philanthropic friend of Queen Victoria and one of the striking figures of the Victorian Age. Though the era of the horse has passed, the parade continues to be held—and televised.[8]

Exploits of dog heroes are not allowed to go unsung by the astute animal friends of the RSPCA. When a chihuahua named Mickey Mouse weighing only five and a half pounds woke up his master and the people living below because the house was on fire, he received the highest award of the RSPCA and international attention. When a boxer named Butch rescued a cat from drowning at sea, the society honored him with its bravery plaque. The fact that Butch got well scratched for his pains by the ungrateful cat did not detract from the human interest of the incident. Perhaps one more example will be sufficient to underline the value of imaginative propaganda to the humanitarian cause. In 1937 the RSPCA established a flying school for birds. The clients were caged birds that had been cruelly confined and taken away from callous owners by the courts. At the RSPCA school the birds learned to use their wings again in a large aviary, and at the official opening of the facility, Miss Pauline Gower, daughter of the then chairman of the society, flew over the farm in Surrey where the birds were practicing, as a salute to the natural aviators who were about to win their wings.[9] So for a century and a half the RSPCA has continued to mingle enforcement, education, and publicity in judicious proportions.

The British society has always been perplexed by a peculiar difficulty: how to curb cruel amusements without interfering with the recreation of persons of wealth and social position who wanted to hunt deer or foxes. Since the Royal Society has always been governed by "noblemen and gentlemen," its efforts to punish cruelists while tolerating fox hunting has sometimes led to unfriendly comment, and even rebellion in the RSPCA itself by members who consider the hunter an anachronism. It all depends, in the view of such outsiders as the National Society for the Abolition of Cruel Sports, upon whose ox, or fox, is gored. The official policy statement of the RSPCA states that it "cannot approve of hunting for sport"—that is, chasing wild animals with horses and hounds. Foxes are made an exception "reluctantly" on the ground that they must be controlled for the sake of agriculture, and alternative methods, in the opinion of the society, cause more suffering than does hunting.[10]

Many Englishmen and women dispute these points. In fact, so much heat has been generated by this issue that there have been some disorderly scenes at annual meetings. At one such meeting, heavily attended by fox-hunting members, the gathering ended in wild disorder, with catcalls, stamping of feet, rhythmic chanting, and cries of "Shame," and at the climax the police had to be called for.[11]

Many observers, however, hope and believe that the end of blood sports in England is in sight, although Parliament lags behind public opinion in this matter. Hare coursing and hunting carted deer (captive animals, trucked to the scene of the hunt and released for the chase) are still legal.[12] But the former is in decline and the last remaining deer hunt, the Norwich Staghounds, has suspended its activities.

Although the English invented fox hunting, the sport has never been widely popular in their country outside a coterie who could bear the high expense and were so placed in life as to reap the psychic rewards of its social importance. Today the pursuit of the fox has become difficult because of suburban sprawl, the web of highways and the extensive use of barbed wire. Furthermore, angry opponents carry placards at the important hunt meetings. One activist group, the Hunt Saboteurs Association, seeks to disrupt the fun by laying down trails of aniseed, which divert the beagles from the fox's scent.[13] A similar instance of direct action discomfited the gentlemen of the Bucks and Courtenay Tracy otter hunt on the Earl of Pembroke's estate near the old cathedral town of Salisbury. Philosophers and professors from Oxford University laid snuff traps along the banks of the Nadder River and the hounds, sneezing violently, stampeded a herd of cattle and two swans flew straight into an oak tree.[14]

Bird hunters detest fox hunters because they don't like to have hounds scattering the pheasants, and they sometimes heatedly accuse fox hunters of perpetuating rather than eliminating the fox population.[15] And those who are politically inclined toward the principles of the British Labour Party are often found in the humanitarian ranks for class-conscious reasons. So they introduce antihunting bills and march under banners protesting the ancient diversion of the aristocracy, although they may not identify particularly with the object of the chase, the victim described by one repentant ex-fox hunter as a "tiny, valiant creature in the face of hopeless odds—small, red, quivering, teeth bared, eyes blazing . . ."[16]

Indeed, in 1948–1949 so many measures affecting the hunting scene were introduced in Parliament—the government was Socialist at the time—that the fox hunters, otter hunters, and beaglers closed ranks and mounted a vigorous counterpropaganda, which included the circulation of petitions and a whispering campaign that the opponents of hunting had adopted Oscar Wilde as their patron saint—a low blow, in view of Wilde's notorious career as a deviate. But Wilde had, after all, categorized the fox-hunting Englishman as "the unspeakable in full pursuit of the inedible." Led by the British Field Sports Society, "mounted fox hunters also sounded their horns in Piccadilly and Regent Street," Mr. E. S. Turner, the British social historian, wrote, "raising echoes even in Soho where hunting horns had sounded centuries before."[17] When the dust had settled, the Protection of Animals Act of 1911, the principal law involved, continued to stand firm and unchanged, denying protection as it always had for those animals which were coursed or hunted.[18]

The Church of England offers no prayer in behalf of animals, nor does it indicate whether kindness to animals is a Christian virtue or cruelty a sin.[19] But some of the clergy observe Animal Sunday on their own motion, and the RSPCA often holds a service in December at St. Martin-in-the-Fields in Trafalgar Square, at which its own Prayer for All Creatures is recited, including the petition, "We pray especially for all that are suffering in any way; for the overworked and underfed, the hunted, lost or hungry, for all in captivity or ill-treated, and for those who must be put to death. We entreat for them Thy mercy and pity; and for those who deal with them we ask a heart of compassion, gentle hands and kindly words."[20]

The service of Blessing the Animals is known in England as well as on the Continent, the collection going to the RSPCA. Young owners of pets clutch cats, dogs, hens, parrots, rabbits, piglets and hamsters, enduring every possible torture from claws and spurs, while wrestling to prevent their pets leaping from their arms to attack an enemy or take French leave altogether.[21]

Vivisection, the overriding animal issue pursued by aggressive ad hoc societies, is not opposed by the RSPCA, if surrounded by precise safeguards. But the society is concerned with the black market in experimental animals and the conduct of laboratory experiments that are redundant or cause animal suffering. It has successfully resisted the introduction of the American rodeo. The handling of food animals remains a problem, including the scratchy question of ritual slaughter.[22] Vegetarianism, which enjoys a degree of public support and respectability in Britain not found in America, is not a part of the RSPCA program, though there is a congenial similarity of view on the abuse of animals reared under stressful conditions by intensive farming techniques. And both vegetarians and meat-eating humanitarians take a sympathetic view of the work of the Right Honorable Lady Muriel Dowding, whose boutiques offer cruelty-free cosmetics under the rubric, "Beauty Without Cruelty."[23]

The society works closely with conservation groups in enforcing the Protection of Birds Act and in meeting the new peril to sea birds from oil spilled or discharged from ships. Prosecutions for cruelty continue when the abuse is flagrant and provable, court convictions covering a broad range of animals, including horses, ponies, donkeys, cattle, sheep, pigs, dogs and cats, caged birds, tortoises, monkeys, and ferrets. The RSPCA, however, knows when to temper vigilance with tact. When Inspector Nolan observed French sports fans enthusiastically waving live cockerels, a favorite Gallic emblem, during a rugby match at the Twickenham football grounds, he was able, despite formidable linguistic complications, to separate the visitors from their unusual patriotic symbols and remand the roosters to an RSPCA animal shelter, including one unfortunate bird that had been abandoned in the wardrobe of a hotel bedroom. In a graceful gesture of consideration for French sensibilities, the RSPCA permitted the chickens to retain their national colors, the tricolor being draped over a tree branch propped up in their quarters.

Today the Royal Society prefers to emphasize its positive role in promoting kindness and the awareness that all life reveals creative wonders that can lift men's hearts. But, with 148 years of experience behind it, the society has become, necessarily, a connoisseur of animal crime. Most violations by adults, it has discovered, entail ignorance, indifference, or neglect, often simply the omission of an act. The tortures that turn the stomach are usually carried out by children, as in the case of the two defendants at Mossley, one a juvenile, who pinned a kitten's ears together and suspended the little animal by a piece of wire in the deep-freeze compartment of a household refrigerator.[24] As a result, an old effort continues, to awaken in children a response to the animal's point of view—anthropopathism in reverse.

The society reviews film scenarios containing animal sequences, especially fake jungle scenes. Unnatural tricks are scrutinized with particular care, where there may have been suffering for the animal in its training, or interestingly enough, where the animal's natural dignity may have been violated.[25] Other areas calling for vigilant concern are conditions in pet stores, the exotic pet trade, the export of live food animals, the cruelties of the fur industry, and the inspection of circus animal acts that the society regards as "pointless" entertainment. It is also critical of zoos for their "quite needless exploitation of animals."[26]

The RSPCA can claim a worldwide influence, since it has branches in Commonwealth countries, maintains close liaison with American organizations and has affiliations with other societies in all parts of the free world. Since animal welfare problems now cross national and geographic boundaries, the RSPCA joined with the Massachusetts Society for the Prevention of Cruelty to Animals some eleven years ago in founding a new agency to meet these conditions, the International Society for the Protection of Animals. Typical of its concerns are seal hunting and whaling, and the impact upon animal life of hydroelectric dams, Asian wars, floods, droughts, and bow-and-arrow safaris.[27]

Members and officers of the RSPCA come from the median to upper levels of English life. Financial support consists of memberships, bequests, and such social fund-raising activities as jumble sales, coffee-and-sherry mornings, gymkhanas, teas, and garden parties. But there have been extraordinary exceptions, as in the instance of a Maltese-born gangster and devoted animal lover. When he was blown to bits by dynamite wired to the ignition of his automobile, the RSPCA found itself, as beneficiary, in control of a chain of twenty-six brothels in Sydney, Australia. Furthermore, the rent was paid in advance.[28]

Problems of the future include some old ones that won't go away: the homeless stray, the abandoned animal, and the appalling surplus population of dogs and cats. Difficult new situations arise that cause stress and suffering, such as long-distance air transportation of wild species and assembly-line methods of animal husbandry, which produce fat but neurotic pigs.[29] Space exploration has added a new martyrdom for animals and a new dilemma for those humans who need no urging from Wordsworth to agree

Never to blend our pleasure or our pride
With sorrow of the meanest thing that feels.

PART

II

Kindness and Cruelty

in the United States

7

Animals in Early America

W hen the English established their plantations on the Atlantic coast of North America, they brought with them, naturally, the tastes of the Elizabethan age in sports and recreation, which included shooting, horse racing, and tormenting animals. These activities were modified and extended as a result of experience in a forested wilderness and contacts with the Indians, who introduced the colonists to spear fishing, deerskin garments, and the ring hunt, a useful device for surrounding game and "varmints."[1]

The ring hunt covered an area perhaps several square miles in extent. Hundreds of men advanced, tightening the lines as they rang bells and sounded horns and rattles, firing their guns, swinging clubs, thrusting with pitchforks as the frantic beasts tried to break through the cordon. Trophies might be in the range of sixty to seventy bears, twenty-five deer, a hundred wild turkeys, innumerable wolves and rabbits. According to one account, the fur shot from the backs of rabbits filled the air like thistledown.[2] As the settlement line moved west there was a change of locale but not of action. Farmer-hunters combined amusement with the gathering of food, while furs and hides were taken for their economic value. In New England men trapped for beaver from earliest times, and until the middle of the eighteenth century Yankee seamen made "feather voyages" to Labrador for eider and other seaduck feathers.[3]

Accurate shooting called for constant practice, and shooting matches became a fixed institution along the border. One technique was to poke the head of a small bird through a hole in a paper, then toss the bird in the air, an excellent diversion for gunnery practice in wet weather, since it could be carried out from the shelter of a shed or barn door. Live targets also spiced the competitive shoots—turkeys, geese, ducks, pigeons, and deer—often held as a feature of stage-tavern life, with the innkeeper providing the target material at so much a shot, with dinner and grog to top off the holiday. As an example of the method, a turkey would be tied to a stake at a distance of eighty or a hundred yards in such a way that only the head and neck were visible and moveable. The prize went to the marksman who first hit the head.[4]

With the passing of the raw frontier, the gunners shot at fixed, inanimate targets to win a beef animal or a barrel of native whiskey.[5] The exciting experience of shooting at something alive still retains its piquancy, and the spirit of the back settlements flourished until 1971—yes, 1971—in Washington County, Wisconsin. For seventeen years before 1971, the Kiwanis Club of Kewaskum tethered turkeys in stalls, with one leg tied to the base and the head exposed to the aim of participants in the annual Kiwanis turkey shoot. The shoot was conducted along the old lines. If the birds broke their wings or legs in their struggles to free themselves, their heads were nevertheless kept jiggling until each fowl was put out of its misery. There were repercussions. Kiwanis International received such massive protests that it threatened to suspend the charter of the local club. With much foot-dragging, the club finally promised to shoot no more at living targets. A bill to impose penalties on persons who use tied or staked birds or animals as targets in a shooting match got as far as a committee hearing in the Wisconsin state senate early in 1971, but further action was stalled by, of all imaginable functionaries, the director of the Wisconsin Bureau of Game Management.[6]

On the frontier there were also such other forms of animal-centered amusement as chasing a greased pig, baiting raccoons, and gander pulling. In this last event, a goose well greased with lard was suspended head down from a pole or crossbar. Competing horsemen galloped past, rising in their stirrups as they tried to grasp the neck and pull the head off the bird. Since the struggling goose was tied by its feet to a slack rope, it oscillated in an arc of four or five feet. As the contestants sped by, their grab produced many wrenches and dislocations and a ceaseless wailing from the bird until it was decapitated. The highest possible accomplishment, accompanied by cheers and a current of excitement sweeping through the crowd of spectators, was when a successful rider pulled off the neck "with the windpipe still screaming after separation from the body."[7] Thomas Gilbert Pearson, early president of the National Association of Audubon Societies, who was later instrumental in putting an end to the trade in bird plumage, witnessed a gander pulling as a boy in Florida. Revolted by what he saw and heard, Pearson remembered the assurance given him by an elderly Negro that the participants were not gentlemen but "pore cracker trash."[8]

Popular taste in the Northeast also ran to baiting animals. Cockfights were staged in the Town House at Salem, Massachusetts, and bull-and-bear fights were advertised in the *Boston Gazette*.[9] New Yorkers were enthusiastic cockers until well into the nineteenth century, and even today evidence occasionally comes to light indicating that the mains are still held in secluded areas of the state. Philadelphians, despite the disapproval of the Quakers, attended cockfights as well as their elegant dancing assemblies, and Pittsburgh in early Federal times was devoted to the fighting chickens, the spectators and handlers willingly risking the three-dollar fine imposed because cocking encouraged idleness, fraud, gambling, and profanity. Dogfights were also available in Allegheny County, and "hog worrying took place without any danger of police interference. . . ."[10]

In the South all the diversions already mentioned flourished under the double impetus of the pioneer mentality and a mimicking of English country life. Especially interesting, therefore, is a letter appearing in the *Virginia Gazette* in the middle of the eighteenth century, protesting against the cockfighting "so much in Vogue here," and denying that a man could use his own property as he pleased if tormenting and killing was what pleased him. So far as hunting was concerned, the abundance of game and the unbounded wilderness effectively prevented hunting, including fox hunting, from becoming the monopoly of those who were gently bred.[11]

Animal populations were decimated without regard for the future of the species, and sometimes, following Indian custom, the settlers burned off the habitat, too. No one knows with certainty the story of early wildlife in Virginia, for example. But it is recorded that three or four men with dogs could kill twenty buffalo in a day, and we know that the passenger pigeon population, vast though it was, reached the point where it couldn't make up its losses.[12] The last buffalo in Virginia was shot in 1797, the last elk in 1855, and the once-abundant cougar or "panther" disappeared in the late eighties. Along the shore, market hunters and trappers slaughtered the waterfowl at such a rate that it was commonplace to fill a wagon box with ducks in an afternoon's shooting. The march toward extinction in the New England towns was no different. Wild animals were hunted relentlessly for meat or fur or to secure the bounties paid on wolves or wildcats. Jeremy Belknap, the historian of early New Hampshire, wrote in the 1790s that deer had actually become scarce in the state.[13]

In the old Southwest—Tennessee, Kentucky, Georgia, Alabama, Louisiana, Mississippi, and Arkansas—where coon hunts and wolf drives were indigenous, the goal was extermination. Out of this climate came the whole corpus of bear-hunting stories and the affectionate names that hunters bestowed upon their guns, "Old Hair-splitter," "Old Blood Letter," or "Old Panther-cooler." A whole countryside would join in the cooperative hunt known as a "squirrel frolic," the winner determined by the tail count. The *Kentucky Gazette* for May 17, 1796, printed the total number of squirrels killed in one day's fun: 7,941.[14] " 'Out West' is certainly a great country . . ." wrote a sprightly correspondent of the New York sporting newspaper, the *Spirit of the Times* in 1851. He continued:

> There is one little town in 'them diggins' which . . . is 'all sorts of a stirring place.' In one day, they recently had two street fights, hung a man, rode three men out of town on a rail, got up a quarter race, a turkey shooting, a gander pulling, a match dog fight, and preaching by a circus [sic] rider, who afterwards ran a footrace for apple jack all round. . . .[15]

One would have to look long and hard to find any trace of compassion toward wildlife. When Friedrich Gerstäcker came to the United States, his head filled with ideas picked up from reading James Fenimore Cooper, wearing his German hunter's costume— forest-green jacket, thigh-high boots—he projected an epic sortie against the native fauna to be found west of the Mississippi. Gerstäcker adopted a jocular tone, calling the bear that fell before his rifle "bruin," and he wrote briskly about bringing down an eagle: "I was pleased with my shot, as it was the first eagle I had killed." He celebrated the moment by putting a feather in his cap. A complete listing of Gerstäcker's trophies—not all of them, unfortunately, clean kills—would comprise most of the fauna of the region, including alligators shot by torchlight. Although he considered them to be "harmless creatures," he was, as he said, "very active in shooting them."[16]

The Far West also turned to the indigenous animal life for its moments of relaxation. When Los Angeles was a Spanish-American town, the Mexican and Indian population assembled in the plaza after Mass to enjoy the cockfights. At Virginia City, Nevada, small boys carried transparencies through the streets on Saturday nights advertising a cockfight at a popular saloon, and in the ranch houses of the Southwest cowpokes relieved the tedium in matching carefully tended tarantulas in finish fights. On the Comstock Lode a rooster provided a variant on the goose pull, and the sports program provided dog-and-panther fights, while the Virginia City Alkali and Sagebrush Sporting Club spurred after greyhounds coursing coyotes.[17]

A flash of compassion for a tormented beast does come through in the account of one observer, John Ross Browne, traveler and author. Browne witnessed what was described as a badger fight at Bodie in which a valiant little beast fought for its life for two hours against successive relays of dogs. Browne begins in light vein, sketching the "very pretty scene," the excitement and jollity of the crowd; but when the badger had bested all the dogs and the spectators finally beat the animal to death with clubs, being unable to dispatch it in any other way, Browne "turned away with a strong emotion of pity . . . there was something about the whole business very much like murder."[18]

In the early national period there continued to be no sharp division between the pastimes of town and country. The cities were still small, the forest and fields easily reached. So urban dwellers also hunted, fished, attended horse races, and enjoyed the " 'Royal Diversion' at the cock pit."[19] The flourishing sporting journals not only reported on bear hunting in the West, but also gave the details of such accessible pleasures as a cockfight held near Hartford, Connecticut, or a pigeon shoot in New Jersey, mingled with retrospective reviews of the last racing season and advertisements of guns, horse goods, and quack patent medicines.[20]

City dwellers were not deprived of the age-old fascination of looking at snakes. At Washington Hall in New York City on July 27, 1821, a diamondback rattlesnake was advertised to strike, poison, and consume a rat; and at about the same time one of the museums of natural wonders in the city was in the market for a hundred rats at six cents each, as snake food.[21] Performances of similar biological interest were available in the City of Brotherly Love. At an exhibition at Masonic Hall in Philadelphia, twelve rats were put in a box with rattlesnakes. One large rat was killed in a minute and later swallowed entire by one of the snakes, "taking the head in first," the *Democratic Press* noted with scientific precision.[22]

Animals figure prominently in American folklore as "apocryphal biology."[23] The impact of the vast, wild, empty continent must have had a shattering effect upon the imaginations of the early planters of the Atlantic colonies. We do not have to guess about this. Persons who had been lost in the forests during the early times reported that they had heard terrible, unexplained roarings, which William Wood, seventeenth-century settler in Massachusetts Bay and author of the rare descriptive work, *New Englands Prospect* (1634), concluded "must eyther be Devills or Lyons." It is significant of the emotional state of the men of the first century of settlement that they commonly described the forest as a "howling wilderness." American notions about the beasts that did the howling have taken two general forms. They relate either to familiar animals behaving in an unfamiliar way or sightings of frightening creatures not previously reported. It is not easy to invent absolutely new animals; everything seems to have been thought of before. But out of the effort to improve upon nature came the distinctive American contribution to the world's store of romantic zoology—the tall tale. Thus in the first century of colonial life, men were titillated by fireside storytellers who described a sea serpent coiled like a gigantic cable on a rock at Cape Ann, or told of a fisherman who saw a merman in Casco Bay.[24]

Later the animal story evolved into a humorous art form. Among those Americans whose names are associated with tales of unlikely beasts are such major figures in American history as Benjamin Franklin and the Reverend Cotton Mather. Dr. Franklin described, for English consumption, we may note, the fatness of life in America in terms of sheep. "The very tails of American sheep," he wrote, "are so laden with wool that each has a little car or wagon on four wheels, to support and keep it from trailing on the ground." He also insisted that whales were so fond of codfish that they pursued them *up* Niagara Falls, making a grand leap, which Franklin said was "esteemed by all who have seen it, as one of the finest spectacles in nature."[25]

More surprising, perhaps, is a bit of nature faking that came from the pen of the Reverend Mather. A bulwark of Boston Calvinism, Mather was presumably no gay deceiver. But he, like all colonial Mathers, had a taste for marvels, especially if they were somewhat gruesome. So we find the great Puritan clergyman, who was enormously proud of being a member of the Royal Society of London, the oldest scientific society in Great Britain, passing on to his colleagues an item of unnatural natural history that he had uncritically accepted. If a rattlesnake bit the edge of an ax, Mather told the society, the color of the metal changed, and the next time the ax was used, the discolored section would chip out because of the power of the poison, leaving a gap where the serpent had struck the blade.[26]

Our oral tradition is rich in myths about beasts, squirrels who have crossed rivers by launching a shingle or piece of bark and hoisting their tails for sails, beavers who used their tails for trowels, alligators whose teeth, if taken from the right jaw, have been found to restore the waning powers of aging human males.²⁷ Not less wonderful than Aesop's animals that could talk, or Pliny's dolphins that carried human riders, or the dragons killed by Beowulf, are the creatures of our own indigenous folklore. "From Maine to Idaho," wrote Ben C. Clough, "from the Adirondacks to Arkansas, unlikely creatures crawl, prowl, whine, and roar through the jungles of the American imagination."²⁸

Marvelous new zoological discoveries followed the opening of the West, among them the hodag, the whifflehoople, the side-hill gouger, the squonk, the gumberoo, and the wampus. In a wild, new land of magnificent distances, reports of fearful and wonderful brutes were not easily verified and not easily dismissed. Why, then, could there not be a snake capable of taking its tail in its mouth and rolling like a wheel toward its prey? Or a reptile able to kill cattle by lashing with its powerful tail?

Let us take a closer look at one genus for a moment, the hoofer, or side-hill gouger, whose scientific name is *Membriinequalis declivitatis*. It flourished in hilly or mountainous country. There the beast evolved most peculiarly, for it had two long legs on the downhill side and two short legs on the uphill side, and looked like a cross between a buffalo and a mountain goat. It was dangerous, but easy to avoid. One took a couple of steps downhill if the animal charged, for it could not turn without falling and breaking its neck.²⁹ Another zoological novelty is the augerino, an enormous worm shaped like a corkscrew. The augerino drills or burrows underground and exists for the sole purpose of letting water out of irrigation ditches. Perhaps you have heard of this rare specimen, the goofus bird, which may have given us the verb *to goof*. The goofus bird inhabited heavily timbered areas and flew backward instead of forward because, said old lumberjacks who were familiar with its habits, "it doesn't give a darn where it's going, it only wants to know where it's been."³⁰

Some of our handed-down beliefs about domestic animals clearly descend from European analogues, such as the opinion that black cats are a sign of bad luck. The folklorist Gordon Wilson collected an item in Calloway County, Kentucky, that is also well known in the Old World, the legend that farm animals kneel at midnight on Christmas Eve. He said, however, that no one in the county had ever gone out to the barn to check on the story. According to a tradition that came down to his mother through her family, an observer would not have seen anything unusual because the animals did their kneeling on Old Christmas Eve, now January fifth. Wilson adds a nice touch in commenting: "It is possible that the cattle and other stock were still living under the Julian calendar."[31]

Although the concept of kindness to animals had no place in the common law, certain species enjoyed a measure of protection because they had economic value. Their abuse, however, had to constitute a public nuisance and any injury be proved to involve malice toward the animal's owner. One instance of humane legislation did exist in colonial America, dating back to the seventeenth century, which places it almost two centuries earlier than similar laws in England. In the spring of 1638 the General Court of Massachusetts turned its attention from exterminating the Pequots to the compilation of a legal code. The work was carried out by the Reverend Nathaniel Ward, a university man, trained as a barrister though he had entered the Church, who then turned Puritan and emigrated to Massachusetts, where he had held a pastorate at Ipswich.[32]

Ward's compendium was formally adopted by the court in the session of November 1641, and was revered for the rest of the century as scarcely less a bulwark of freedom than the common law of England or the Magna Carta. The work, called "The Body of Liberties," was more than a codification, for it included new principles. The ninety-second section, entitled "Off the Bruite Creature," provided that "No man shall exercise any Tirranny or Crueltie towards any bruite Creature which are usuallie kept for man's use." The following section added, "If any man shall have occasion to leade or drive Cattel from place to place that is far of, so that they be weary, or hungry, or fall sick, or lambe, It shall be lawful to rest or refresh them, for competant time, in any open place that is not Corne, meadow, or inclosed for some peculiar use."[33]

Thus Massachusetts takes first place among the governments of the Western world for having elevated mercy into law. Yet one must remember that the Boston Puritans were men of their own time. They had discarded the saints, but not the Devil. They continued to believe in the reality of an invisible world in which witches operated against mankind, sometimes entering the bodies of animals to accomplish their malign purposes. It was logical, then, if the premises are admitted, in that horrible episode at Salem in the hot summer of 1692, that two dogs were hanged along with nineteen Massachusetts men and women for refusing to make any answer to the indictment charging them with the practice of witchcraft.[34]

Let us turn to a more pleasant subject. "With the exception of an occasional hanging," wrote the late scholar, bibliographer, museum director, and circus buff, R. W. G. Vail, "our robust ancestors had very little in the way of entertainment until the arrival of the menagerie and equestrian show," and Vail then proceeds with great urbanity and erudition to assemble the evidence.[35] Wild animal exhibitions began when a hunter who had captured a young animal turned it over to a tavern keeper, precursor of the gas station zoo operator. Wandering showmen presented a dancing bear act on the village green or exhibited a horse trained to "make his manners to the ladies and gentlemen." Sometimes the solitary showman penetrated the back country with a monkey and hand organ. A stroller would drift into a taproom and play the fiddle or a flute while his dog did tricks to the tune. One man, one animal.

Then little menageries were formed, managing to be present on market or court days to astonish a country-bred audience happy to stare at a tame bear or the "Cattamount" which was viewed at the Gray Hound in Roxbury, Massachusetts, with "a Tail like a Lyon, its legs are like a Bears, its Claws like an Eagle, its Eyes like a Tyger, it's Countenance . . . a mixture of everything that is Fierce and Savage." Furthermore, the advertisement said, the animal could leap thirty feet at one jump though only three months old. All of this constituted "a great Moral and educational exhibition" and could be seen for only a shilling.

A camel appeared in New York City in 1739. Admirers were reminded that the camel figures frequently in the Scriptures, which made a visit to the show practically obligatory as an act of piety.

While an occasional monkey came into the Atlantic ports as the

pet or property of a common seaman, it was the shrewd Yankee
captains who introduced the larger animals from distant lands.
Boston was the first town to see such exotics. A "Lyon" was on
show "at Mrs. Adam's at the South End" in the first quarter of the
eighteenth century, then shipped out for the West Indies in 1726.
Happily, he returned to pay further visits to Philadelphia and
New York, still known simply as "*the* Lyon," which strongly
suggests that there was no other. There are similar reports that a
camel reached our shores in 1721, a polar bear in 1733, and at last,
in 1796, the Yankee nation gaped at its first elephant. The colonial
schoolboys had read descriptions and seen crude woodcuts of
pachyderms in their geography books or the almanac that hung in
the family kitchen. Now, at long last, came the thrilling word of
the safe arrival of a two-year-old female from Bengal.

The hero of this event was Captain Jacob Crowninshield, one of
the young scions of the great sailing and trading family of Salem.
The energetic captain, who at the age of twenty-four years had
already made several voyages to India, bought the beast at Calcutta
as a speculation, paying $450 for it. He wrote to his brother of his
unique purchase, "It will be a great thing to carry the first elephant
to America."

The young captain was obviously well aware that the exhibition
of animals was a growing form of entertainment. Crowninshield
left port in his ship, *America*, in December 1795, carrying coffee,
Indian textiles, the elephant, and a large gallonage of water, stopping at Saint Helena to take aboard, according to the ship's log,
"greens for the elephant." There were adventures and alarms. In
the Caribbean the *America* was hove to by four British warships
patrolling the Bermuda station, England and France being at war
at the time, but the search party permitted the *America* to proceed.
On April 13, 1796, the ship docked at New York with the elephant
safe and sound, a whopping six feet and four inches high. Captain
Crowninshield had hoped the beast would bring him perhaps
$5,000, but it went for $10,000, netting a handsome $9,550 profit on
the original investment. The *New York Argus* reported that this was
"the greatest price ever given for an animal in Europe or America." Crowninshield rather looked for a psychic profit, too, in the
form of credit and fame for his coup. But his name was never
mentioned in the advertising of the animal during its later travels,

despite the fact that the captain became wealthy and a congressman.

A Philadelphian named Owen purchased the elephant, which
was described in the *Aurora* as possessing

> the adroitness of the beaver, the intelligence of the ape, and the
> fidelity of the dog. He is the largest of quadrupeds; the earth
> trembles under his feet. He has the power of tearing up the
> largest trees and yet is tractable to those who use him well.

The people of the Atlantic states saw the elephant for years, from
a crossroads hamlet in North Carolina through the seaboard cities,
then eastward along the coast of New England. On one occasion
the big animal hurried to attend the commencement exercises at
Harvard College, later played a stand in Boston "at Mr. Valen-
tine's Market Square," where admittance was half a dollar, after-
ward reduced to a quarter.

The reader will notice that the beast was referred to as "he," but
the Reverend William Bentley of Salem was not misled by "the
common language" as he confided to his diary: "It is a female &
teats appeared just behind the fore-legs." Little is known of the
later life of the first American elephant, but she may have been
killed in 1822. She bore no name, nor needed any, for as her
admirer, Dr. Vail, said, "She was *the* elephant." It was the spectacular career of this unnamed yet famous creature that may have
given us the folk expression *to see the elephant*, meaning to see the
sights, or to gain experience in life.

Strange animals reached the United States in increasing numbers in the first half of the nineteenth century: royal tigers, an
orangutan, ostriches, a live seal, an ape that appeared in the costume of a sailor, dromedaries, rhinos, giraffes, and anacondas. The
peripatetic wanderer gave way to the caravan, the caravan to the
modern circus. A quite separate attraction was the equestrian
show, which by about the middle of the century merged with the
menageries to form the one-ring tent show.

The animal performers were, of course, prisoners, trundled
about in a life of unremitting exploitation. They were still, as a
practical matter, Descartes' clocks, there to be used. This was the
standard attitude in all levels of society. At the top, let us take

Professor Louis Agassiz, the Harvard College zoologist. Lecturing on "The Animal Kingdom," Agassiz declared that men have a body and a soul, a body similar to that of animals, but a soul participating in "the Divine Nature." The earth existed for man, who "stands at the summit of animal being . . . the head of Creation. . . ."[36] At the other end of the social scale may be cited the words of a veteran plume hunter who was being criticized for slaughtering terns on the beaches of North Carolina. Objecting to the objection, the old man replied: "The good Lord put us here and the Good Book says, 'man shall have dominion over all creatures.' They're ourn to use."[37]

The universe was still made for men only.

8

The Trek to the Cities

When Americans in significant numbers began to make the great transition from farm to city, they were shaped by a rural tradition and found it natural to bring their animals with them. The rural code for the treatment of animals was not especially humane. But a code of sorts did exist, based upon a degree of respect and the exchange of services when a man fed and milked his own cow and raised his own pig. Economic self-interest introduced some rudimentary consideration of cats as protectors of the grain bin, and of chickens, dogs, goats, geese, and horses. All of these satellite companions moved into town with their owners as a matter of course.

New York City furnishes a paradigm of the problems that arose. When the island of Manhatten was still New Netherland, little more than a fort and a trading post, ordinances were passed prohibiting domestic animals from roaming the streets. In the English period that followed, laws were piled one on the other, passed and repassed, but the complaints continued of the damage done to

76

orchards and gardens and of the absolute need for penning. But the
laws were easier to pass than to enforce.

In all seaboard cities the dog population soared during the eighteenth century, and rangy, long-legged town hogs were continuously at war with what the despairing selectmen of Boston called "curst & unruly doggs & bitches." Newport's roadways must have resembled a barnyard, for the town records for 1703 noted that there were so many hogs on the loose that children were "in danger of being destroyed by them," and the town fathers made a special effort to "get some Persons to bury all the Dead Doggs . . . that lye in ye streets of this Town." Boston at about the same time tried to cope with the nuisance by applying a means test for the ownership of a dog, requiring an annual income of twenty pounds, and permitting only one pet to a household. The Philadelphia authorities ruled out absolutely any "great Dogs" within the city limits. All attempts to control the dog population ended in failure until the fear of rabies became widespread. Then, the incidence of hydrophobia after the middle of the century led to Draconian methods of control.[1]

Animals, dead and alive, continued to plague the city inspectors of New York throughout the nineteenth century. The metropolis grew too fast for sanitation methods to keep up with its expansion, and the populace continued to ignore the stock laws. Dead animals lay where they fell or were carted off to vacant lots or dumped on the shores of the once-sparkling Collect Pond. In 1842 an estimated 10,000 hogs ranged the streets and sidewalks of the city.[2] "Take care of the pigs," Charles Dickens warned when he tried to cross lower Broadway, and he added, "a select party of half a dozen gentlemen hogs have just now turned the corner. . . ."[3]

On the eve of the Civil War, most of New York's piggeries, which were concentrated on the West Side, had been moved north of Eighty-sixth Street, except for small sties of less than four pigs, which were permitted to remain, and it was ordered that cattle could not be driven in the streets south of Forty-second Street except at night.[4] The human population soon after the end of the war approached the million mark. Nearly half of the city's inhabitants lived in squalid courts, rookeries, alleys, cellars, and "fever nests" known by such pejorative names as "Cat Alley," "Cow Bay," "Rag Picker's Row," "Murderer's Alley," or "Bummers'

Retreat." Some 10,000 abandoned children lived on the streets as outcasts and existed by blacking boots, peddling, and stealing.[5]

Public transportation was by horse-drawn street cars or omnibuses, most lines converging at the Astor House and City Hall, with route markings displayed on the outside of the vehicles. At night they were illuminated by colored lamps, which formed a perspective of long lines of red, green, and blue lights, rising and falling with the motion of the coaches and the contours of the cobblestone pavement.[6] Along Broadway, in the neighborhood of Fulton Street, there was a continual churning of carts, carriages, trucks, drays, and omnibuses wedged together as some 18,000 vehicles passed a given point each day. The city was noisy. But the noises were different from those we know now. Iron tires rang on the granite-block paving. Horses neighed. The curses of the carmen mingled with the shouts of the "Broadway squad," swinging their whips to disentangle blockades caused by locked wheels.

Added to the din was music of a sort—the tootling of a German band, the mechanical notes of a hand organ. Hawkers cried their wares—apple women, newsboys, vendors of peanuts, hot chestnuts, or maps of Ireland—working the city's main stem from the Battery north to Grace Church. Alarm bells clanged suddenly in the fire department's watchtowers, and a riot was always a possibility when the Irish paraded the Fenian flag. If New York had become a city of noise, it might also be characterized as a city of smells. Chatham Street (now Park Row) was known for its junk and scrap metal yards, its fetid rag and bone depositories. Near the island's water boundaries, one caught the whiff of bilge water, sewer gas, and that necessary consequence of the Horse Age, immense dumps of rotting horse manure. The odor of ammonia from the street railway stables was widely diffused, since the street railroad corporations violated the Sanitary Code with impunity.[7]

Offensive trades were distributed all through the city: slaughterhouses, stables, swill-milk nuisances, and gut-cleaning establishments that manufactured sausage casings. An ordinary nose could detect the presence of one of these concerns "for a full mile and a half from the building".[8] Most of the smells of animal origin have been eliminated from American cities by pesticides, modern architecture, which offers poor harborage to inquilines, and the disappearance of horses and livery stables, flies and sparrows. Whether the tail-pipe odors of unburned automobile hydrocarbons are less harmful or disagreeable is an arguable proposition.[9]

As New York pushed northward in the 1860s, the streets below Central Park were, according to George Templeton Strong, lawyer, Columbia University trustee, and Trinity Church vestryman and diarist of the period, "a rough and ragged track . . . rich in mudholes, goats, pigs, geese and stramonium [jimson weed]. Here and there [stood] Irish shanties . . . composed of a dozen rotten boards and a piece of stove-pipe for a chimney." Trash and refuse were collected by shanty boys who drove dog or horse carts. Swill and garbage were fed to the squatter-town goats and hogs, especially the hogs, for pig raising was an active form of animal husbandry in the area. According to a survey made in 1865, there were eighteen pig pens in the one block bounded by Sixth and Seventh avenues and Fifty-first and Fifty-second streets.[10] Only recently—work began in 1857—had Central Park ceased to be the setting for squatters' huts, stagnant marshes, hog farms, and open sewers. Notices, enclosed in a rustic frame, were mounted at the entrances of the park to warn: "All persons are forbidden to turn cattle, horses, goats or swine into the Park."[11]

Rarer zoological specimens could be inspected by visiting "a large and peculiar-looking building near Sixty-fourth street . . . formerly used by the State as an arsenal . . ." It was fitted up as a museum of natural history and surrounded with cages of live animals and birds.[12] There one could catch the exciting smell of the wild. Strong, a frequent visitor at the Central Park zoo, scoffed at it nevertheless as consisting "of donations sent in and received without any system; sundry bears, black bears and a grizzly bear, priarie dogs, foxes, beautiful ocelots, owls, eagles, two meek camels, pheasants, monkeys, macaws, etc."[13] Yet it is interesting to notice that the diarist was always going back to see the animals again, writing after one such occasion, "No man can look at a menagerie, without the dim, awful perception of a great mystery . . . when you watch, for example, the cruel eyes of some living leopard or tiger, the kindly expression of the antelopes. . . . The animal creation is a mystery of mysteries."[14]

Other animal-oriented diversions available to New Yorkers included P. T. Barnum's well-publicized American Museum, where his beasts paced away the tedium of their lives in cages, which it was thought, by those who thought about it at all, were entirely too small. Another common sight around 1870 was a performing bear, muzzled and wearing a ring through his nose. The animal, imported from Austria, roamed the streets with his master, who sang a song while the bear, rearing up on his hind legs, moved in circles in clumsy imitation of dancing. At about the same time a showman was exhibiting "Wicked Ben," a learned pig. This entertainment took place in a basement in Broad Street. It became quite a fad for stockbrokers, after the close of the market, to play cards with the animal. The beast stood upon a dias and played euchre and poker with his human adversaries by pointing to his card with his snout. According to the recollection of a contemporary, the hog was a frequent winner.[15]

The Bowery boys and the "fancy"—sporting gentry—patronized hidden arenas devoted to various forms of bloodletting. These *recherché* entertainments were carried out, necessarily, in the rear of stables, in cellars, or in the back rooms of saloons, since dogfights, ratting, and cocking mains had been outlawed in New York State since 1856. Animal fights also flourished in New Jersey, where at Ludlow's Hotel in Union Hill the impresario of the cockpit called out regularly, "Come, gentlemen—come out with your tin: the main is goin' to begin."[16] These events were not peculiar to New York. Philadelphia offered a spectacle in which a man joined the dogs in a rat killing, and a report from Saint Louis on a Christmas Eve described how one Patsy Brennan, a pugilist, fought a Siberian bloodhound for forty-five minutes, the man emerging from the battle with dreadful lacerations, the dog so badly maimed that it died within an hour.[17]

On a higher level, socially speaking, heavy swells retired to Long Island to course rabbits with greyhounds or shoot pigeons tossed into the air from traps. The birds were often first damaged in a wing or blinded in one eye, to create interesting flight patterns for the gun. It is a reminder of the element of coarseness that ran through metropolitan life in the last century to leaf through the *Recollections of Old New York* as set down by Frederick Van Wyck. Van Wyck recalled, in what may be regarded as a kind of bar mitzvah rite among the old aristocracy, that at the age of seventeen he saw his first stag show in a livery stable on Eighth Street in Greenwich Village. The performances included a dogfight as a curtain raiser, a cockfight, a ratting, a butting match between two goats, and a boxing match starring two topless human females.[18]

The most abundant bird in American cities was the so-called English sparrow, which was neither English nor a sparrow but a European house finch. The bird was first introduced in Brooklyn in the 1850s as a sentimental importation from England. For a time the messy, quarrelsome birds were the objects of a craze. "I feed our dear little Gramercy Park sparrows every afternoon now from the library windows," George Templeton Strong wrote in 1870. But by the eighties the "sparrow mania" had passed, and the bird was universally detested. A schoolboy with a slingshot may have been compelled to learn that Henry Wadsworth Longfellow had wept when he shot a robin, but he also knew that no tears would be shed for the fall of an English sparrow. In fact, in 1887 it became a misdemeanor in New York State to give food or shelter to the noisy bird whose domestic habits definitely did not conform to the standards of Victorian morality.[19]

Dogs were regularly used to pull milk or rag carts or operate a moving display in a shop window. An animal that was a picturesque feature of urban life was the capuchin monkey, the sprightly and clever assistant of the street-organ musicians. The monkey, decked out in the colorful uniform of a Zouave, was an effective collector of pennies from servant girls who lolled over area railings and the delight of little boys hanging out of upper-story windows, enthralled to see that a monkey could climb the drainpipes of the smoothest brownstone front, take off his cap, and hold it out for small coins.[20] Account must also be taken of the forms of life that moved into the city without assistance or encouragement from man—rats, mice, silverfish, clothes moths, and the like. Nor can one exclude from mention the internal parasites of man, which also made the trek to the city.[21]

Hard-faced curbstone pitchmen stood along Broadway, often wearing costumes that made them look like awnings or barber poles, offering bear cubs and puppies in baskets or holding cage birds in their hands, trusting to their merchandise to make its own emotional appeal. In the wholesale meat trades, dealers in fowl carried their ducks and chickens head down and plucked them while the birds were still alive, while calves, gagged and tied, were handled in piles at the ferries of New York and carted like bags of grain to the abattoirs. There calves were bled up to six times before the slaughter because of a belief that a slow death produced whiter veal.[22] A similar indifference to suffering marked the transportation of food animals by rail. These abuses were only ameliorated some twenty years after the time period of this chapter by the intervention of Congress, using its power to regulate interstate commerce.

When cattle arrived live from the West in the post-Civil War period, they were driven into New York City from the North River, hustled, beaten, prodded, and screamed at while the frantic animals dashed through the streets with lolling tongues and bloodshot eyes, raising a dust storm and sweeping pedestrians from the sidewalks. "Through the very busiest part of the town they go, stopping business, frightening horses, filling eyes, mouths and clothes with dust, stopping travel"—it is *Frank Leslie's Illustrated Newspaper* speaking in 1866—"getting even into Broadway, and at last reaching the pens of the slaughterhouses on the east side . . . to be turned into beef. . . ."[23] Not all of the steers reached the end of their journey. It was frequently said that no drover could expect to herd his cattle past "Rotten Row" in Laurens Street and leave the neighborhood with the same number of animals he had when he entered it.

For many years cattle remained a hazard of New York life. As late as 1889 a Mrs. George O. Foster, wife of a salesman, was knocked down by a runaway cow, which broke her collarbone and two ribs. In the same year an ox escaped from a cattle boat at the foot of West Fortieth Street. The animal was chased and shot at by a mob, which harried it east and south as far as Fifth Avenue and Twenty-fifth Street. The beast was finally subdued by the police, with generous participation on the part of the citizenry. At the end of the affair, the animal was bleeding from thirty bullet wounds. It died, however, for a quite different reason. A stranger quietly cut its throat.[24] Industrious pigs continued to investigate uncollected garbage as of yore, and straying horses constituted a real peril. We know this was the case because it was legally determined that if a horse on a sidewalk kicked a passerby, "it is immaterial whether its act was vicious or merely playful: the owner is liable in either case."[25]

Tradition has it that Mrs. Horace Greeley, wife of the famous newspaper editor and candidate for the presidency, kept goats in the backyard of the Greeley residence on Nineteenth Street. But the real domain of goatdom in the 1880s extended from 110th Street to 125th Street, and from Morningside Drive to Riverside Drive on the west. One disenchanted observer once counted sixty-seven goats visible at one time in the neighborhood of Riverside Drive and 110th Street dining on park grass, private shrubbery, flowers, and in one instance, lace curtains.[26] Jacob A. Riis, in his classic work of social reporting, *Children of the Tenements*, describes a scene on West Forty-sixth Street in which thirteen goats were dozing in doorways, foraging in gutters, and knocking over the ash barrels. It was decided by the residents of "Hell's Kitchen" that the goats were a nuisance and must go for mutton. But at the last moment they were pardoned. Public opinion, it turned out, could not be effectively mobilized against Jenny. As a Mrs. Buckley said: "She ain't as bad as they lets on."[27]

Present but less visible on the animal scene were the large, whiskered, brown wharf rats (*Epimys norvegicus*), which had displaced the black rat in the Western world some two hundred years earlier and reached American shores during the Revolution. The big brown rats infested the waterfront, the cellars, drains, and dark tenements where the only touch of greenery was a cabbage leaf wilting on a broken flagstone or the mold on the bedroom wall. The brown rat was vicious. Often an old buck was capable of putting up a fight that would make a cat forget all about dining on fresh rat meat. No one knows how many rats there were. But recently the New York Health Department has concluded that the number of rats in New York today is about equal to the city's human population. A century ago there were probably more rats than people, because of the larger slum areas, more succulent garbage, and the number of wooden buildings then existing.[28]

It should be pointed out that the rats were not without some redeeming social and economic value. They helped to reduce the piles of refuse in the streets when the sanitation department failed to appear. And they had a modest monetary value, being worth a nickel each at the dog pits, where a good ratting terrier could dispose of a hundred rodents in thirty to thirty-five minutes. One gifted dog, named "Jack Underhill," once finished off a hundred rats in eleven and a half minutes in Secaucus, New Jersey.[29]

A large distilling industry flourished in New York in the fifties and sixties, producing as a by-product spent mash or "distillery slop." This was a watery substance that contained cereal nutrients useful as cattle feed. But it had to be consumed quickly. So the swill was turned into milk at slop dairies maintained near the still houses; for example, at Johnson's distillery at West Sixteenth Street and Tenth Avenue there were two to four thousand cows tightly confined in low sheds with no exercise, no litter, slurping up the warm mash, often mixed with restaurant kitchen scraps and sweepings from the slaughterhouses[30]. One stable in the Williamsburg section of Brooklyn was found where the cows were chained to their troughs with a lateral play for their heads of six inches. For such beasts there was no hope of release until their teeth dropped out, their tails rotted off, and the dead cart came for them[31]. Officially, there was nothing to be done. The city departments that had jurisdiction were blocked by political influences from carrying out serious inspections or from prosecuting violators of the regulations.

These conditions led to a severe arraignment of the dairy industry in *Frank Leslie's Illustrated Newspaper*, which combined a rowdy tone, effective pictorial journalism, and a social conscience in attacking the twin issues of venal public officials and cruelty to animals. Angry citizens and the New York Academy of Medicine joined the crusade, which became known as the "stump-tail cow" campaign, against the dairy interests that sold distillery-mash fluid, made and watered in New York City, but offered to the public as "Pure Orange County Milk," or "Ridgwood Grass-Fed Milk." Grateful citizens presented the publisher, Frank Leslie, with a watch and chain "whose gold links were shaped to resemble the lost tails of the martyred cows." The attached charm showed three aldermen whitewashing a stump-tailed cow[32]. The revelations of municipal corruption during this affair were utilized by Paul Leicester Ford in his popular sociological novel, *The Honorable Peter Stirling* (1894), dealing with the fight of a "practical idealist" against political grafters and the swill-milk vendors.

A universal feature of urban life in the nineteenth century was the annual rabies scare, occurring in July and August when, according to an ancient superstition, dogs went mad. Homer refers in the *Iliad* to a disease that was probably rabies, and it was recognized by Democritus and Aristotle. In the minds of the ancients, the affection was associated with the incidence of the "dog days" in the summertime when Sirius, or Canicula, the great white star in the constellation Canis Major, brightest in the heavens, rose and set with the sun in the latitude of the Mediterranean basin. It was a spooky time. Ponds stagnated, snakes went blind, and any dog that ran when chased and opened its mouth to perspire was deemed to be rabid. A more realistic interpretation is that the infection appeared to occur especially in the late summertime because more animals were then in circulation.

It was a season of indiscriminate slaughter. New York City waged a war of extermination against the dogs. The efforts of official dogcatchers were supplemented by those attracted by bounty payments available to all at fifty cents for each dog. Dog killers scoured the streets and alleys, clubbing every animal found, spattering gore in a relentless search for victims. The system produced an active trade in family pets as well as strays. Street boys used a decoy dog to attract others, and even raided Brooklyn, Hoboken, and Jersey City for new supplies to be sold in New York at no expense except a five-cent ferry ride.

The animals that reached the city dog pound alive were drowned each evening at sundown at the foot of East Thirty-first Street, in what a reporter facetiously called "a comfortable tank." One New York resident reported having redeemed his dog at the pound eleven times in five weeks. He finally made a deal with the thief not to steal his animal upon payment of a dollar a week. When the control program became a public scandal, the bounty was reduced to twenty-five cents. The young dog peddlers, who sold their catch to middlemen at a discount, complained indignantly that canocide didn't pay at only a quarter for a dog[33].

Stories about biting dogs were regularly reported in the press without investigation of what the human who was bitten may have done first, but when a policeman shot a dog it was described routinely as being mad. Old newspaper files do disclose one serio-comic affair in which an excess of zeal on the part of the dogcatchers collided with a segment of the New York public that was enthusiastically pro-dog. It was a hot July afternoon in the late eighties. Three men with a load of captured dogs spied Nathan Weisbaum's little spitz investigating a fish head in front of Weis-

baum's fish store at 53 Hester Street. Two of the catchers took off
in hot pursuit of the spitz, which fled up two flights of stairs at
number 51 to take sanctuary in Jacob Kraus's bedroom. Meanwhile, a hostile crowd had gathered around the cart, which the
driver unwisely left unattended to chase a boy who had snatched
his whip. When the panting agents returned from an unsuccessful
effort to seize the Weisbaum pet, they found that their horse had
vanished and a cheering crowd was happily releasing the wagon-
load of dogs. There was some pistol play, and one bullet creased
Nathan Weisbaum's wrist. The dogcatchers landed in the neo-
Egyptian splendors of The Tombs prison, in default of bail. It was
a glorious afternoon for free men and free dogs at the corner of
Hester and Essex streets![34]

9

Horses Are Cheaper Than Oats

The most visible of all city animals in nineteenth-century America were the hundreds of thousands of horses that turned the wheels of commerce and provided public and private transportation. Nowhere was this more evident than in the elongated parallelogram of the city and county of New York. In the early part of the century longshoremen, clerks, ship chandlers, sailmakers, coopers, and employees of ropewalks, shipyards, distilleries, and sugar refineries lived near their work. Small merchants had their living space above their shops. With the development of large-scale trade and manufacturing, the old residential areas of the lower island were squeezed out. Workers who insisted upon living within walking distance of the harbor had to accept cramped, dark, squalid tenement-house life. For "the old walking city" could no longer contain the metropolis. Twenty-six steam ferries were bringing in a large working population from Brooklyn and New Jersey, and solid blocks of row houses pushed north so steadily that by 1860 Manhattan island was heavily settled to Forty-second Street and somewhat beyond. By 1867 a large, urban population was living as far as four miles from City Hall.[1] During the business day the streets were choked with traffic, and at night some 30,000 drays, vans, and express wagons stood in the roadways, an interference with street cleaning and fire protection, a dumping place for ashes and garbage, and a home away from home for the city's goat population. It was the duty of the Bureau of Incumbrances to remove the vehicles to "the corporate yard"— New York's first towaway program. But the bureau, it was complained, never got on top of the problem.[2]

Mass transportation was urgently needed. The first facility was the omnibus. The French term *omnibus* came into American usage in the 1830s to describe a horse-drawn vehicle, also popularly called the "city stage." It carried about a dozen passengers over a fixed route.at a fixed fare of six cents, later reduced to a nickel because of the competition from the horse-drawn streetcars.[3] The stages were a compromise between the long-distance stagecoach and the expensive hackney coaches, forerunners of the taxicab. They developed as a means of moving people in other places as well as New York, in Philadelphia, Boston, Brooklyn, and Baltimore. Decorative panels were painted on the sides of the New York stages, and they bore distinguished names, such as "Lady Washington" or "De Witt Clinton." But they were dirty and crowded and raced madly to compete for passengers, zigzagging from side to side of the street to pick up or discharge fares. Often there were surreptitious races, which left the vehicles hopelessly wedged together and caused "barricades."

The stage drivers were known in journalism as "jehus." There was no need to explain the reference to a generation steeped in biblical lore: ". . . and the driving *is* like the driving of Jehu, the son of Minshi, for he driveth furiously." Today's subway riders may derive a crumb of comfort from knowing that martyrdom was defined as riding in a New York omnibus, whose progress over the cobblestones was "a perfect Bedlam."[4] "Life," wrote one woman visitor to New York in 1854, after dodging wheels and hoofs, "is so fearfully insecure;" and a young father, returning to America after a long stay in Paris, wrote to a friend in anxiety, "Is it really necessary to carry a pistol in New York? . . ."[5]

The usual motive power for the stages was a team of horses. But there were also immense stages available for custom work, great arks pulled by twelve horses and capable of transporting the Ninth Ward Chowder Club to Sheepshead Bay for a go at the clams.[6] It was in New York that the idea first caught on of laying rails in the streets. One horse could do the work of three or four in drawing a vehicle over the smooth rails. The horsecars traveled a third faster than the buses, and could carry from forty to seventy-four passengers with fearful overloads beyond that during rush hours.[7]

There was resistence to the horse railroads. Right-thinking Philadelphians were outraged at the idea of railroad tracks in Chestnut and Walnut streets. But the politicians found the awarding of street railroad franchises an agreeable and profitable activity, and the horsecars, offering a new mobility at a democratic price of five cents a ride, were soon accepted as "the improvement of the age." For some forty years they dominated American urban transport, until they were succeeded by the cable car and the electric streetcar.[8] In New York after the late fifties the City Council required that the steam railroad cars be pulled into the central city by horses and mules, preferring animal power, manure, and sparrows to the noise, smoke, and danger of the locomotives. At one time the horses dragged the coaches all the way to Chambers Street, preceded by a man on horseback carrying a flag.[9]

The horsecars were not luxurious. They had no cushions, no heat, no floor covering except a scattering of musty straw. But in their peak period there were 1,500 of them in New York, and 12,000 horses labored to keep them moving.[10] For the country as a whole there were in 1882 415 horse railroads, with 100,000 animals trotting and clopping along the "horseway" between the rails, pulling 18,000 vehicles after them.[11]

Horsecar crews were supposed to be polite and courteous, the conductor throwing off drunks and dead beats with exquisite tact and judgment and only when the car was not moving. The rule book said the driver was to "speak pleasantly to teamsters . . . who may be in the way, kindly requesting them to move. . . ." Horses were to be treated with consideration, too, walked around curves, never galloped uphill, their hooves to be continually scrutinized for loose shoes, wounds from nails, or signs of spavin in the legs. Most cars were double-enders pulled by two or sometimes four horses, although the papers frequently described and deplored an economical "nuisance" called the "bobtail" or "jigger" car, which had only one horse and no conductor. The jiggers were finally discarded and sold off to begin a new life in Jersey City, Syracuse, Lowell, Allentown, Pennsylvania, and Findlay, Ohio.[12]

It was a matter of common observation to one who cared to look that New York was a hell for car horses. On the evening of February 11, 1868, for instance, a Third Avenue car was seen carrying sixty persons inside the car, with forty on the platforms and others both on the roof and hanging out the windows. The weight of the load was estimated at 21,000 pounds, with two feeble horses struggling to move the car up the steep grade that then existed between Twenty-second and Thirty-sixth streets.[13] Sometimes a pedestrian with an ear attuned to that kind of thing could hear the labored breathing of the horses as far as a block away. Yet the streetcar companies seemed to exercise a mesmeric influence upon the legislature at Albany when the question arose of placing a legal limit on the number of passengers a horse might transport, and the magistrates pondered long and abstractly over such an arcane question as, "Is it overloading a horse to overload a streetcar and then attach it to the horse?" A favorite trick of the railroad companies was to bring out the lame animals for duty at night, when their condition would be less evident.[14]

Car company horses were habitually underfed. Dirty, unventilated stables made the animals easy victims of such equine diseases as glanders and farcy. Salting the car tracks for snow removal was illegal, but it was done, with the result that the hooves of the horses often sloughed off from the irritation. On one occasion 122 horses passed City Hall in an hour's time with fetlocks wrapped in bandages as a result of working in the salty slush.[15] Straining to start overloaded cars produced spavins, so that the American Society for the Prevention of Cruelty to Animals, the pioneer animal welfare society in America, was impelled to furnish neatly printed cards to those city railroads which would accept them, to be mounted in each horse car. Their message:

SPARE THE HORSE

To relieve the Horses from the severe strain of starting the cars, Passengers are requested to get on or off only at the street corners.[16]

Wounds from rocks, nails, and poorly fitted shoes were daily experiences for the horses, as well as sunstroke in what the Victorians called "the heated term." Even the best animals lasted only four or five years.[17] In railroad circles the beasts were regarded merely as the necessary engine for turning wheels, and a very expensive one, since a horse cost from forty to sixty cents a day for his keep. The point of view of the railroad lines was well put by one manager, who once remarked, "Horses are cheaper than oats."[18]

And so it was that the animals arrived, handsome and healthy, only to leave broken and crippled, usually passing to new owners for a nominal sum, often farmers who bought up town horses for whatever strength they had left and literally worked them to death on the farm.[19] According to one bit of horse folklore, which does great credit to the sagacity of the car horses on the Fourth Avenue line, when they were pushed beyond their endurance they pulled up in front of the ASPCA building and waited patiently for the humane officers to come out and arrest their tormentors.

Were callous indifference and outright cruelty more prevalent in New York than elsewhere in America? The president of the American Humane Society once said so at a convention held in Cincinnati in the 1880s. In this instance Henry Bergh, founder of the ASPCA, defended New York "rather warmly," replying that in proportion to population there was just as much animal abuse in Cincinnati, Chicago, or Boston. "Cruelty," he declared, "has no particular home."[20]

In a survey of the life of the streetcar horse, *The New York Times* reported:

> His time of misery must be held to date from the time he enters that service, when his "poor feet" never know what it is to be off those horrible cobblestones. By the end of three years the ruin of the legs of most of these car horses has been completed, and then they are sold off to the large class who understand extracting the maximum of work with the minimum of food. All over the City may be seen animals attached to junk carts and dilapidated expresses, which literally have not a leg to stand upon. Watch the poor things for a moment standing, and you will see them shift painfully from leg to leg, so as to give one an occasional rest. Many are lame of both a fore and a hind foot, and cannot move without great distress

... A long way up town, near the East River, there is a market
for animals of this kind, and any humane person attending it
must reflect that the existence of horses is one of the most
inscrutable in the arrangements of Providence. Here are animals, presumably innocent of offense, condemned to long
years of the extremest misery without remedy or appeal. For
can any misery be much greater than, with a weak, sick old
body and terribly tender feet, to be attached to a heavy load
driven by a man with a heavy whip, day after day. . . ?

The investigative reporter concluded that the horse was truly "a
martyr to the industrial age."[21]

News accounts of mass cremations of horsecar horses were once
almost routine. The animals were kept in cellars or on the upper
floors of wooden stables, above the cars and the hay. There was
little chance of rescue in case of fire. As a form of property the
horse was no different from the car, but the car was definitely
ahead of the horse. And so the dismal record reads: forty-three
horses dead on West Fifty-third Street; 275 perished in the stables
of the Eighth Avenue Horsecar Company; 1,200 roasted alive in
the stalls of the Belt Line, which circled Manhattan island below
Fifty-ninth Street.

"There is no reasonable doubt," Henry Bergh, the president of
the American Society for the Prevention of Cruelty to Animals,
wrote after studying a report by the New York Fire Department,
"that had these poor animals been stabled upon the floor on a level
with the street, every one of them would have been saved. . . ."[22]
But the traction companies blocked every attempt to reduce the
hazard through legislation. The railroad corporations, *The New
York Times* said, regard public opinion only when it is "expressed
in the form either of law or of riot."[23]

The insurance companies constituted another obstacle to the
compassionate treatment of horses. "Mercy killings" were not covered or permitted under their contracts. As a result a horse, fright-
fully injured in a stable fire, wandered for days up and down
Fulton Street in Brooklyn, the hide nearly burned from the body,
the mouth and eyes hard as a crisp. The suffering of the animal
before it finally died was unavoidable, in the owner's view, since
the insurance company refused to pay the claim if the beast was
put out of his agony.[24]

"Fashionable cruelties" were also practiced upon the private carriage horses who pulled the smart landaus, phaetons, and victorias of the well-to-do classes. The short checkrein, which forced the head into a high, unnatural position, produced a prancing step, greatly admired as evidence of a spirited animal. Tailbones were broken and reset, tails docked for stylish effect, and winter coats clipped close, which removed the animals' natural cold-weather protection. Bits were also used that made the horse seem hard-mouthed, such as the burr bit, armed with tacks, or worst of all, the chain-and-leverage bit, which was capable of fracturing the jaw. Thus the fiery toss of the head, the jaws flecked with foam, merely signaled that the creature was in anguish.[25]

Transit by animal power began its decline in the eighties. In New York the elevated trains took over on Second, Third, Sixth, and Seventh avenues, with "elegantly finished and furnished cars," which, according to a circular letter issued by the New York Elevated Railroad Company, "take no more than can be seated." The horse railroads fought back with injunctions and double-decker cars, but horsepower finally had to yield to speed overhead and the electric surface car.[26] Electric power in Baltimore, Denver, Detroit, Los Angeles, and other cities released thousands of horses from their burdens, clearing the urban environment of stable odors and the manure-pile problem. The last horse-drawn city stage was replaced on New York's Fifth Avenue in 1907, and the jingle of the horsecar bells was heard no more anywhere in the borough of Manhattan after 1917. A curious footnote to the social history of New York is the fact that the employees on the Third Avenue elevated line were rough and rowdy characters, like the drivers on the old horse railroad, while the crews on the Sixth Avenue "el" were mannerly in the tradition of the Sixth Avenue streetcars.[27]

Progress in humane feelings is hard to discern during the decades when 25,000 streetcar horses died annually. Poverty and frustration in human society multiplied animal suffering. When laboring men earned $1.60 for working a twelve-hour day, with penalties frequent and jobs scarce, little compassion remained in the weary driver of a dray or streetcar for the feelings of a horse that was not even his. So human dilemmas triggered many instances of cruelty. Neither the moral nor the emotional aspect of the helplessness of animals appeared to have touched the public mind.

Yet the humanitarian view was quietly gaining in influence. The ASPCA was firmly established in New York by the eighties. Colonel M. Richards Mucklé was in the field in Philadelphia. James S. Hutchinson had started the San Francisco SPCA because he saw two vaqueros dragging a hog by their lassos over the cobblestones of Washington Street. And in St. Louis a "tiny ninety pound Mrs. Anderson," as William Alan Swallow tells the story, "always carried a rolled up umbrella when riding a horse-drawn streetcar. Whenever the driver would start to beat the horse she would hit him over the shoulders with her umbrella and ask him how he liked it!"[28] And in Massachusetts (see Chapter 11) the organized protest against the mistreatment of animals found its leader and voice following an instance of spectacular cruelty to two fine horses in connection with the settlement of a gambling bet.

10

Don Quixote of Manhattan

O n an unseasonably warm evening in April 1866, a well-
tailored gentleman with a drooping mustache and a long,
thin face, obviously a member of the "Upper Ten," stood
at the intersection of Fifth Avenue and Twenty-third Street in
New York City, watching the tangle of traffic where Broadway
slants across Fifth Avenue. A wilder individualism than we know
today prevailed among the horsecars and omnibuses, the struggling carriages, drays, vans, and butchers' carts.[1] Suddenly the
observer stepped off the curb and threaded his way toward a teamster who was giving his horse an unmerciful beating. This dia-
logue followed, as the pedestrian recounted the incident later:

"My friend," said I approaching, "you can't do that any
more." The man paused in sheer amazement.
"Can't beat my own horse," he exclaimed,"——the devil I
can't." And he fell to again. Again I ordered him to stop and
added:

"You are not aware, probably, that you are breaking the law,
but you are. I have the new statute in my pocket; and the horse
is yours only to treat kindly. I could have you arrested. I only
want to inform you what a risk you run." The fellow stared
at me with open mouth, and exclaimed:
"Go to hell—you're mad!"[2]

Thus Henry Bergh began, quietly and politely, a twenty-two-
year effort to arouse the American conscience to the plight of
fellow creatures who cannot protest or explain their predicament.
Earlier that same day, the nineteenth of April, the New York State
legislature had passed a law punishing an act, or omission of an act,
that caused pain to animals "unjustifiably." It was a historic step
forward in the nineteenth-century movement toward the protection of animals.

It became one of Bergh's most effective arguments to emphasize the *cost* of cruelty to the more than eighty-five million animals "contributing in one way or another to the daily support
and enrichment of the people of this country." Cruel treatment
of cows resulted in contaminated butter, cheese, and milk. The
horrors of the cattle train endangered the meat supply. And the
aphorism that "horses are cheaper than oats" lost its specious
appeal when in 1872 two-thirds of all the horses in the city of
New York were stricken with a deadly respiratory disease, producing, in Bergh's words, "a panic among the human inhabitants." Thousands walked, and the flow of urban life slowed
almost to a standstill.[3]

There were laws to protect animals on the statute books of
several states, including New York. But they were narrowly
drawn. Machinery for enforcement was lacking. They were
largely ineffective.[4] Just a few days before the New York legislature passed the animal protection act of 1866 entitled "An Act
better to prevent cruelty to animals," it had also chartered a humane society, a private corporation exercising delegated police
powers.[5] The new organization, first of its kind in the Western
Hemisphere, was called the American Society for the Prevention
of Cruelty to Animals.

The sponsors who signed the petition for the chartering of the
ASPCA were representative men of New York, leaders in finance,

commerce, the law, and politics. But the driving force behind the idea was Henry Bergh. He was the founder, president, inspirer, advocate, diplomatist, lecturer, writer, administrator, fund raiser, and tireless propagandist for the protest against the abuse of animals. "To plant, or revive, the principle of mercy, in the human heart," Bergh said, would be "a triumph . . . greater than the building of the Great Pacific Railroad."[6]

The cause became known as "Bergh's war." The ASPCA was the "Bergh Society," its agents "Bergh's men."[7] The tall, muscular figure and long, sad-eyed face of Henry Bergh himself, as he patrolled the streets, appeared in courtrooms, or stopped in at the American Museum to see how P. T. Barnum, the circus impresario, was treating his menagerie, became as familiar to New Yorkers as William Cullen Bryant's magnificent white beard or Horace Greeley's long, flapping duster and high, white hat.[8]

There was nothing in Henry Bergh's heritage or earlier life to suggest his remarkable ability to imagine the psychological states of the beasts pacing their narrow cages in the Central Park Zoo, or his empathy with the biblical Balaam's ass, which, when the Lord opened her mouth, reproached her master: "What have I done unto thee, that thou hast smitten me these three times?" Bergh's forebears had emigrated in the eighteenth century from the Lower Palatinate to the mid-Hudson Valley. Henry, the youngest of three children of Christian Bergh—a prosperous shipbuilder in New York City whose yard produced sailing vessels of advanced design during the first forty years of the century—was born on August 29, probably in 1813, in a homestead that stood in an orchard of oxheart cherry trees at the northeast corner of Scammel and Water streets. (There is some uncertainty about the year of Bergh's birth, to which he himself contributed by treating the event in his later years as a movable feast.) The two-story frame home stood within hearing distance of the axes, adzes, saws, and hammers at the shipyard on Corlear's Hook, where the island of Manhattan shouldered out into the East River toward Williamsburg and the Navy Yard.[9]

Bergh entered Columbia College in 1830 with some thought of a career in the law. Meanwhile he lived as a young man of fashion, enjoying the balls and the company of the town wits. Preferring the pleasures of foreign travel to the life of study, Bergh dropped out of Columbia, and after tasting Europe, turned his thoughts to marriage. In 1839 he married Catherine Matilda Taylor, daughter of an English architect practicing in New York.[10] Following Christian Bergh's death in 1843, the shipyard was closed, and Henry and his wife, childless and well off, traveled and lived for extended periods in Europe. A hint of the future came at Seville, where the Berghs attended a bullfight and were revolted as eight bulls were killed and twenty horses eviscerated.[11]

During their visits abroad the Berghs received social attentions at the American legations, at the Elysée Palace during the presidency of Louis Napoleon, and at the Tuilleries after Bonaparte assumed the imperial role as Napoleon III. In search of a calling, Bergh's thoughts turned to literature and diplomacy. In his literary endeavors Bergh was, unhappily, a poet *manqué* and an unsuccessful though persistent playwright. Ignored as a writer, he was, briefly, more fortunate in diplomacy. In the spring of 1863 President Lincoln named him to succeed Bayard Taylor as secretary of legation at the court of Czar Alexander II. In St. Petersburg Bergh served under the colorful fire-eater and southern abolitionist, Cassius Marcellus Clay. Bergh enjoyed his life in Russia, but disillusionment came when Clay resented his popularity with the Russians and summarily dismissed him. Clay said, in fact, "Go, God damn you!"[12] Bergh lingered in London for several months while he maneuvered for a new appointment, but it never came.

During his tour of duty in Russia, Bergh had watched the peasants beat their horses and had, from the legation carriage, directed his splendidly liveried Vladimir or Alexander to order the droshky drivers to stop it. "At last," he commented, "I've found a way to utilize my gold lace."[13] Bergh often admitted that previously he had never been particularly interested in animals. Once when he was calling upon Clara Morris, a leading emotional actress of the period, Bergh drew back when her small dog put a friendly, inquiring paw on his knee. Miss Morris asked him if he objected to her pet because it was small, but Bergh said no—it was because the dog was a dog.

Not as one devoted, then, to the beast world or out of a sentimental flinching at happenings that caused animals pain, but rather because of a kind of abstract concept of justice, Bergh seems to have undertaken his life work. Yet one wonders if that quite covers it. Horses must have been his secret passion. His lectures and reports were filled with affectionate praise of "that generous and faithful servant, the horse," or "that noble creature, the horse." Why else did this gentleman, who looked rather like a blend of Quaker and French count, wear a gold horse-head scarfpin in the folds of his black satin cravat, and recall, in one of those classical allusions of which he was somewhat too fond, how "Darius . . . owed his crown to the neighing of a horse?"[15] "What struck me most forcibly," Bergh declared, "was that mankind derived immense benefits from these creatures, and gave them in return not the least protection."[16]

Before leaving London for home in June of 1865, Bergh met the Earl of Harrowby, president of the Royal Society for the Prevention of Cruelty to Animals, then in its forty-first year. Stimulated by what he learned of the service rendered by the RSPCA, Bergh resolved to found a similar institution in the United States. The advancement of "merciful principles," he assured Lord Harrowby, was the "long cherished dream of my heart." After careful preparatory work, Bergh unveiled his proposal in February 1866 to a small but carefully chosen audience, which included the mayor and later governor of New York, John T. Hoffman, and other figures of importance in the life of the city and state.[17] Noticing in a quick historical survey what happened to animals, and humans, too, in the Roman arena, the tortures inflicted in the Spanish bullring, and the brutalities of modern vivisectionists, Bergh denounced the blood sports still popular in New York, the abuse of the streetcar horses, and the barbarities that accompanied the transportation and slaughter of food animals. "This is a matter purely of conscience," Bergh concluded. "It has no perplexing side issues . . . it is a moral question . . . it is a solemn recognition of . . . mercy."[18]

The response was positive. As a result of the meeting and the circulation of a paper outlining the objectives of the proposed society, the ASPCA came into being with Henry Bergh as president. Bergh now had at his disposal an effective law and a private society clothed with public authority. Bergh himself was empowered by the attorney general of the state and the district attorney for the city to represent them in all cases involving the law for the protection of animals.[19] In later years educational activities and relief work became more important than punishing offenders. This gain was due in part to the spread of a social gospel, which included a new attitude toward inferior creatures, and in part to another circumstance: the ASPCA was able to secure convictions in over ninety percent of all cases that reached the courts.[20]

President Bergh hoped that the word "American" in the name of the society would come to stand for a national organization. But the charter, under New York laws, was not appropriate, and the idea of branches outside New York state proved impractical. The ASPCA's influence, however, was national, as other humanitarian societies quickly came into being. Within five years, an astonishingly short time for the diffusion of a new idea, nineteen states and the Dominion of Canada had established societies of similar character.[21]

There was plenty of work to be done in New York. Wealthy sportsmen held live pigeon shoots. The gambling fraternity repaired to Kit Burn's Sportsmen's Hall at 273 Water Street, just north of Peck Slip, to see bulldogs fight a black bear. Terriers dispatched wharf rats in a zinc-lined enclosure for the delight of the Bowery boys, and as a special afterpiece, Kit's son-in-law, William Varley, alias Reddy the Blacksmith, pickpocket and thief, would, for the price of a glass of beer, bite a live rat in two.[22]

The president of the ASPCA carried a cane that could be used as a weapon of defense. But usually a lifted finger and a glimpse of his official badge were sufficient to tame his adversaries. Bergh spent long hours in the Court of Special Sessions, where he was formidable in cross-examination, or in climbing the bleak hill to the Capitol in Albany, where he frequently appeared before legislative committees. Meanwhile he carried on the routine business of the society, cajoled the editors of the fifteen daily newspapers then exisiting in New York, and beat the bushes for money. "My time by day and night," he told a correspondent, "is devoted to the Institution which I have founded."[23] Yet the strenuous life was not without its rewards. Bergh clearly enjoyed the exercise of his very considerable authority and had in his temperament that focus on a single purpose necessary to the accomplishment of any great reform. As one newspaper editor remarked of him, "He who doeth one thing is terrible!"[24]

Bergh was always urbane, but he was also always precise. When he wrote to the police captain on West Thirty-fifth Street about a horse that had been abandoned in the gutter to die, he gave the name of the owner, the name and address of the man who committed the act, and the name and address of a witness. When he complained to William H. Vanderbilt about a "dead lame" horse owned by the New York and Harlem Railroad, he gave the date and identified the horse as being attached to Fourth Avenue car number 30. "I have adopted a habit through life," he warned a judge who was delaying unreasonably on a horse-abondonment case, "of always pursuing a subject until it is brought to its legitimate conclusion."[25]

Early on, Bergh undertook to stir up the city through working on a spectacular case: the elimination of torments visited upon green turtles. The turtles, source of delectable soup and succulent steaks, were transported by sailing vessels from the tropics to the Fulton Fish Market in New York. The turtles lay on their backs for several weeks, without food or water, held in place by ropes strung through holes punched in their flippers. Bergh boarded a schooner engaged in the turtle trade, arrested the skipper and crew, and marched them off to The Tombs prison. He reinforced his case with a letter from Professor Louis Agassiz. The famous zoologist assured the ASPCA that turtles could feel hunger, thirst, and pain and had, besides, certain minimal rights. However, a skeptical judge acquitted the defendants on the grounds that a turtle was not an animal within the meaning of the law. The trial was a nine-day wonder, with the newspapers making extensive facetious comments on the nature of turtles and aggressive humanitarians.[26]

"The day following," Bergh told a lecture audience later, "a morning paper [it was the *New York Herald*] devoted six columns to an account of the trial; and to the funny fellow who wrote the account I have always felt grateful, for it at once placed the Society before the public and let them know that there was a Society for the defense of the inferior animals."[27]

Bergh tried on several subsequent occasions to come to the aid of Florida turtles, but the cases were always dismissed. It was one of his few failures. Even his best friends were embarrassed. Americans were not ready to extend their concern about animal suffering to a cold-blooded species. People could get excited about cruelties visited upon such domestic friends as dog, cats, and horses. But not turtles.

The ASPCA was a constant threat to Barnum in connection with his zoological activities. A typical incident occurred when the head of the anticruelty society heard that the boa constrictor in the Broadway menagerie was being fed live toads and lizards in the presence of paying customers. The resulting pressure from Bergh was so heavy that at one time Barnum had to send his snake to Hoboken in a suitcase to be fed beyond the reach of the ASPCA.[28] But Barnum found a way to punish Bergh. He obtained the support of Professor Agassiz, who told him that snakes require live food, and expressed the doubt that the members of the ASPCA "would object to eating lobster because the lobster was boiled alive, or refuse oysters because they were cooked alive, or raw oysters because they must be swallowed alive." The president of Barnum's & Van Amburgh's Museum and Menagerie thereupon demanded an apology from the president of the ASPCA, and released the complete correspondence concerning the proper feeding of reptiles to the press.[29]

Some years and several incidents later, Barnum tormented Bergh again when he announced that Salamander, the Fire Horse, would jump through fire as one of the main attractions of the Barnum, Bailey & Hutchinson show. Bergh rose to the bait and sent Superintendent T. W. Hartfield of the ASPCA with five agents and twenty policemen to stop the act. But the flames, it turned out, were artificial, produced by a harmless chemical. Barnum, ten clowns, Salamander, and finally even Superintendent Hartfield himself, all leaped through the burning hoops unsinged.[30]

Respect and even liking developed between the two men after Bergh defended Barnum on an occasion when the latter was attacked for using elephant goads. The circus impresario began contributing to both the New York and Bridgeport, Connecticut, SPCAs, and announced that he was "the Bergh of Bridgeport!" When Barnum died in 1891 he left a bequest to the city of Bridgeport for the erection of a monument to Henry Bergh. The memorial was duly constructed, with water troughs on two levels for animals of various heights, and was topped with a statue of a horse. The horse was damaged beyond restoring when an automo-

bile crashed into the memorial in 1964, but the rest of the monument still stands.[31]

As the years passed, the ASPCA kept a vigilant eye on the
operation of the city dog pound, on the treatment of horses and
mules along the Erie Canal, and on the handling of dairy cows in
Brooklyn and on Long Island. Bergh intervened successfully when
it was proposed to make a circus horse walk a tightrope stretched
over the rapids below Niagara Falls. He is also credited with
devising derricks and slings for raising large animals that had
fallen into excavations and with the invention of the clay pigeon
to replace live birds in trap shooting.[32]

In 1874, a case of flagrant brutality toward a child known as
"Little Mary Ellen" aroused widespread interest and sympathy
after the emaciated girl appeared in court clothed in rags and
displayed a mass of scars caused by repeated beatings. As a result
of this affair Bergh and his associates launched the first organized
movement in the United States for the defense of children from
those who have, or claim to have, a legal right to control them. The
new society, organized separately from the animal welfare work,
was known then, as it is now, as the New York Society for the
Prevention of Cruelty to Children. It, too, "stirred the public
conscience," Jacob A. Riis wrote in his *The Children of the Poor*, as
it extended protection to exploited waifs who were beyond the
reach of the existing child care societies.[33]

Henry Bergh's newsworthiness, his frequent entanglements
with powerful commercial interests, and his striking personality
and appearance all served to keep the ASPCA and its president in
the news. Because of his sad-eyed countenance and what the comic
press saw as his wildly romantic objectives, the cartoonists of the
day inevitably delineated him as a nineteenth-century Don Quixote, mounted upon a bony Rosinante.[34] The *New York Sunday Mercury*, which represented the point of view of sportsmen, assaulted
Bergh editorially as "An Ass That Should Have His Ears
Cropped."[35] Using the technique of the *reductio ad absurdum*, the
humorous newspaper *Wild Oats* suggested that the ASPCA had
created a new social atmosphere in which "Cockroaches . . . insist
on sharing the best. . . . Rats insist on having a chair at the table.
. . . goats put on airs . . . hogs grunt delightedly . . . [as] unlimited
sway is given to the very humane Bergh."[36] But the significance

of the satire aimed at the animal cause was this: while ridicule papered over the disturbing ethical challenges, the laughter masked a queasy conscience.

According to sprightly anecdotes circulated after Bergh had become a celebrity, he had as a child manifested a special sensitivity to the welfare of animals which included an earnest effort to persuade his parents to give up mousetraps, insect powder, and flypaper, and it was reported with relish in the New York weekly review of metropolitan life and the arts, *The Arcadian,* that young Bergh had once cured an aged mouse of neuralgia with Mrs. Winslow's Soothing Syrup. The journal also announced that Bergh would shortly introduce a bill in Congress to make it illegal to eat oysters.[37]

A rumor often appeared in print that Bergh was a vegetarian, which granted him a theoretical consistency while neatly categorizing him as a crank. But it was not true. Bergh allowed in his philosophy for what he termed "necessary killing." At one time, indeed, he tried to introduce horsemeat as an article of diet. Characteristically, the move was attempted in the interest of the horse, a quick death being preferable to Bergh's eyes to the fate that awaited the victims of the horse dealers.

The physical courage of the president of the ASPCA was often tested. He received numerous threatening letters advising him to leave town. One postcard named the day and hour when he would be assassinated. A drayman, arrested for overloading, took a cut at Bergh with a piece of strap iron, but fortunately missed. And the society was always accused of choosing the wrong targets. The "dairymaids" thought Bergh ought to confine his attentions to the butchers. The butchers favored vigorous action against cockfighting. Kit Burns, the impresario of the dogfights, warned: "Your society is doing a noble work, sir, yes, a magnificent work, but let me tell you, when it interferes in dog fighting, it digs its own grave."[38]

The ASPCA was also charged with bearing down on the poor while excusing the rich. But Bergh found his path full of tacks when he tried to call to account members of the business and social elite. The courts held, for example, that unless an officer of a corporation that owned horses personally hit a horse on the head with a shovel or personally abandoned it in the street, he could not be held accountable. But on the whole, the press came to support the ASPCA, accepted Bergh as a sage, and printed his views on things in general.

As president of the society, Bergh received no pay for his work, and in fact turned over a substantial endowment to the society. New York City always remained his special domain, and its citizens came to regard indulgently, even proudly, the old gentleman with the kindly yet dyspeptic face, low voice, and old-school manners who, when he stopped a teamster and saw a crowd gathering, would seize the opportunity to deliver a little talk on Americanism. It always included the thought that free men who make their own laws ought to obey their statutes. In all that he did for animals, he always had a further objective in view, which he wrote out in French just three years before he died: *Les hommes seront justes envers les hommes, quand ils seront charitables envers les animaux* ("Men will be just to men when they are kind to animals").[39]

The criticism was often leveled against the ASPCA that it was more concerned with improving the condition of animals than of men. This still remains a stock argument advanced by the opponents of animal protection activities. Bergh pointed out in reply that if the animals had to wait their turn until all human affairs were perfectly adjusted, they would still be waiting at the Second Coming. Neither the movement to alleviate the suffering of the lower animals nor justice for men, he insisted, excluded the other.

Henry Bergh kept bachelor hall during his later years in his brownstone house at 429 Fifth Avenue, with two nephews, a clutter of objets d'art, and his long memories.[40] His wife had been an invalid for years, living at a home in Utica, New York, where she died in 1887. During the blizzard of '88 Bergh died in his Fifth Avenue home, and was immediately recognized as a man who had created a profound alteration in the moral climate of nineteenth-century America. James Gordon Bennett's *New York Herald*, which had gotten so much mileage out of Bergh's foibles, eulogized him. The *New York Citizen*, an old antagonist, announced "the man who loved his fellow animal is mourned by his fellow man. . . ."[41]

Recognition took many forms. Milwaukee, like Bridgeport, erected a monument.[42] Columbia University became the seat of a Henry Bergh Foundation for the promotion of humane education, and Henry Ward Beecher, the popular pulpit orator of the period, thought it both proper and probable that the founder of the ASPCA and his furred and feathered wards would be joyfully reunited in a human-animal heaven. It is a success story quite outside the rags-to-riches tradition that Henry Bergh, born to affluence, achieved his fulfillment in the role of "mediator," as he himself once said, "for the upper and lower animals."[43] There is no evidence that Henry Bergh was especially well grounded in the speculative origins of humanitarianism. He was not a zoologist, theologian, or thinker absorbed in theoretical questions. He resembled, rather, the "righteous man" of Proverbs who regarded the life of his beast because that was the way of life of a just and good man.

11

How Mercy
Came to Massachusetts

An extraordinary horse race made Washington's Birthday, 1868, a red-letter day for the sports of New England. Starting from the Charles River House, at Brighton, two trotters, Empire State and Ivanhoe, each drawing two men, raced forty miles over rough roads to Worcester for a purse of one thousand dollars. Empire State won, making an average speed of more than fifteen miles per hour. Both horses died. They had been, in the exact meaning of the expression, driven to death.[1]

The next day a letter appeared in the *Boston Daily Advertiser*, signed by George T. Angell, a prominent attorney, in which Angell declared, after describing what had happened:

It seems to me that it is high time for somebody to take hold of this matter in earnest, and see if we cannot do something in Boston, as well as others have in New York, to stop this cruelty to animals . . . I, for one, am ready to contribute both time and money; and if there is any society or person in Boston

107

with whom I can unite, or who will unite with me in this
matter, I shall be glad personally or by letter to be informed.[2]

The appeal won quick response. The timing was right. With the
slavery issue settled, it was possible to consider other claims for
social justice, and the animals were among the first to benefit.[3]
Cruelty was on the increase, or at least was increasingly to be seen,
because of urban growth, the arrival of masses of immigrants who
had desperate lives to live, with little tenderness to spare for ani-
malkind, and who easily acquired established American attitudes
of indifference. Nor can the New England Brahmins be excused,
those privileged to live out golden years in Beacon Hill, Nahant,
Bar Harbor. They showed no concern with the problem until
George Angell pointed the way.

Among those who rallied around the Boston proposal were such
leaders in New England life as Nathan Appleton, manufacturer,
banker and father of Mrs. Henry Wadsworth Longfellow; the
Reverend James Freeman Clarke, Unitarian clergyman and a
prominent cultural figure in Boston; also Samuel G. Howe, cham-
pion of the disabled; George B. Emerson, influential educator; and
Amos A. Lawrence, the merchant-philanthropist. An especially
welcome caller was Emily W. (Mrs. William G.) Appleton, who
had already, on her own initiative, traveled to New York to observe the animal protection work there. Scattered individuals had
long been thinking about the problem. Mrs. Appleton's father, for
one, Dr. John. C. Warren, a leading surgeon of his day, had spoken
out against the harsh treatment of workhorses.[4]

On March 23, 1868, the Massachusetts Society for the Prevention of Cruelty to Animals, hereafter called the MSPCA, was incorporated under a state charter with George T. Angell as
president, an office he filled until his death. The names of the
directors reflected the interest shown in the project by Boston's
representative men. Mrs. Appleton, whom Angell regarded as co-
founder, was not a member of the board. Why? This was the Age
of Victoria, when it was not "deemed judicious" as Angell explained, "to make this use of a lady's name." But the omission was
repaired when the climate of opinion permitted. Mrs. Appleton
later received appropriate recognition from both the Boston and
New York societies for her devotion to the brute creation.[5]

The new society needed a law to give it the power to act in cases of flagrant cruelty. This was provided by the legislature on May 14, 1868. Also urgently needed were members and money. Angell enlisted the aid of the mayor, the chief of police, and the city attorney, and got seventeen patrolmen in uniform detailed to canvass Boston. They produced twelve hundred of the sixteen hundred members with which the MSPCA began operations.[6]

There was plenty of work to be done. In Boston, as in New York, the patterns of living and working required the horse railroads, with consequences for the horse that we have already seen in the survey of New York.[7] The surplus animal problem was most pressing, and a particular horror was the annual hydrophobia frenzy, when the dogs of Boston were muzzled, chased, shot at, and killed or wounded.

But the most widespread offenses were connected with the economics of the marketplace. They were the same ones already identified. Said Angell:

> Take the city of Boston, alone, and *one* animal, *the horse*. . . .
> Take into consideration all the overloaded teams, the over-
> loaded omnibuses, the overloaded horse-cars, the cases of fast
> driving, over-driving, over-working, and under-feeding, ne-
> glect to water, neglect to properly shelter and protect from the
> weather, tight check-reins, sores worn by harness, twitchings,
> beatings, kickings, bad shoeing, bad pavements, bad stables,
> bad feeding, bad harness, bad grooming, *bad drivers*. . . . Then
> extend the estimate to the whole wide circle of dumb creatures
> . . . let it include all the cattle-trains . . . the bagging of cows;
> the starving at the cattle-markets . . . the cruel plucking of live
> fowls . . . the cruel transportation of calves *tied* . . . the abomi-
> nable treatment of . . . worn-out horses; the short feeding of
> cattle . . . the cruel methods of slaughtering . . . the dog-fights
> and cock-fights . . . the unnecessary dissection of living ani-
> mals.[8]

One of the first endeavors of the MSPCA was to install drinking fountains.[9] The president also tackled the sensitive subject of bloody amusements. The shooting of live pigeons from traps was banned in the state as a result of Angell's dramatization of the suffering of wounded birds.[10] He could be firm when prosectuion was indicated, but he put education ahead of punishment. Psychopathic cruelty was, fortunately, comparatively rare. The background of most of the cases that came up was usually ignorance, thoughtlessness, a property interest, or some kind of human frustration being worked out at an animal's expense.

Angell tended to emphasize the similarities between men and amimals. This view was a part of the larger shift away from theological explanations of the universe, and toward the evidence turned up by the natural sciences. Although not affiliated with any church, Angell could quote the Bible fluently when it expressed humane sentiments: that it was a sin to abandon the injured ass to die, to rob birds' nests, or deprive a working animal of its Sabbath rest. From childhood George Angell had been extremely fond of animals, and in his mature years he had often personally intervened in instances of cruelty. In fact, before there was an animal welfare society anywhere in America, Angell had drawn up a will by which he gave a substantial portion of his considerable property to be used to prevent the abuse of the lower creation.[11]

Born June 5, 1823, in Southbridge, Massachusetts, the only child of the Reverend George Angell, a Baptist minister who was a good man but a poor provider, the boy was reared by a widowed mother who supported herself by teaching school, while the boy was passed around among relatives and friends in various parts of New England. He worked for a time in a Boston dry goods house, then attended a school in Meriden, New Hampshire. He entered Brown University but changed after a year to Dartmouth College, from which he graduated in 1846. Returning to Boston, he studied law and was admitted to the bar in 1851. His professional progress was spectacular, and after seventeen years of practice, Angell was able to retire with a fortune. In 1872 he married a widow, Mrs. Eliza Martin, of Nahant, who shared his sympathies and philanthropic interests.[12]

When the MSPCA was organized, Angell knew that his personal destiny was set. "It was already clear to my mind," he wrote, "that I was entering upon my life's work." People who loved their companion animals and treated all lower animals with kindness had always existed in New England, as elsewhere. It was, after all, a New England poet, John Greenleaf Whittier, who affirmed that mercy includes "every creature endowed with life." Dr. Oliver Wendell Holmes pitied "the caged lion," and Emerson asked,

"Hast thou named all the birds without a gun?" Longfellow, too, demonstrated his deep concern for animal life in "The Birds of Killingworth" and "The Bell of Atri." But Angell was after more than this, the recognition of animal rights and a systemized effort to educate youth in the principles of kindness, for he understood that each generation has to reinvent the world and find its own humanity. Impressed by the fact that none of the inmates of a Boston prison had ever owned a dog or other pet as a child, Angell launched a companion agency to the MSPCA, the American Humane Education Society.[18] It undertook to modify prevailing cultural attitudes of children and to publish a magazine, *Our Dumb Animals*, the first periodical in the world devoted to disseminating humane attitudes. This publication, which still flourishes, reached not only children but thought-leaders here and abroad. Editorial contents included true incidents of animals rendering services to the human world, stories about faithful dogs and noble horses, and news reports of cruel pastimes broken up by MSPCA agents.[14]

The American Humane Education Society brought out the first edition of *Black Beauty, His Grooms and Companions*, a little paperbound version of Anna Sewell's "autobiography of a horse." Angell called the book "the 'Uncle Tom's Cabin' of the horse," and the tale became a best seller, with sales of 226,000 within two years' time.[15] The society also sponsored Margaret Marshall Saunders' *Beautiful Joe*, a dog story that has sold steadily for nearly eighty years. Its total sales have exceeded a million copies and generations of young readers have shed copious tears over one or both of these animal narratives.[16] The work of the society with children was carried on, and still is, through Bands of Mercy, an adaptation of an English idea that has proved to be as effective in the United States as in Great Britain.

Although his health was always somewhat uncertain, and his work load astonishing, the president of the MSPCA traveled far beyond the confines of his own state, carrying the message of fair play to animals. There was a fruitful missionary journey to England, which in many ways sharpened the vision of the RSPCA, and at home Angell made wide-ranging speaking tours, appearing before state legislatures and college and university audiences; in churches and normal schools; before humane society conventions, city police, and mass meetings of teamsters. The importance of these visits may be estimated from the fact that they were followed by the formation of animal welfare societies in such diverse locations as Connecticut, Florida, Illinois, Louisiana, Maryland, and Wisconsin. In Philadelphia Angell spoke against the use of the checkrein. On an incognito visit to the Detroit stockyards, he observed how dead and dying meat animals were processed, and remarked drily that he had told an audience at the Detroit Opera House "much more about their meats than they had previously known." Chicago impressed him as "certainly one of the most cruel cities in the world," but he was able to assist in the establishment there of a vigorous Illinois Humane Society. And during a visit to New Orleans the Yankee crusader was instrumental in stopping a bullfight.[17]

He was often in Washington, testifying in favor of legislation aimed at regulating the treatment of livestock in interstate commerce. A portion of President Rutherford B. Hayes' inaugural address dealing with this subject came from Angell's hand. Later he denounced President Theodore Roosevelt for his well-publicized exploits as a bear killer, pointing out that if the scene of his assaults upon the bear population had been Massachusetts he could have been fined and jailed. In reprisal, Washington authorities barred *Our Dumb Animals* from the city's schools.[18]

It was frequently used as a stick against Angell that he was a one-idea man. He recalled one editor who "compared me to an old clock which *once wound up would never stop striking.*" He added, genially, "I liked the simile."[19] The fact was quite otherwise. Angell's reforming interests ranged widely, including the cause of peace and the prevention of crime. He was interested in pure food legislation and carried on an aggressive attack against worthless patent medicines. He also worked for strict limitations upon vivisection, although he did not fully satisfy those who were opposed to the practice under all circumstances.[20]

Angell knew and mingled with the men of his time who represented what used to be called "the Standing Order": lawyers like Daniel Webster and Rufus Choate; musicians like Ole Bull; political figures like United States senators Sumner and Hoar; literary lions like the poets Longfellow, Whittier, and Dr. Holmes; William Lloyd Garrison and Wendell Phillips among the reformers of the age; the gifted Mrs. Julia Ward Howe; influential clergymen like D. L. Moody and Phillips Brooks; and among men of science, Professor Agassiz. But Angell was far too deeply engrossed with the mission to the animals to mingle in general society except as he might have incidental contacts. "Our society holds its annual meeting this year at the Music Hall, Friday Evening, April 9th," the president of the MSPCA wrote in 1880 to Longfellow. "Can we have your presence? Can you aid us with a contribution of poetry or prose? *Anything* you may *say* or *read* or write will help us *and those we represent.*"[21]

There is no denying that Angell had his own way of conducting the affairs of his two societies, which is to say he ran a taut ship. Tall, spare, handsome, with a shock of white hair in his old age, Angell combined strength with a gentle tact and a feather-light touch. He possessed a ready wit and a feeling for timing that often turned the balance of an argument in his favor. His humor and modesty were bywords among his associates. On one occasion, when he had been referred to as "Doctor" by a magazine, Angell wrote to the editor, " . . . as I made *in the practise of law* the money which has enabled me to work for dumb animals the past eighteen years, without pay, and was never a doctor—either of divinity, medicine, philosophy, or anything, will you kindly say so, and much oblige . . . ."[22]

During his last years Angell occupied an apartment in the Westminster Hotel, at the corner of Copley Square, where he labored at a work-piled desk, only occasionally going to the offices of the society to attend board meetings. Death came peacefully, after a brief illness, on March 16, 1909. Notable in the funeral procession were thirty-eight splendid horses wearing mourning rosettes consisting of black satin bows with long streamers attached to the bridles. The horses, led by Old Ned, thirty-five-year-old winner of many medals in the traditional Boston workhorse parades, followed the hearse in double line from the Second Unitarian Church to Mount Auburn Cemetery in Cambridge, drawing up on both sides of Massachusetts Avenue to let the cortege pass between them.[23]

The unique quality of Angell's personality was widely remarked upon when the moment came to close the books on his long and busy life. It has frequently been asserted that animal lovers are people haters. But it was not so with Angell, who never lost confidence in the essential goodness of mankind. More than a thousand publications paid tribute to his practical humanity. "Our dumb animals also mourn," the *Boston Transcript* said, and a newspaper artist caught the moment well when he sketched the monument over Angell's grave with the grieving animals he had championed gathered before the stone, which was marked "Our Friend."[24]

So far as Boston was concerned, by the turn of the century an ill-used animal was a rarity in the city. The MSPCA still extends its influence, still reacts vigorously to local and out-of-state problems while increasing its influence on a global scale. Since humanitarian problems and issues now cross national and geographical boundaries, Dr. Eric H. Hansen, then president of the MSPCA, in 1959 led the society into an association with the RSPCA in forming a new facility, the International Society for the Protection of Animals, to cope with "one world" problems.[25] The American Humane Association later entered the arrangement as a founder member of the ISPA. Activities include advancing the cause through diplomatic channels when such action is indicated, initiating humane educational projects in undeveloped countries, and the introduction of merciful slaughter techniques. The ISPA has provided financial assistance for hundreds of thousands of animals all over the free world when their lives have been threatened by floods, fires, earthquakes, food shortages, drought, or such man-made hazards as the trade in captive animals or the flooding of jungles to provide water for hydroelectric dams.[26]

The Massachusetts society remains, like Saint Paul, "instant in season and out of season," and like its founder, the good angel of our animal associates who live for their own sakes yet do gladden the spirit of man.

12

Kindness Gains
a New Dimension

Although in both speech and writing people constantly refer to *the* SPCA, as though there were a single agency exercising national jurisdiction, there is in fact no such institution in the United States. The American experience had been that the most practical area of operations for private animal aid societies exercising police powers is the city or county, because of the great size of the country and because each state makes its own animal protection laws. There are in addition many other kinds of associations that do no prosecuting but carry on many forms of animal assistance and public education. Often they overlap in scope and function. But the names reflect their variety—animal rescue leagues, refuges, shelters, anticruelty societies, humane societies, welfare societies. Childrens' auxiliaries are conducted under such rubrics as the Boston-based Bands of Mercy, the Chums Pet Club of the San Francisco SPCA or the Tail Wagger's Club in Washington, D.C., which operates a clinic and a lost pet service and publishes a pet directory.[1]

Many humane groups perform special tasks that grow out of their history or circumstances. A random sampling that serves to make this clear includes the Canadian and American Wolf Defenders and the Committee for the Preservation of the Tule Elk. For many years the Animal Rescue League of Boston searched summer cottages and patrolled the beaches of Boston and Cape Cod in the autumn to collect the abandoned pets that lighthearted vacationers had forsaken.[2] Similarly, the San Francisco SPCA provided overshoes made of pieces of carpet for the street railway horses to wear on the slippery slopes of the city's famous hills. A special function of the Humane Society of Rochester and Monroe County, New York, was at one time keeping a vigilant eye on the treatment of the horses that worked on the Erie Canal.[3]

Local groups do federate for certain purposes, the exchange of information, coordination of policies, comparison of operating methods and so on. The Humane Society of the United States works through branch societies. The American Humane Association, founded in 1877 by John G. Shortall, then president of the Illinois Humane Society, first gave its attention to widespread abuses that cut across local political lines of authority. It grew to be a national federation of more than seven hundred local societies, as well as attracting thousands of individual members, and is concerned with the protection of children as well as animals.[4] By the 1880s more than three-fourths of the states had general anti-cruelty laws in effect, and most of them domiciled societies for education, propaganda, and the prevention of cruelty. It is an interesting point that at this same time complaints about cruel episodes were rising in volume. This was not because of a sudden upsurge of inhumanity but rather a sign of changing times. The community at large was demonstrating a new standard of feeling and awareness about the treatment of animals.

Today there are a thousand-odd animal protection organizations in the United States alone, with a membership that runs into several million persons.[5] Some of these supporters take the compassionate position on religious grounds, some on philosophical, others because of an emotion they feel, still others from the psychological point of view that kindness is a beneficial, integrative attitude. For most persons it is probably a matter of pure emotion. Dr. Karl A. Menninger identifies three types of love for animals:

a generic feeling for all life, such as has made the memory of Saint
Francis of Assisi so appealing down through the centuries; a solicitude for animals as a means of preserving man's own moral worth,
as exemplified in the life of Henry Bergh; or a repentance for
previous cruelties and an anticipation of those yet to come, as
represented by the celebration of the Mass on November 3, feast
day of Saint Hubert, patron saint of hunters. It is customary, even
today, in Sologne, for example, a region south of Orléans favored
by French hunters, to bring hunting dogs into the church. "A
member of my own family who hunts in Sologne," writes Pierre
Courtines, president of the French Folklore Society, "tells me that
at this special Mass the hunting horn is sounded and all the dogs
begin to howl!" The same kind of expiation on an individual basis
occurred in the case of Louis Bonnard, a fur trapper, who made
the first important bequest received by the ASPCA. Dr. Menninger thinks it significant that one of the incorporators of the
ASPCA was John Jacob Astor, whose grandfather had industrial-
ized the trapping and marketing of animal skins.[6]

Since more people can be reached through their feelings than
through intellectualizing, the animal welfare societies early
learned that the way to raise the humanitarian standards of the
general community was to dramatize situations where kindness
was obviously needed, backed up by pressure upon the law-making
process. Some of the forms of animal abuse that were commonplace a century ago are rare or of little consequence now, such as
the mistreatment of draft horses, lack of provision for watering
troughs in cities, or such blood sports as dogfighting and rabbit
coursing.

A colorful phenomenon of the past was the workhorse parade.
Such ceremonial events were held in many cities in the early years
of the twentieth century under the direction of associations
formed for the purpose. Well-groomed horses with shining har-
ness joined the line of march, drawing equipment representing a
good cross section of transportation at the time, the milk and ice
wagons, the brewery trucks and express carts. This amiable feature of urban life, once a sure sign of spring, has, of course, long
since disappeared. In Chicago the national prohibition law ban-
ning alcoholic beverages had a curious impact upon the city's
horses. Before Prohibition, that is, before 1920, saloonkeepers had

erected horse-watering troughs near their establishments as added attractions to teamsters. After the saloons were closed these oases fell into neglect, and the city's Anti-Cruelty Society took over their management.[7] The end of the Horse Age may perhaps be identified as *circa* 1930–1931, when the Humane Society of Washington urged its membership to write to the newspapers protesting against the parking of automobiles in front of the city's watering fountains.[8] The brutality connected with the transportation and slaughter of food animals early focused the attention of the humane movement. Livestock moved from the feedlots of the Middle West to the eastern seaboard cities packed tightly in cattle cars without food, exercise, or water, and often exhibited savage wounds inflicted by the handlers. Slaughterhouses were "an inferno of nauseous smells, pools of blood and screams of terrified animals," in which pigs were scalded alive and calves hung by their heels for up to an hour, waiting for the butchers. Often it took a man with a heavy hammer ten minutes and many unsuccessful blows to poleax a steer. Every scandal that developed in the packing industry, however, and there were a goodly number, was used by the humanitarians to bring about improvements.[9] The ASPCA, the American Humane Association, and the Illinois Humane Society were in the thick of a fight that had economic consequences and technological overtones as cattle-car interests fought the shipment of meat in refrigerator cars, while the railroads heaped slander and ridicule on those who tried to relieve the suffering of livestock en route.[10]

Other cruelties of the time were excessively deep branding of cattle and the slaughter of birds for commercial purposes. Humanitarians also opposed the use of animals in laboratory experimentation. This, the more radical aspect of the animal protection movement, is still a part of the program in England, but the general societies in America do not press this issue.[11] They do try to place controls over the trade in laboratory animals and to defeat legislation that would compel humane agencies to turn homeless beasts over to the experimenters. They make a common front against experiments on living creatures in the secondary school biology classes and the glorification of home-basement animal surgery projects by Little Leaguers.

Vaccination was also a sharp issue among the first generation of humanitarian leaders because the manufacture of vaccines was accompanied by cruelty to the animals that produced the serums. This position brought the movement into contact with some out-landish medical cultists, such as the still-remembered Henry Lind-lahr, graduate of a low-grade medical college in Chicago, who for reasons quite apart from compassion for animals warned the women of America that vaccination "dries up the mammary glands."[12] Humane workers and conservationists shared the same position toward the decimation of the buffalo herds and the depre-dations of the plume hunters. Henry Bergh, for example, was an early vice-president of the Audubon Society.

The two groupings still share humane principles, but today there are differences of emphasis.[13] The National Audubon So-ciety is not opposed to hunting unless a species is in danger of extinction, and does not find it inconsistent to denounce the clubbing of baby seals off Canada's eastern coast while it en-dorses as good conservationist practice the taking of the skins of Alaska seals in the Pribilof Islands. This position is unac-ceptable from the anticruelty point of view. "The achievement of economic, social or political objectives," says the Interna-tional Society for the Protection of Animals, "cannot justify the deliberate imposition by mankind of suffering upon the seals . . . ." This difference in philosophy has moved the presi-dent of the Friends of Animals, Inc., to acerbic comment: "The Audubon Society is strictly for the birds . . . ."[14]

Animal welfare societies tend to rise and fall with the energies, vision, and sense of mission of a strongly motivated leader or closely knit group, then lose their forward push because of age, death, or failure to attract broad support. Thus, many societies have come into existence, done useful work and then faded away, only to rise again in a new form. The now-forgotten Association for the Prevention of Cruelty to Animals, which once existed in the District of Columbia, illustrates this cycle of decline and renewal. Chartered by act of Congress in 1870 for the city of Washington, the society's early records, it has been observed with modest understatement, "were not well kept . . . ." The association languished, was revived by George T. Angell on a visit to Wash-ington, and rose again as the Washington Humane Society, taking on at the same time the added responsibility of protecting children while energizing the police and judges inclined to treat animal cases with levity.[15]

A similar evolution may be traced in New Jersey. There the state permitted the organization of district, that is to say county, societies after 1873. An SPCA came into being in Hudson County, died, and was born again in 1895, although operating upon so fragile a basis that at first its physical equipment consisted of one rented room, a kerosene lamp, a desk, one cane-bottomed chair, a three-legged bench, and a rusty horse pistol.[16]

A few of the pioneer agencies survived the passing of their founders and were successfully institutionalized. Instances that come to mind are the SPCAs of New York, Boston, Philadelphia, and San Francisco. All have continued through the decades to encourage, as Henry Bergh said toward the end of his life, "that most engaging of the human virtues—mercy."[17]

From the earliest days of organized kindness to animals, when the ASPCA hit upon the happy idea of supplying free straw hats for cab horses in the hot months, the animal friends have made their cause known through actions that generated publicity. Newspaper editors learned to keep an eye on the SPCAs as a standard source of news like the police court, fire department, or city hall. The reunion of a boy and his lost dog, the plight of a cat trapped in a drain, a snake found slithering around an apartment, an animal-related court decision—for a century such incidents have been journalistic staples. Some news accounts, it is true, are essentially frivolous, offering a joking kind of insensitivity mingled with condescension. This still goes on. Thus the Associated Press was pleased to distribute a photograph of Texas Tom, a gray-and-white striped cat described as having won the fashion show segment of the 1970 All-American Glamour Kitty Pageant at Miami Beach, Florida, wearing a Texas cowboy hat and a red, white, and blue cowboy costume with the star of Texas on the side.[18] And even *The New York Times*, which usually lines up editorially with animal causes, will on occasion print a photograph showing an elephant doing a headstand on the streets of New York. Such buffoonery grates upon the perceptions and feelings of those who have grasped the innate dignity and essential innocence of the lower animals. Speaking generally and charitably, however, one can say that animals get a good press in America, with the message of mercy indicated at least by implication if not always spelled out. Zoologists may shudder, but the anthropomorphic anecdote has made more friends for the animal kingdom than they have.

Thus we are pleased to learn the following facts, and from time to time others of similar import:

That there is a dog of uncertain ancestry named Rinny who attends the Campfield Elementary School at Baltimore and gets a report card showing a grade of A in participation, conduct, and singing.

That there is a dog named Ralph who has been attending Drake University for nine years and is in graduate school, now majoring in business administration. Ralph holds an ID card that admits him to college sports events and other cultural activities.

That Ralphine, a cat residing in Tacoma, Washington, has a Texaco credit card. Her occupation on the application was given as "chasing mice."

And finally, that a couple were married at the Henry Doorly Zoo in Omaha, Nebraska, with an orangutan holding a bouquet of petunias as flower girl. The groom explained: "Sharon said that the zoo was the first place I brought her on a date."[19]

The approach to humane education initiated by George T. Angell continues today in the school classroom, the schools often using teaching materials supplied by animal welfare organizations. Twenty-nine states have passed legislation requiring the teaching of humane attitudes. Some carry out the provisions of their laws and some do not.[20] A modern dimension of fair-play-for-animals may be observed in the position taken by scoutism toward the power human beings hold over animals. "A Girl Scout is a friend to animals," the *Girl Scout Handbook* declares, and a Boy Scout is not only trustworthy, loyal, helpful, friendly, courteous, obedient, cheerful, thrifty, brave, clean, and reverent, but he is also "a friend to animals. He will not kill or hurt any living creature needlessly, but will strive to save and protect all harmless life." Of increasing importance in recent years as a force for education in the fundamentals of compassion is the Kindness Club, which admits young people from eight to eighteen years of age. A Canadian idea, the club is now international, with branches all over the free world and its own journal, *Fur and Feathers*. The Club emblem is a raccoon. The leader is a Raccoon Captain, and each branch is named for an animal, such as beaver or chipmunk. A child who wants to be kind to animals but has to do it all by himself can join anyway. He is known as a Lone Raccoon.[21]

Among the promotional days and weeks that crowd our calendar, Be Kind to Animals Week has been a fixture since 1915, encouraging good care and proper handling of animals and focusing public attention on the services of humane societies. Some eight hundred of them celebrate the week in song, story, and graphics, on radio and television programs, assisted by sententious proclamations by mayors of cities and governors of states. The idea grew out of Mercy Sunday and was the brainchild of Henry F. Lewith, a modest printer and animal lover of Charleston, South Carolina. The slogan "Be Kind to Animals" was Lewith's invention. Neatly wrapping up humanitarian teachings, the sentence has traveled everywhere English is spoken and has been translated into many foreign ladguages. For years the Charleston printer wrote long, tedious, impassioned, handwritten letters to humane leaders, one of whom, Dr. Francis H. Rowley, then president of the Massachusetts SPCA, took hold of the plan and gave it the sponsorship it needed. Lewith died many years ago, in 1926, and was followed to his grave, according to a memoir that appeared later in the *News and Courier* of Charleston, by his collie dog, Beauty, who refused to eat after the death of his master.[22]

A major civilizing influence has come from people in the arts, especially the performing arts, who have shown a remarkable empathy with animals. Madame Lillian Nordica, the operatic soprano and ideal Brünhilde, is known to have cherished and later mourned over a clever parrot, and Frieda Hempel, the Metropolitan Opera soprano, was often seen smuggling table scraps into New York's Central Park to provide a meal for a mongrel dog of her acquaintance. The pets of Fritz Kreisler and Gene Krupa, two virtuosos who occupy rather different positions in musical history, lie in the Canine Cemetery at Hartsdale, New York. Harry Lauder, the Scottish comedian and singer, who had been a "pit lad" in his youth, dragging trucks of coal from the mine face to the shaft, worked for the passage of the English Coal Mine Act, aimed at improving the lot of the pit ponies. Mrs. Minnie Maddern Fiske, the American actress, supreme in light comedy yet a great interpreter of Ibsen, protested against the steel traps that provide women with their furs, the treatment of mules in the oil fields, and the suffering endured by the stock on western ranges. With her it was a matter of personal ethics. "I would go to the rescue of a rat," she said, "if I saw it being tortured."[23]

Mrs. Fiske was militant. Actresses who played with her were forbidden to wear furs or articles of clothing decorated with feathers. On tour she would scour the town for stray animals and board her train, according to legend, with assorted tails protruding from under her cloth coat.[24] It was to oblige Mrs. Fiske that Mark Twain, who believed that the animals, like the angels, never sinned, wrote "A Horse's Tale," to aid her crusade against the Spanish bullfight.[25] More recently, but in the tradition of Mrs. Fiske, Mrs. Irene Castle Enzinger devoted herself from the 1920s to her death in 1969 to the care of stray animals. The famous ballroom dancer of the World War I epoch made her primary interest the animal shelter she founded, Orphans of the Storm, at Deerfield, Illinois. "It comes from my heart," she said of this work, and directed, "When I die my gravestone is to say 'Humanitarian' instead of 'Dancer.' "[26]

In the period of the great international actresses, Sarah Bernhardt kept a whole menagerie—cheetahs, pumas, dogs, cats, monkeys, fish, and a tortoise named Chrysagère, whose gold-tinted shell was set with pale blue, yellow, and rose-colored topazes, all of which sounds more like animal exploitation than affection. So do the habits of our contemporaries: Adamo—singer, movie star, and idol of the French public—who takes his leopard with him when he strolls the boulevards, and Salvador Dali who keeps, contrary to all humanitarian counsel, an ocelot. This handsome beast is reported as having attended an intimate dinner for twenty-five at the artist's apartment at the Hotel Meurice in Paris and at midnight went on with Dali to help pop the champagne corks at Maxim's, accompanied by a bevy of no less faithful and pretty bipeds.[27]

Because there are so many degrees of cruelty and so many subtle shadings of exploitation and so many clever rationalizations men indulge in to justify doing what they want to do, the advance made by animal welfare programs has always been a sort of two-steps-forward, one-step-backward rhythm. Man, philosophizes Cleveland Amory, social historian and president of the Fund for Animals, Inc., "has an infinite capacity to rationalize his rapacity, particularly when it comes to something he wants to eat or wear."[28]

Sometimes humanitarian groups get taken over suddenly by a special interest bloc that has some other aim in view than the animals' welfare. This happened in rather spectacular fashion to the Dane County Humane Society of Madison, Wisconsin, in 1967. Some sixty individuals associated with the University of Wisconsin Medical School, the Veterinary Science Department, and the Primate Laboratory swamped the annual meeting of the venerable society and by bloc voting elected as directors a medical student, the typist of an assistant professor, and the "buncher" who drove the truck that collected the dogs for the laboratories. This episode was widely assessed as an attempt to turn a respected humane society into an agency for the procurement of raw material for the dissecting rooms.[29]

People generally have a vague but comforting impression that animals are adequately protected from inhumane treatment in law and in fact. But laws often have loopholes, laws have to be enforced to be effective, and animal-protection agencies often run out of steam, or funds, or bend to pressures. They can, under circumstances of stress or the adoption of differing strategies, give each other a vigorous clawing. It is not the way of the humane professionals to take the cash and let the credit go, for they know that in their benevolent work he who gets the credit is likely to walk off with the cash, too. Thus money and mercy march hand in hand.

Human nature being what it is, a humane organization can easily acquire a vested interest in kindness, as one can in religion, in the oil depletion allowance, in holding public office, or in any other attractive activity. One can easily be too cynical about this. The fact is that, so far as animal suffering is concerned, both the ethical commitment and money are necessary. A danger should be mentioned, however. It arises when an SPCA-type organism prospers through catering to pet lovers who remember it generously in their wills. The society may then take on the insurance company mentality and direct its warmth to its fiduciary duties rather than its speechless clients. When such a situation occurs, there is bound to be criticism. In this context new groupings of humanitarians often come together with a broader and more dedicated program.

So it was in 1899, when a number of Chicago women headed by Mrs. Theodore Thomas, wife of the conductor of the Chicago Symphony Orchestra, concluded that the Illinois Humane Society was getting fat and lethargic. So they started a new endeavor, the Anti-Cruelty Society, whose "main impetus . . . was mistreatment of work-horses and mishandling of meat animals . . . ." As this chapter is being written, New York's ASPCA is being charged by an ad hoc group, the Committee to Protect New York City Animals, and a coalition of humane societies, with slackness in carrying out the society's mission.[30]

Among the societies of today that are the lengthened shadow of a man or woman may be mentioned the Animal Welfare Institute, Mrs. Christine Stevens, president, which is especially concerned with the treatment of animals utilized for food, fur, and experimentation. The Defenders of Wildlife under Miss Mary Hazell Harris joins together the two areas of kindness and conservation. The Friends of Animals, Inc., Miss Alice Herrington, president, documents the cruelty present in the slaughter of livestock and the annual seal "harvest." The National Catholic Society for Animal Welfare, Miss Helen E. Jones, president, is a lay, nonsectarian agency that also works on the problem of humane slaughter, points the finger at the brutalities of rodeo, and does not hesitate to take cruelists to court.

The societies mentioned and many others not mentioned practice a degree of specialization because they cannot fight on all fronts at once or because they are well situated for performing some particular task. The Wyoming Humane Society, out in the cattle country, concentrates on the animal suffering caused by the rodeo industry, and Mrs. Elizabeth Sakach, of the Animal Welfare League in Reno, Nevada, brings behind-the-scenes knowledge to bear on the same problem. Cleveland Amory's Fund for Animals goes anywhere to meet crises and sudden needs, though Amory's bête noire is the bullfight. The Texas Council for Wildlife Protection, under Mrs. Ann Gough Hunter, has been successful in campaigning against raccoon baiting, a popular amusement in some southern states since pioneer days. The Unexpected Wildlife Refuge, Inc., of Newfield, New Jersey, makes a specialty of preserving beavers.

All of these societies, and many others, run on the energy and skills of a leader who has the calling for animal rescue work. The directing heads observe no office hours, fear no controversies, including controversies with each other. Reformers at heart, the humane leaders of our time aim at nothing less than arousing the conscience of the whole human community and so modifying the total culture of our society. They form the cutting edge of humanitarianism today. Whether the quite personal societies will in time become institutionalized, and whether that would be desirable, is a matter only the future can determine.

13

Going the Whole Way:
Vegetarianism

Those who support humanitarian efforts are frequently asked how they justify eating the objects of their compassion. The answer is that some eat meat and some don't and some occupy a kind of shaky middle ground, as did Mrs. Minnie Maddern Fiske, the celebrated actress and staunch *amie* of animals, who shared the vegetarian principles of George Bernard Shaw and Count Tolstoy, but admitted, "I myself often fall off the vegetable wagon. . . ."[1]

"We're just like other people, only we don't eat meat," the earnest president of the New York Vegetarian Society protested some years ago.[2] But there is abundant evidence that the more than five million persons in the United States who gather under the vegetarian banner are quite special people.[3]

As an organized Western movement, the no-meat doctrine came into public view about a century ago; the word *vegetarian* dates from 1842. Yet the idea it represents is endemic. In the long perspective of history, vegetarianism represents a form of perfection-

127

ism, touching the mind, the body, and the spirit. This view of man's nature is both pessimistic and nostalgic, blending the dream of a vanished Golden Age with the Hebrew story of the fall from a state of grace. To this legendary inheritance is added a romanticism that seeks to recapture a lost innocence and calls up visions of straw-eating lions and tigers, no longer red in tooth and claw.

Although the vegetarian movement is a kind of melting pot, bringing together reformers, ascetics, hippies, pacifists, raw food crusaders, utopians, mystics, poets, millenarians, idealistic individualists, as well as zoophilists, its central idea is the ethical obligation not to inflict pain upon any form of sentient life. "We are the species uniquely capable of imagination, rationality and moral choice," writes Brigid Brophy, the Anglo-Irish author (and vegetarian), "and that is precisely why we are under the obligation to recognize and respect the rights of animals."[4]

The emotional revulsion against eating flesh foods is summarized in the question, "How can you eat anything that has *eyes?*"[5] The question was often asked by Dr. John Harvey Kellog, dynamic health reformer, founder of the famous Battle Creek Sanitarium, and inventor of some eighty ready-to-eat cereal foods, including the ubiquitous cornflake. Dr. Kellogg, a superb publicist, kept a morose chimpanzee, which he used for a stunt. The doctor would toss a juicy beefsteak to the suspicious animal. The chimp would examine it and quickly slam the meat right back at him. Then Dr. Kellogg would offer a banana, which the ape munched with evident enjoyment. Kellogg drew the conclusion: "Eat what the monkey eats . . . our nearest relative."[6]

Closely joined to the emotional objection to meat is the aesthetic. To a vegetarian, the emanations from animal and fish carcasses are revolting, and vegetarian writers have often suggested that each meat eater should have to kill and eviscerate his own animal. One pamphleteer has advised that when a child asks questions about the source of meat, the honest parent will not "conceal the origin of 'mutton' or 'beef' from a child." Combining the emotional and aesthetic retreat from meat, Voltaire asked, in his article on *viande* in the *Dictionnaire philosophique*, whether, if animals had speech, we would dare to kill and eat them. The philosopher saw in his imagination a lamb at the slaughterhouse imploring the butcher "not to be at once assassin and cannibal."[7]

In support of their position vegetarians employ vivid images of "the pitiful organs and limbs of the creatures" freshly slaughtered. Dr. Kellogg never failed to allude, with gut realism, to any carcass displayed in a meat market. In his lectures, the doctor gleefully recited unappetizing statistics on disease, gathered at the Union Stock Yards in Chicago, or he would whirl on his audience to bark, "How would you like to eat a dead hen?" Vegetarian publicists also discuss—with a certain relish—the parasites that inhabit animal flesh consumed by humans, including the tapeworm, and the occurrence in pork of the nematode *Trichinella spiralis.*[8]

Mel Morse, former president of the Humane Society of the United States, who advocates mercy toward animals but is not personally a vegetarian, remarks in his *Ordeal of the Animals,* as he sketches a slaughterhouse scene, "If every one of our slaughterhouses were constructed of glass, this would be a nation of vegetarians."[9]

The animal defense movement and vegetarianism often pursue parallel aims, although the SPCAs and humane groups do not usually object to what they call "necessary killing," provided humane procedures are followed in the slaughter. In contrast to this position, the vegetarians do not recognize the concept of "necessary killing." They often meet life's complexities with versatile responses. One prominent vegetarian, whose wife discovered that she missed the taste of breakfast bacon, developed a type of smoked yeast that tasted like bacon, then found that he had a prosperous new business on his hands. Another, when asked what he would do about the plague of rabbits in Australia, replied, "If I could not live in the country with the animals, I should go somewhere else."[10]

The ethical vegetarian, who refuses to eat meat or take life on moral or philosophical grounds, appears in the person of Bronson Alcott, the New England sage and mystic, most transcendental of the Transcendentalists. When he went to the meat shop to market for his wife, Alcott shuddered, "Death yawns at me. . . . The death-set eyes of beasts peer at me and accuse me." At his vegetarian communal farm, "Fruitlands," Alcott forbade the use of woolen clothing because it deprived the sheep of its coat. Nor did he approve of his fields being cultivated by oxen or horses, since such slave labor would have violated the natural rights of animals. Thomas Carlyle, who both loved and laughed at Alcott, described him as a man "bent on saving the world by a return to acorns and the golden age."[11]

This same line of reasoning has led idealistic vegetarians to reject shoes and gloves made of leather and to avoid soap and cosmetics made from animal fats. When the International Vegetarian Union met in London some years ago, one of the delegates wore a derby hat made without silk. Another displayed "vegetarian" furs. Exhibits included pocketbooks of vegetable origin, and dog collars, "tortoiseshell" combs, and strings for tennis rackets and violins for which no cat made any sacrifice.[12]

The vegetarian draws conclusions from man's tooth structure, which are opposed to those of the anthropologists, who find that the biting incisors, tearing canines, and grinding molars indicate that our species is designed to draw on all food sources. The vegetarian is a moralist and reformer before he is a physiologist. Historically, he connects sympathetically with other altruists in such groupings as the antifur-wearers, the antitobacco and temperance movements. Vegetarians occupy a position near to that of the opponents of vivisection and compulsory vaccination and are frequently stern critics of orthodox medicine. They emphasize that their diet promotes world peace. Meat makes men want to fight, according to some vegetarians who believe that we become what we eat. Carnivores are killers, say the vegetarian thinkers; men who eat meat take on the same characteristics. Actually, the grass-eating African buffalo is more vindictive than the lion. Why are tigers fierce? Simply because they are tigers!

Vegetarianism must be viewed in part as a theological attempt to explain the cosmos, for it contains elements of pantheism, metaphysics, yoga, yin and yang, and Vedic mysticism. For example, Mrs. Annie Besant, the nineteenth-century theosophist and author of a vigorous little work, *Vegetarianism in the Light of Theosophy*, is still cited in the literature read by vegetarians. She describes how she felt a profound depression of spirit when she was coming into Chicago because she was receiving astral messages of reproach from the spirits of thousands of beasts murdered in the South Chicago stock yards.[13]

A revered father figure of vegetarianism is Sylvester Graham (1794–1851), a verbose and belligerent promoter of the nutritional values of the whole-grain cereals. At the same time he denounced meat as a stimulant of sexual vigor, an attack that probably had quite a different impact upon his lecture audiences than he contemplated.[14] Physiologically, man stands between the highly specialized herbivores, which have long, capacious intestines and a large cecum, and do little but browse and rest, and the carnivores with their shorter tract and small cecum.[15] Some vegetarians are strong and healthy men. So are some people who rely upon beef and bourbon.

Yet the vegetable diet has ranked up many impressive accomplishments. One has to look, however, at more than the dietary regimen to find the reasons. Attention to health, backed by a theory and a scheme, usually brings in such supplementary factors as rest, a better environment, and an improvement in general habits. As Dr. L. Jean Bogert wrote in *Diet and Personality*, "The suggestion and belief that benefit will be derived is . . . a strong force making toward health."[16]

The true spiritual vegetarian, as distinct from the stomach vegetarian, believing that each animal has its place in the evolutionary order, its own life to live, its own joy and purposes, considers that it is unethical to consume *any* product of animal origin. Thus from the strict point of view, those who use milk, butter, cheese, eggs, and honey are regarded as no more than demi-vegetarians, to whom the undefiled say crossly, "You may as well eat the Devil as drink his broth." For those who are sympathetic in principle but unreliable in practice the Vegetarian Society of New York provides a special, but inferior, class of membership.

There are other subgroups. Fruitarians eat only what the term indicates. Some vegetarians have survived on nuts. Others eat only plant life that is organically grown. Another division subsists on raw foods only, while some will eat only the "aspiring" vegetables that grow in the light of the sun—no tubers or root vegetables allowed in the pot. Those vegetarians who look at flesh eating from the standpoint of the animals that get eaten, join gladly with the animal welfare societies in the celebration of Be Kind to Animals Week or of World Day for Animals. They look with distress upon those brothers whose introspective vegetarianism is concerned only with their own dietary salvation. But the extensive literature of vegetarian cookery, recipes, health treatises, and works on herb therapeutics suggests that the majority of the adherents are primarily concerned with the state of their insides rather than the crisis of conscience that may erupt when a merciful man dines upon a fellow creature.

There is a religious element in vegetarianism which rests upon Old Testament authority and emphasizes selected passages, literally interpreted. Man, looked at from this vantage point, is not at all at the top of his development but rather has suffered, after the Garden of Eden incident, a physical as well as moral Fall. One can also find warrant in the Scriptures for eating meat if he wishes to —see Genesis 9:3. But the vegetarians, like all particularistic interpreters of sacred documents, display a marvelous ingenuity in explaining away whatever commands fail to fit the thesis.

The first organized vegetarian religious group to arrive in the United States left Manchester, England, in 1817. Searching for a Heavenly City, they found Philadelphia. There they established a "Bible Christian" church, which practiced vegetarianism in the spirit of the Psalmist: "He causeth the grass to grow for the cattle, and herb for the service of man." And the congregation sang with the great vegetarian poet, Oliver Goldsmith:

> No flocks that range the
>   valley free
> To slaughter we condemn;
> Taught by the Power that
>   pities us
> We learn to pity them.

The Bible Christian church lasted for nearly a century, initiated the American vegetarian cult, and shaped its theories. The line of descent from this little band of English fundamentalists to the religious-health-medical tenets of today's powerful Seventh-Day Adventist denomination can be clearly traced.[17]

Although vegetarianism has flourished in the social environment of the last century and the present one, all of its ideas and assumptions are thousands of years old and find expression in various Eastern religions: in Brahminism, Buddhism, and Zoroastrianism. In the West, from at least the sixth century B.C., the practice was incorporated into the thought of the Orphic societies, drawing strength from the doctrine of the transmigration of souls. This idea has persisted into the modern era as a half-believed myth, comforting to men of sensitive feeling who see animals suffering and are solaced by the hope that injustices of the present world will be compensated for in another life.

In classical literature, Pythagoras advocated asceticism in eating, and Porphyry in his *De Abstinentia*, where he viewed men as more than beasts but less than gods, also shrank with abhorrence from the practice of engulfing the entrails of our animal brothers into our own. Vegetarianism claims Socrates and Plato, Plutarch, Leonardo da Vinci, and Saint Francis; and coming down the centuries, Rousseau, John Wesley, and the poets Burns, Cowper, Shelley, and Thomson. The poets celebrated the unity and sacredness of all life, and decried the disastrous effect upon men, as well as beasts, when human bellies have no ears to hear the agonized cries of the doomed. Domitian, the Roman emperor, as Seneca says, started by killing flies and ended by killing men. This thought has been repeated many times and given new applications down to the present moment, when vegetarians relate the diet question to the search for world peace. Vegetarians further contend that theirs is a practical philosophy, in light of the relationship between world population and the utilization of agricultural land. A vegetarian needs only about one-third as much land to support himself as does a meat eater.

Famous men of more recent times whose eating habits are praised at vegetarian festivals include Count Tolstoy, Gandhi, Richard Wagner, the composer-conductor; Wilhelm Fürtwängler, great interpreter of Beethoven and Brahms; and George Bernard Shaw, who chided his English compatriots for a misplaced confidence in beef tea and declared that meat eating was "cannibalism with its heroic dish omitted."[18] In nineteenth-century America most of Emerson's circle, as well as Horace Greeley, Dr. Oliver Wendell Holmes, and the sprightly and scandalous Victoria Woodhull, all adopted vegetarian dining. In the present century Henry Morgenthau; John D. Rockefeller; Lucy Page Gaston, the nemesis of the cigarette; Gifford Pinchot, the conservationist; John H. Patterson, who invented high-pressure American salesmanship; and Horace Fletcher, "the Great Masticator," who put the verb *to Fletcherize* in the dictionaries, all have been claimed as fellow members by the vegetarians. Possibly best-known of all is Johnny Weissmuller of Tarzan fame. Weissmuller, after only a few weeks on the meatless diet (according to news released from the Battle Creek Sanitarium), was able to hang up six world swimming records.[19]

It is widely believed that Hitler was a vegetarian. But the *Vegetarian News Digest*, which has looked into the matter, indignantly rejected any association of the Führer with the cause. "We have no information to indicate that he eliminated flesh foods from his diet for humanitarian reasons," the magazine concluded. The avoidance of meat or fish, it was pointed out, does not meet the definition of vegetarianism, "which is a philosophy of life and not a mere way of eating."[20]

Critics of vegetarianism never tire of teasing the faithful by pointing out that if a cruel and relentless war was not waged on such insects as bean beetles, cabbageworms, aphids, and leafhoppers, there soon would be no vegetables and no vegetarians to eat them.[21] Because of the humor and even hostility directed toward the vegetarian way of life by the "gentile" world, members of the cult tend to yard up for creature comfort in societies and lecture halls, and at festive dinners where they dine enthusiastically on soybean cutlets, carrot pie, and alfalfa tea. Meat eaters seem to be endlessly fascinated with the vegetarian menu, especially on our great feast days. *The New York Times* regularly satisfies this morbid interest by reporting what the adherents of the Vegetarian Society of New York nibbled, munched, chewed, and quaffed for their Thanksgiving Day dinner.[22] And those of congenial views meet in the pages of coterie magazines, often advertising for suitable mates: "Vegetarian woman wishes to correspond with spiritually oriented vegetarian man, 40 to 55."[23]

Vegetarians tend to marry vegetarians. Exogamous unions are called "mixed marriages." In a number of instances, vegetarians have withdrawn from the frenetic world of flesh eaters into quasireligious communities. One such venture was the Octagon Settlement scheme, in which an idealistic group attempted in the 1850s to set up a colony on the Neosho River, near Fort Scott, Kansas. To the rhetorical quesion posed by their leader, the Reverend Henry Stephen Clubb, "Is Edenic life practical?" the answer turned out to be no. At least in Kansas.[24]

Oregon and Florida have also been suggested as suitable sites for vegetarian colonizing; and a few years ago a Dr. J. Waterman Rose, director of the Bronx Vegetarian Center, drew up plans for a vegetarian city, where it would be illegal for the residents to eat meat. The new town was to be called something appropriate to the central idea like Vegetonia or Vegetaria, and the location thought of was near Middletown, Connecticut.[25] But the plan died on the vine.

There are more vegetarians in the United States today than ever before, each responding individually to some combination of the emotional, moral, or physiological arguments advanced in support of the vegetable mystique. They support hygienic havens such as the eight-acre Shangri-La Health Resort at Bonita Springs, Florida, which offers mental and emotional poise, nude sunbathing, watercycles, organically grown fruits, but no meat or dairy products.[26] Vegetarians support a national network of health food stores that supply fruit juicers and vegetable graters, soya cookies, roasted dandelion roots, nutrition charts, unsprayed rose hips, and the writings of the late Symon Gould, who put an American Vegetarian party into politics and himself ran for President.[27]

Vegetarianism remains at bottom a form of sensibility, despite its scientific trappings. It has undoubtedly influenced the large, uncommitted public, which, while it appreciates the satiety value of prime roast beef and has never seen the inside of an abattoir, yet is ill at ease over such topics as calories, cholesterol, and sometimes, cruelty to animals.

PART

III

No More Room in

the Ark?

14

Declining Contact
Between Men and Animals

M an has been described as a cooking animal. He has another characteristic almost equally distinctive. He keeps pets. But aside from our special relations with our domestic beast companions, human attitudes still contain elements of fear, a fascination with killing, a general indifference to animal life and death. Since ninety-five percent of us are now metro-Americans, it follows that the respect that comes from intimate contact is dissipated.[1] It can be argued, indeed, that as modern man knows less and less of the forests, the stream margins and meadows, or the psyches of the commonest farm animals, our sensitivity to the world of nature is probably less than it has ever been in recorded history.

Contact with other living creatures is actually difficult to achieve. The impulse must be largely satisfied by some means compatible with living in flats: a bowl of tropical fish, a gerbil, or an afternoon at the zoo. When the Assembly of the State of New York voted to make the bluebird the official state bird, the only lawmaker to vote against the measure was Seymour Posner of the Bronx. He explained: "Those of us who are city dwellers don't know the bluebird . . . How are we going to go along with a bird we never saw?"[2]

Once there were important roles in human affairs for the horse, the dog, the cat, and other animals whose services are for the most part now forgotten. Ferrets, for instance, were good at pulling telephone wires through long conduits. The French still use pigs to sniff out truffles, but not every pig has the true vocation for locating these aristocratic relatives of the mushroom, and truffle entrepreneurs are seeking alternative methods of discovering the delectable tubers. Birds now out of work include the homing pigeon and the miner's canary, and we no longer need the purple martin as mosquito control. Sheep and donkeys are still useful for animating nativity scenes at Christmas time, but this is seasonal employment of limited duration.

Animals have much to teach us. This has always been recognized. "Were it not for the animal world," Buffon, the French naturalist, observed long ago, "men would find themselves more incomprehensible than ever."[3] Yet twentieth-century philosophy is out of touch with animals, since it follows the way of introspection rather than observation, "a method obviously not applicable to the animal kingdom."[4] In recognition of the sense of alienation experienced by today's urban masses, educators are calling for the introduction of environmental studies in elementary schools, most of whose students may never know "the satisfaction, stimulation, romance, adventure, excitement, fun, richness and inner tranquility that comes from experience with the natural world."[5] Ghetto children are bussed to green areas, museums, and botanical gardens to meet the birds and bees. Mice and rats are, of course, quite easily encountered.[6]

"A number of these inner-city children have never seen a hamster or lizard," says Mrs. Lena Ransdell, librarian for both books and animals at the Englehard Elementary School in Louisville, Kentucky. "You should see them carrying out science books now," she added. The animals are taken to the classroom but not to the students' homes.[7] For many years the Animal Rescue League of Boston has conducted an Animal Friends Summer School at Cape Cod, where children learn to wash dogs, remove ticks, hatch duck eggs, handle live snakes, and release herring gulls under the eye of a state conservation officer.

Despite such ingenious efforts, for the most part we observe wild life behind bars or in the circus. In the circus rings an uncomprehending public watches wild creatures perform eccentric tricks, often in violation of the anatomical structure and deepest instincts of the animal: horses dancing on their hind feet, bears roller-skating, dogs pushing prams, cats firing off cannons, tigers jumping through hoops. One elephant, trained to dance and to play "Yes Sir, That's My Baby" on the harmonica, was described not long ago as being probably the meanest elephant in the United States. Perhaps he had reason.

It is all so preposterous when one really thinks about it. Furthermore, the only quick, commercially feasible way of breaking the spirits of animal prisoners, according to critics and trainers who have discussed the subject, is by using whips, electric shocks, sharp hooks, loud noises, and as a last resort, starvation. The training is done in seclusion, often in a foreign country where anything goes so far as animal treatment is concerned. "Animals," says the RSPCA, "do not learn to do unnatural things merely by listening to words."[8] The Performing and Captive Animals' Defence League of London has a standing offer of a thousand pounds to anyone who will train any animal to perform a circus trick on demand without cruelty. The prize remains unclaimed. Deeply imbedded as it is in our culture, the circus is, nevertheless, in a sharp decline. The movies and television have about done it in. Now most circuses exist as adjuncts of charities, which use them as fund-raising devices.[9]

The public zoo—colloquial word for zoological garden—has been known in the Western world since 1793, when the menagerie at the Jardin des Plantes was opened in Paris. In the United States the Philadelphia Zoological Garden claims to have been first because of the date of its charter, but the Central Park Zoo in New York City was actually the first to open its gates. Zoos have been a controversial wildlife topic ever since.[10] We badly need two new words in connection with this emotion-charged subject, one for zoo lovers, one for zoo haters. "Zoophile" and "zoophobe" won't do, since they have already been applied to the love or hate of the animals themselves.

Pro-zoo literature emphasizes that "mainstream zoos" save endangered species from extinction, advance the science of zoology,
are a primary means of widening knowledge in the field of veterinary medicine, and offer the only means by which most Americans
will ever see a wild animal. Thus the zoological park introduces
the charm, grace, and beauty of wild creatures into the city habitat
and fosters an appreciation of wildlife and the need for conserving
it at our point in history when even the barnyard stock has disappeared from the scene.[11] It is also argued, from the animals' point
of view, that few animals die of old age in their natural environment, and that the captives, after all, are assured of food and safety
and some degree of freedom from parasites. Most zoos today have
recognized the symptoms of "cage fatigue," and have advanced
beyond white-tile caging to provide rudimentary habitat facilities
such as mud wallows, cement "mountains," scratching posts or
logs for clawing. Furthermore, we are assured by Dr. Heini
Hediger, animal behaviorist and director of the Zurich Zoological
Garden, that it is a mistaken idea to attribute human reactions,
such as a longing for liberty,[12] to subhuman beings. Zoo directors
do not dwell upon the subject of animal deaths in zoos or the
methods employed by "beachhead dealers" in collecting wild
beasts. In general, the strategy is to shoot a young mother and
catch her baby, which may or may not survive crating and shipment. The total effect upon animal populations is appalling.[13]
    Zoo critics see these places of amusement as just another in-
stance of man's willingness to deplete the natural world for a
shallow pleasure, all done in the name of education.[14] Henry
Bergh raised the question long ago, "What is the use or sense of
penning those poor beasts up to gratify the curiosity of idle gazers
. . . in the miserable shed in Central Park?" Bergh never wavered
in his opposition to the exhibition of caged animals by which, he
said, "neither public taste, education, nor morals are benefited
. . .'.[15] This attitude has a continuing history. It appears in John
Galsworthy, the English playwright and novelist, who called captive eagles "statues of winged grief," and in the eloquent contemporary writings of Julia Allen Field, who declares, "We cannot
glimpse the essential life of a caged animal, only the shadow of its
former beauty . . . "[16]
    Yet people of sensibility and concern do not speak with one

voice about the zoo concept. The attitude of humanitarians is ambivalent, with a leaning toward acceptance of zoos when they are well administered. However, Brigid Brophy doesn't give an inch. She has even suggested that it would be less cruel to cage the human visitor in an English zoo than the animals, because the animals can know only raw terror, while a British subject in such circumstances could read a book, reason and reflect upon his misfortune, and write to the Home Secretary about it.[17] Miss Brophy would appreciate the acquaintance, from a safe distance, of Rebecca, the beautiful jaguar of the Central Park Zoo, of whom the head keeper has been quoted as saying: "She's never adapted . . . she refused to adjust . . . she just never hauled down her colors."[18]

Zoo animals necessarily share the consequences of violence when human affairs go awry. The Parisians, starved out by the German army during the siege of the city during the Franco-Prussian War, ate not only "salmi of game" (rat) but kangaroo, English wolf, camel, and elephant from the zoological gardens. Only the monkeys were still alive after three months of short rations because, as one English observer wrote, "these are kept alive from a vague and Darwinian notion that they are our relatives, or at least the relatives of some members of the Government." And the philosophic Briton noted further that stark hunger produces a new tolerance of otherwise unattractive dietary novelties.

Germany's zoological stock was hard hit during World War II, a destruction of innocents mourned by the naturalists of all countries. Much of the great London Zoo perished. The lions got the best of it—a good ration of horsemeat, since this war was fought with gasoline and the horse was no longer an engine of war. Marine life went into the frying pan, and the zoo restaurant served giraffe cutlets, which, one diner recorded, were "deemed inferior to Barbary sheep."[19]

Today in America the zoo animals suffer along with the rest of us from the sickness and alienation in our society. A tiger smashed its skull against the wall of its prison after someone exploded a cherry bomb inside the cage. A nighttime rifleman shot two lions at the Portland, Oregon, Zoo, after the beasts had mauled a nineteen-year-old youth, high on beer and wine, who had clambered into the lion pit and kicked the lions. This phenomenon of abuse of zoo animals is nationwide. At the Dallas, Texas, Zoo, someone stuck a monkey in the stomach with a four-inch nail, while at Baltimore vandals killed thirty-one animals in one rampageous period by stoning and feeding them glass, drugs, and pesticides.[20] Faced with similar problems, the Zoological Park at Topeka, Kansas, has put on display a Museum of Human Stupidity, in which is assembled actual objects that have been used to harass the animals—pencils, bottle caps, paper cups, plastic bags, wires, string, and can openers.[21]

One facility of a repulsive sort for satisfying our curiosity about animals is the roadside zoo. It is a zoo in name only. These animal slums, conducted by filling stations, "trading posts," motels, souvenir stands, and snack bars, are not wholly a modern invention. They descend from the colonial tavern, which attracted customers by chaining a bear to a post in front of the premises. The zoological come-on experienced an extraordinary expansion as a side effect of the automobile in the 1930s, when coyotes, bears, and monkeys were confined in cages to draw motorists to the gasoline pumps.[22]

Now this filthy business befouls the landscape for miles along important highways with its sensational signs. "Bear Likes Pop," reads a crudely scrawled placard attached to the bars of a cage in North Carolina. There are similar lures in New York's Adirondack region, various "monkey jungles" and "alligator farms" in Florida and Arizona. "Donations Help Feed the Animals," says a sign in New Mexico. No donation, no food? One wonders. Misery, heat, cold, dirt, and stress is the portion of the victims who drag out their weary lives beneath the beckoning signs and tattered banners. Even water is a scarce commodity at these "Indian villages" and "wishing wells."[23]

Only eighteen states at present writing issue permits for roadside menageries. Of this number only nine prescribe minimum standards. Where regulations do exist, they are often drawn so as to cover only narrow categories, such as migratory birds, wild native animals, or endangered species. Most states simply ignore the problem or rely upon the SPCAs.[24]

Quite aside from the usefulness of animals or the exploitation of beasts for profit, man still likes to have furred, finny, and feathered

creatures close to him. No one claims that canaries, parrots, turtles, or tropical fish are useful, and, as Marston Bates says, "There
are easier ways of catching mice than by keeping cats."[25] Clearly,
a pet is a psychic outlet, a source of emotional gratification, a
consolation to the aged who extend through the animal their grip
on life, a channel for aggressive feelings if the pet is a large dog
of fighting ancestry. Or the animal may be a substitute child that
shows appreciation for favors rendered and never smokes pot or
calls its "parents" "Establishment freaks."

The enormous importance of pets is a phenomenon that deserves more analysis than it has received. But psychologists have
identified animals in this kind of personal relationship with humans as a love object, a challenge to responsibility, an aid in the
sex education of children, a vehicle for teaching toilet training, a
longing for dominance through the control of the life and destiny
of another being. Or sometimes, just something to attract attention
and talk about. Some such attachments, Dr. Karl A. Menninger
believes, are of an "essentially sexual nature."[26] The possession of
more than one pet often doubles the pleasure or gives the ego an
extra fillip. As the animal warden of the town of Poughkeepsie,
New York, expressed it: ". . . if you don't have more than one pet
in this town, boy, you're just not 'in.' "[27]

Pets are part of "the American way," an official of the American
Humane Association has pointed out to the audience of the Voice
of America. Their number in the United States is about 50 to 57
millions of owned animals, distributed over 12.5 million
households. The figure for the dog population, between 22 and 26
million, is fairly accurate because of the licensing system. The
number of owned cats, disregarding the homeless, is perhaps
slightly less. But no one really knows. The idea of licensing cats
comes up from time to time, but never gets anywhere. It is doubt-
ful if anyone truly owns a cat. And besides, there just isn't any
place on a cat where a license tag can be securely attached.

Horses are making a comeback. There are more of them in the
United States today, according to the Census Bureau, than ever
before, and the two-car family now has to bow socially to the
family with a stable and an acre, or at least a good-sized back yard,
for the horse. Contributing to the expansion of this seven-billion-
dollar-plus industry is Wayne Newton, the singer, who with a

partner paid $150,000 for a prize Arabian stallion, and Lee Carpenter, former automobile dealer of Los Angeles, who keeps his three Arabians "in an anthropomorphic atmosphere that includes piped-in stereo music. . . ." But bridle paths are being steadily extended, and the horse is going democratic. By 1977, according to the American Horse Council, approximately 82 million Americans are expected to ride a horse for pleasure at least once a year.[28]

For those who don't have room for a horse, a parakeet fits well into today's efficiency apartment. Turtles and hamsters are also suggested by the ASPCA for situations where space is limited and the pet owner goes to work all day. And right now there are hundreds of snakes in New York City apartments, appreciated by their owners because they do not have to be walked, vaccinated, licensed, or fed on a regular schedule and they will not claw the upholstery or bark.

From the economic point of view—and do we ever wander far from it?—pets represent a market in the United States that is growing faster than computers, electronics, or communications. Animal medicines, garments, toys, accessories, grooming, feeding, burial, and the trade in pets themselves add up to to a sum slightly greater than the gross national product of Ghana. There is a National Dog Groomers Association, which believes that not just anybody should be allowed to pick up a pair of clippers. There are dog perfumes such as Le Chien No. 5 and Arf-Peggio, and a company in New York markets Sani-Panti, a sanitary belt "for your dog's trying days." I shall pass on hastily with no more than a mention that there are tiny cotton snap-ons for the parakeet that is not housebroken.[29] These and other examples that could be easily extended represent frivolous merchandise, to be sure, but perhaps they should be looked at charitably: they do reflect a desperate human need to love and to be loved.

Since pet animals have the same basic needs as people—food, companionship, freedom from worry—and since they can experience fear, frustration, hate, shock or homesickness, it follows that with the unprecedented numbers that exist today there is also bound to be an increase in suffering.[30] The RSPCA offers counsel to meet this situation. It discourages the importation of animals not native to England or the keeping of caged birds. But the society accepts it as a fact of life that people will have such pets. So it provides information on their housing and health requirements.

Spectacular pets from far corners of the world help relieve identity crises for their owners. They are advertised, therefore, "for their unusual color, habits, or status value for the person who wants to be a real individual." Unfortunately, the cunning little boa constrictor becomes a big snake, the ten-pound chimpanzee soon weighs fifty pounds or more and develops a marked tendency toward jealousy, biting, and frequent urination. So, too, enthusiasm for iguana lizards, acquired as an impulse purchase, can quickly vanish. But the problem of the biological needs of such creatures remains, and the danger of serious diseases communicable to humans is always present.[31] Owners of exotic pets find that they have opened a real "can of worms." "Adult monkeys," John Hunt points out in his readable *A World of Animals*, "are not furry little people . . . they are wild animals."[32] Most exotic animals that fall into private hands die of lack of proper diet, abnormal environment, or inadequate facilities. Those that don't die find their skid row in a roadside zoo.[33]

Although animals should be valued for what they are—instinctive creatures of marvelous complexity, beauty and mystery—mankind cannot resist the fallacy of reading human values into their lives—and their deaths. And so, in England, pets are sometimes buried with the full Christian commitment ceremony and placed under headstones that announce *Toppie Waits Here* or something similar. Nearer home, a Texas woman had the entire Episcopal service read over her deceased dogs. The humanitarian movement, which has its hands full trying to prevent cruelty to living animals, and does not believe in running two rabbits at the same time, is not overly concerned with the idea that animals will take part in the Resurrection. Yet there are approximately 400 pet cemeteries in the United States, with more than 40,000 animals buried in the celebrated Canine Cemetery at Hartsdale, New York, and some 15,000 animal bodies filling four cemeteries in and around Baltimore, with a thousand more added every year. They lie beneath such epitaphs as *The Angels Were Lonely*, or *Bye-Bye, Molly—See You Later.*[34]

This kind of thinking, or feeling, leads to bequests whose recording has become a genre of daily journalism—news stories about the richest cat in Chicago, who dined on pot roast, or the seventy-year-old tortoise that will finish out its life nibbling on such delicacies as strawberries and bananas, due to the thoughtfulness of an English widow. At the demise of a Boston parrot, which had had its own trust fund, *The New York Times* remarked, with perhaps unconscious resentment at such arrangements, "Almost any boy would have wrung the bird's neck for ten cents."[35]

Our speech habits show how animal traits are still borrowed to illustrate human qualities—harebrained, for instance, or as an example of an admired characteristic, lionhearted. Indeed, the language is loaded with animal referents, some complimentary, some neutral, most pejorative. In the proverbial wisdom our friend the dog, curiously enough, measures humanity at its worst or weakest —that is, " dog in the manger," "dog eat dog," and "dogsburg," which means a squalid town. Sometimes the rhetoric is neutral or humorous, as in "dog tired" or "autograph hound" (one diligent in collecting the signatures of well-known people). But in each instance dog equals man.[36] "Bitch," once a taboo word, is bandied about freely in novels and the theater, but it is still ambiguous and unsafe, though not slanderous legally. And "son of a bitch" is probably our hardest-worked term of insult.

It is safe to call a man a hog (except in Wisconsin), but it is actionable to compare a neighbor to a skunk or call him "an itchy old toad."[37] John Kieran, who has written so perceptively on nature, greatly deplores the use of the word *toad* as a term of disgust, finding such disparagement a libel on this gentle, tailless amphibian. "Familiarity with toads," Kieran says, "will not breed contempt—nor warts, as the ancient fable has it. . . ."[38]

Of greater consequence is our deep aversion to our commensal, the Norway rat. When Mrs. Morris Caffritz, the Washington real estate heiress, wanted to convey her reaction to an early-season charity event, which brought out high society in force, she put it this way: "The rat race has begun."[39] And speaking of rats, it is now necessary to turn to a topic that cannot be postponed, the unwanted animals and the unpopular animals.

THE ANCIENT WORLD: A MAN, SOME BEASTS, AND GOD

To survive together, live together — Noah's Ark. Ecology mythologized.
Painting by Edward Hicks.

For various offenses, animals of all kinds were tried in courts of law, as in this case concerning a sow and piglets at Lavegny, France.

In early medicine, knowledge of anatomy was gained largely through the vivisection of animals, as shown on the title page of an edition of Galen's *Opera Omnia,* Giunta edition, 1541/2.

hile various Scenes of sportive Woe
The Infant Race employ,
d tortur'd Victims bleeding show
The Tyrant in the Boy,

Behold! a Youth of gentler Heart,
To spare the Creature's pain,
O take, he cries — take all my Tart,
But Tears and Tart are vain.

Learn from this fair Example — You
Whom savage Sports delight,
How Cruelty disgusts the view
While Pity charms the sight.

To the CURIOUS.

To be seen at Major Leavenworth's Stable, opposite Mr. Lothrop's, State-Street,

Two CAMELS,

Male and Female, lately imported from

A R A B I A.

THESE ftupendous Animals are moft deferving the Attention of the Curiou being the greateft natural Curiofity ever exhibited to the Public on th Continent. They are Nineteen Hands high; have Necks near Four Feet long have a large high Bunch on their Backs, and another under their Breafts, in th Form of a Pedeftal, on which they fupport themfelves when lying down; th have Four Joints in their hind Legs, and will travel Twelve or Fourteen Da without drinking, and carry a Burden of Fifteen Hundred Weight; they are r markably harmlefs and docile, and will lie down and rife at Command.

Price of Admittance for a Gentleman or Lady, NINE-PENCE *eac*

A 1790 broadside advertising exhibitions of camels, early imports into the United States. America's first elephant followed soon after in 1796.

Entertainment in the eighteenth century — "THE SOLITARY SHOWMAN" does his act with a dancing bear and other animals in the American colonies. From Richardson Wright's *Hawkers and Walkers in Early America,* Lippincott, Philadelphia, 1927.

PHOTOGRAPH, COURTESY NEW YORK STATE LIBRARY

And a bear is baited in a London bear garden. From *The Sporting Magazine,* London, January, 1795.

COURTESY, YALE UNIVERSITY PHOTOGRAPHIC SERVICES

A contemporary depiction of a dog fight at a popular New York "arena" and gambling hangout of the mid-nineteenth century.

COURTESY, THE NEW-YORK HISTORICAL SOCIETY, NEW YORK CITY

Manhattan cattle drive, 1866, from *Frank Leslie's Illustrated Newspap* April 28, 1866: "CATTLE DRIVE IN THE STREETS — WHO CARES FOR WOM AND SMALL CHILDREN?"

COURTESY, NEW YORK STATE LIBR

"THE SWILL AND GARBAGE GATHERERS OF NEW YORK CITY"— and "friends" — in the nineteenth century. Dogs were widely employed as beasts of burden. From *Frank Leslie's Illustrated Newspaper,* September 1, 1866.

SOME EARLY FIGHTERS FOR ANIMAL RIGHTS...

Richard ("Humanity Dick") Martin

James T. Angell

Henry Bergh

(Above) The enemy: mindless cruelty. "CITY ENORMITIES — EVERY BRUTE CAN BEAT HIS BEAST." From *Frank Leslie's Illustrated Newspaper*, 1865.

COURTESY,
NEW YORK STATE LIBRARY

(Right) The enemy: bestiality. This man entertained large crowds with his act of killing rats by biting them. From *Frank Leslie's Illustrated Newspaper*, December 22, 1866.

COURTESY,
NEW YORK STATE LIBRARY

"John Gay was pleased with the thought that the coachmen of London would through transmigration of souls be transformed into hackneys and that draymen would have bits put in their teeth." From *Animal World*, August 2, 1875.

ANIMALS FOR FUN . . .

RODEO—SALINAS, CALIFORNIA, 1969. Enraged because this frantic horse refused to be mounted, a cowpoke took vengeance, as shown above.

FAMILY GAMES—GATESVILLE, TEXAS, 1968. Men, women and children watch delightedly while a dog drags a leashed raccoon from a keg. The raccoon was used time after time until it died.

...AND PROFIT...

SAN FRANCISCO, CALIFORNIA, 1913. Horses pulling a heavily laden horse-car down Market Street. Fortunately, this was San Francisco's last horse-car. From *Our Animals,* April, 1943.

CANADA, EVERY YEAR. A baby seal dies to become money and a coat.

...AND UNSPEAKABLE TORTURE...

The coyote (right) was killed at tax-payers' expense by government poisoners who jump when the wool and sheep trade associations whistle. The rabbit (below), may have lived for days before dying of pain, loss of blood, thirst or predators. Many traps are found with just a paw still in the steel teeth, the trapped animal having gnawed through it in desperation.

(RIGHT) COURTESY,
DEFENDERS OF WILDLIFE

(BELOW) COURTESY,
FRIENDS OF ANIMALS

No movement allowed, a monkey is kept in a restraining device during an experiment attempting to make it an alcoholic. One monkey has been an unwilling participant in such an experiment for three years.

Through a tube inserted in its windpipe, a dog is forced to smoke cigarettes to show that smoking is bad for people. It's also bad for dogs. Many have died in such experiments conducted by Veterans Administration doctors.

COURTESY, NATIONAL CATHOLIC
SOCIETY FOR ANIMAL WELFARE

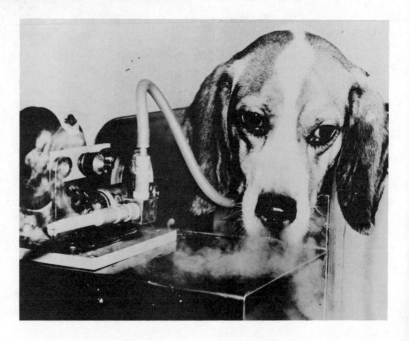

The famous dancer, Irene Castle, became famous also for her work in animal welfare. She is shown with four dogs adopted from Orphans of the Storm, the animal shelter she founded at Deerfield, Illinois.

COURTESY, MRS. RICHEY B. WATSON

The Bishop of Reading at St. Stephen's Church, Upper Basildon, England, blesses the local animals. This rite has been celebrated in many countries to remind men that "nature is part of our humanity." From *Animal World*, October, 1970.

COURTESY, *Evening Post*, READING

15

The Unwanted Animal

Since man is the principal environmental force on our planet, the animal population depends in large measure upon human decisions. Frequently the result has been extinction. In the present century alone we have eliminated an average of one bird and one mammal species each year, and the memory remains that the bounty system once included a payoff on the scalps of Indians as well as wolf hides.[1]

Meanwhile man is unable so far to control his own numbers or those of the animals closest to us, the dog and cat, which increase at a frightening daily rate, so that we have among us 15 million dogs as homeless strays and between 18 million and 25 million cats.[2] The female cat can produce three litters a year, averaging four to five kittens per litter. The dog can whelp two litters a year, averaging out at about six puppies. To the natural fecundity of these animals must be added the consequences of the trend to suburban living, the desire of more and more people to own pets, and their irresponsible willingness for them to breed. As a result,

149

some 25 million unwanted puppies and kittens die in each year
from disease or by starvation, by clubbing, drowning, shooting,
gassing, poisoning, or are crushed by automobiles after being
dropped on a busy highway. Animal life is cheap. A two-dollar dog
or a cat that cost nothing is easily abandoned, for as Ogden Nash
once observed:

> *The trouble with a*
> *kitten is that*
> *Eventually it*
> *becomes a cat.*

It has been determined mathematically that if all the progeny of
one female cat over a period of ten years survived, she would have
84,652,644 descendants. We would be overwhelmed with these
creatures except that they are being executed almost, but not quite,
as fast as they are born. The direct, traceable cost in tax money and
in the funds collected by private humane agencies engaged in
rescue and control work is in the range of $65 million to $100
million dollars a year. This takes no account, of course, of the
ethical issue that is involved.[3] The situation becomes ironic when
one reflects that animal rescue leagues, SPCAs, and shelters, which
are supposed to improve our civilization by introducing principles
of mercy toward all living creatures, in actual practice become
animal Auschwitzes.

One refuge in the Chicago area estimates that the annual "kill"
of animal waifs in the city and suburbs is more than a quarter of
a million, and sadly describes each victim as "a living, loving, loyal
creature, eager to shower its affection on some responsive human."
At the Montgomery County Animal Shelter in Maryland, about
120,000 animals in a year are given lethal doses of sodium pheno-
barbitol, which means killing about ninety percent of all animals
that pass through the shelter. Only ten percent make it to new
homes. The Pennsylvania SPCA also has figures to show the
futility of adoption as the ultimate solution, reporting in March
1969 32,331 animals taken into its shelters in a twelvemonth, homes
found for only 7,708.[4] The Humane Society of the United States
calls our careless overbreeding of dogs and cats a consequence of
our "toy" concept of animal life, and "the greatest cruelty facing

the humane movement." Other social problems flow from the first one, a disturbing increase in free-running dog packs in city streets and the spread of disease.[5]

"Today's unwanted animals are mostly the result of suburban negligence toward pets," says one scientist who is working on the problem of animal sterilization, and he notes as a psychological fact "the strange identification of male dog or cat owners, who enjoy their animals' 'going over the fence' and doing what they are not allowed to do."[6] Legitimate criticism may also be directed toward some local humane societies, which permit adoptions without spaying and altering because a reduction in the number of animal placements would mean a lower income. Veterinarians who charge high fees are also a contributing factor. Because the expense of spaying or altering can start at ten and twenty-five dollars and run to more than double those amounts, *Modern Veterinary Practise*, an influential professional journal, has suggested that veterinarians have as great an obligation to the less affluent pet owner as to those who can pay "upper echelon" fees. But the profession reacts coolly to this social service concept of their occupation. When Los Angeles established a municipal clinic to spay and neuter dogs and cats at seventeen dollars and fifty cents for female dogs and cats and eleven dollars and fifty cents for males, the Southern California Veterinarian Association recommended higher fees and withheld its endorsement of the program to alleviate what one member of the Los Angeles City Council describes as "the heart-breaking animal population explosion." Efforts to get prices down to a reasonable level through the establishment of clinics have been made by humane organizations in California, Illinois, Massachusetts, Michigan, New York, Pennsylvania, and other states. Legislation has also been introduced in several states to let the penalties for irresponsible breeding fall on owners rather than the animals. "If you can afford to KEEP a pet," runs one humanitarian slogan, "you can afford to SPAY it."[7]

Naturally, the question of "the pill" for animals comes up. Products to inhibit animal reproductive functions are on the market in Great Britain and France.[8] A good deal of work has been done in the United States on antifertility agents, but according to Dr. Wolfgang Jöchle, vice-president and director of the Institute of Veterinary Science, Syntex Corporation, ". . . at the present time there are no mechanisms available which would allow to interrupt pregnancies in pets, although work is also being carried on in another direction, the use of sex hormones to control the male libido."[9] There is reason to suspect that veterinarians would object strenuously if agents that block dog and cat reproduction were dispensed to the general public without going through a licensed veterinarian. In other words, it would have to be made available by prescription only.

Long years ago the editor of the *New York World* took Henry Bergh to task for wasting his time on cruelties to snakes and turtles and admonished him to work on "those inhumanities to animals which everybody recognizes to be inhumanities. . . ."[10] This is a good example of the "ugh complex," which repudiates certain forms of life but lavishes affection and concern upon others. We all have this trait to a greater or lesser extent. It is part of our accumulated inheritance. Enemies of humanitarian work, and they are numerous and articulate, like to ask loaded questions. Must we regard as sacred, they ask, the life of the sucking louse, which can carry the typhus virus within its body and has killed more humans than all our wars and weapons? The question posed is the familiar one of the pseudoproblem. There is no ethical obligation upon man to commit racial suicide by tenderly guarding the life of the typhus louse or any other form of animal life that constitutes a genuine threat to human survival.

The late, distinguished bacteriologist Hans Zinsser, famous for isolating the typhus germ and developing a protective vaccine, was a louse respecter if not exactly a louse lover. He called it "this not unattractive insect" and one of "the many important and dignified things that are made the subjects of raucous humor. . . ." Professor Zinsser was displeased to note that his *Encyclopedia Britannica* gave only two-thirds of a column to the louse, about one-fifth the space allotted to Louisville, Kentucky, which he thought was unfair to lice.[11]

Many beneficial animals, such as skunks, hawks, and spiders, have suffered because humans make zoophobic judgments about the animal kingdom. Yet nature doesn't know any animal as vermin, and all animal names are, or ought to be, respectable. We should examine ourselves: why do baby opossums arouse the protective instincts in most people, while the slothful adults are viewed with marked distaste? Most predators are hated, although they are an integral part of the drama of nature and serve to balance off the natural populations far better than any fish and wildlife bureaus have ever been able to do. They do it, moreover, without lust or hate, which is beyond the emotional reach of most human killers.[12]

The regard in which a particular animal is held varies enormously according to time, circumstance, and location. Madame Roland, who was guillotined by the radical majority of the French National Convention in 1793, said, "The more I see of men, the better I like dogs," and the dog is almost worshipped in Britain; yet this same animal is held in such low esteem by Muhammadans that "dog of a Christian" has had a wide currency as a common epithet. Another contrast: the cow, sacred in India, is just a milk machine in the Western world. When respect and affection are found, these feelings seem not to rest on any principle but on some kind of sentiment or aesthetic judgment.[13] Robins are pleasing; caterpillars are squashy. Speaking generally, the larger the beast, the better we like it.

Since we dislike insects, many of which are working with us, making possible among other amenities honey, coffee, tea, trout, chocolate, ginger, castor oil, and typewriter ribbons, we choose to dislike a large portion of our fauna.

Many people fear snakes. A few love them. But the detestation humankind feel for rats is universal. We no longer believe that the Devil is the "lord of rats and eke of mice, of flies and bed-bugs, frogs and lice", as Goethe expressed it in *Faust*, but we must acknowledge that the striking similarities between the social behavior of rats and men do not add to the popularity of this intelligent rodent. In fact, the unsettling thing is that rats do act so much like people. We can hardly overlook the analogy between ourselves and these successful competitors. Consider the following:

Both rats and men eat almost anything, including, under stress conditions, their own kind.

Both breed at all seasons.

Both hybridize easily, and judging by the way the brown rat has persecuted the black rat, both have social and racial prejudice.

Both adapt to all climates.

Both can organize armies and make war on their own kind.

The first rat to arrive in Europe from the Orient was the black or ship rat, *Mus rattus*, which may have been brought back, inadvertently, by returning Crusaders. At any rate, it was common in England in the time of Geoffrey Chaucer, for he wrote in the fourteenth century:

> *And forth he goth, no lenger wold he tary,*
> *Into the toun unto a Pothecary,*
> *And praied him that he him wolde sell*
> *Some poison that he might his ratouns quell.*

The ferocious brownish-gray rat, *Mus decumanus*, short of nose and tail, also called the "Norway rat," reached England as a camp follower of commerce in 1728–1729. Since to many Englishmen of the period anything unpleasant arriving from the Continent was associated wth the reigning royal family, recently arrived from Hanover, *Mus decamanus* was inaccurately called the "Hanoverian rat." Actually it is believed to be a native of the Caspian region, so, reflecting the political tensions of our own time, we might describe this uninvited guest at our table as the "Russian rat." The brown rat multiplied so rapidly that it soon became a major pest, and the trade of ratcatcher was as important an occupation in the eighteenth century, Professor Zinsser wrote, as that of realtor or mortician in ours.[15]

There is no reliable rat census. But it is estimated that there are as many rats in American cities today as there are people, and that each rat does about ten dollars' worth of damage in a year. Their depredations include killing young poultry, starting fires and floods, and eating the United States mail. They also nibble at babies and gnaw the feet of elephants in zoos.[16]

Rats live a hedonistic existence in Washington, D.C. Experts on the rat counterculture say that they have never seen a skinny rat in the District of Columbia, and the rats along the Potomac are so healthy they probably do not carry the fevers, infections and parasites that afflict humans. This information should comfort the 2,000 Washingtonians who are bitten each year.[17] New York rats have certain advantages going for them: people who put out grain and bread scraps for the pigeons and suspicious tenants who refuse to admit the exterminator because he might be a bill collector in disguise. New York rats are tough. Neighborhood Youth Corps members on a clean-up campaign refused to enter a lot on East 109th Street because they feared the rats, five of whom were visible at the time, and when a Long Island man took a dozen kittens to New York's City Hall to help in the battle against the rats, the director of Mayor John V. Lindsay's Action Committee handed them right back, explaining that the New York rats would do in the cats.[18]

A plague of rats, it would seem, is scarcely a laughing matter. But that conclusion is to underestimate the robust sense of humor displayed in the Ninetieth Congress by members who opposed federal aid for rat extermination in city ghettos. Fear was expressed by some southern Democrats that the "civil rats" bills would create a new "rat bureaucracy," and a representative from Virginia addressed the chair in these words: "Mr. Speaker, I think the rat smart thing for us to do is to vote down this rat bill now." The bill eventually passed, however, but was inadequately funded.[19]

Since this book is pro-animal in its orientation, I have searched diligently to find something constructive and cheerful to say about our ancient enemy, the rat. But the results are meager. All I have been able to turn up is the declaration of a Philippine provincial official who says the flesh of rats is superior to dog meat, if properly prepared; and a captivating moral fable, written by La Fontaine and illustrated by Theodore Rousseau, the poetic landscapist, about "a pious rat who retired from the world into a large Dutch cheese and refused to have anything to do with a league against cats."[20] La Fontaine's charming conceit doesn't tell us anything about wild rats, and is not supposed to. But perhaps under the cover of the fabulist's gentle and sage rodent we can read his purpose: to suggest to mankind the ideal of a more peaceable biological community than any that has yet been achieved.

16

Rodeo: Cruelty
Packaged as Americana

Ride 'em, cowboy! Bite 'im, cowboy!
The crowd roars. The bell clangs. The chute gate swings wide and a beleaguered animal dashes into the arena to put on an exciting exhibition of pain and panic. Presented as a colorful epic of the range cattle industry in the days of the Chisholm Trail, evoking the sturdy values of frontier life—or, as the Pendleton, Oregon, Round-Up rephrased the idea recently, "Four Big Days of Fun in the Ol' West"—what is rodeo, really?

The answer varies, depending upon one's environment and personal background. The spectators see a show and read into it what they will. The riders and ropers and stock contractors, who represent a culture in which beasts are here to be used and used up, see the money and notoriety that go along with mass entertainment. The humane societies do not present a solid front on how to deal with rodeos, though no national animal protection society approves of them.[1] Some SPCAs and humane groups, however, are silent and uninvolved for reasons that will appear shortly.

But whatever rodeo is—stirring historical pageant; nostalgic symbol; wholesome, red-blooded entertainment; or commercialized brutality—it is undeniably Big Business. More than 41 million spectators paid to see one or more rodeos in 1970 and the industry is confident that television exposure is going to boost the gate receipts if some way can be found to silence such critics as Bob Cromie of the *Chicago Tribune* or Mrs. Elizabeth Sakach, who once played in a rodeo band but was sickened by what she saw and heard. Rodeo now operates on a twelve-month schedule, beginning with the season's opener on New Year's Day, and ending with what are called the National Finals, an indoor event held in recent years at Oklahoma City in December and promoted as "rodeo's World Series."[2] Nomadic professional athletes to the number of 3,000 to 4,000, whose home corral may have been New Jersey or the Bronx, pull down earnings that can approach $60,000 a year, and swing around the rodeo circuit by automobile, truck, or camper, pulling a horse trailer. And some make their hops by private plane.[3]

Substantial extras are donated to consistent winners by pant-and-shirt manufacturers and boot-and-saddle makers. Local firms add more modest gifts—hats, ties, wristwatches, jackets, gloves, scarves and scarfpins, cigarette cases and lighters, ropes, spurs, and as one laureate of rodeo has written, perhaps inadvertently, "silver-mounted brides." And profitable sidelines include acting as horse dentists, modeling for photographers, and giving testimonials for whiskey and tobacco products.

Also present at the arenas, and a part of the multimillion-dollar economics of rodeo, are stock contractors, who provide the animal raw material, stock foremen, Indian chiefs, beauty queens, sales agents for accessories, hillbilly singers, concessionaires, arena directors, bandsmen, juvenile gunslingers, owners of dog acts, photographers, public relations men, judges, timers, baton twirlers, trick ropers, Roman riders, comedy mules and monkeys—and, of course, the bawling, apprehensive, restless livestock, indispensable yet expendable.

Such romantic types as press agents have seen a resemblance between rodeo and the knightly tournaments of the Middle Ages, in which high personages jousted in the European tradition of courtly love. Less friendly observers of the rodeo scene are reminded of the Roman populace in the Circus Maximus, lusting after the blood of man and beast.

Neither of these rather loose analogies can be pressed very far. There is nothing aristocratic, certainly, about rodeo, although some of the "rastlers" are college material, having attended Northeastern State College at Tahlequah, Oklahoma, on a football or basketball scholarship; or have wrangled their sheepskins from Sam Houston State or Olds Agricultural and Vocational. As for the bloodlust, it may be there, buried in the crowd's id. But the thoughts of the ticket holders are usually under the firm control of the man at the microphone who guides them into happy, constructive channels. Or, if there is a mishap in the calf-roping contest, for example, and the animal has to be sledded out of the arena and pistoled back of the holding pens, the soothing voice on the loudspeaker quickly relieves the anxiety of the squeamish: "Don't worry about him, folks. He's just had the wind knocked out of him."[4] Between their tours of duty up in the crow's nest, the rodeo announcers deliver inspirational talks to schools and service clubs about how rodeo preserves the heritage of the Old West, and they also make radio and television appearances to promote the, as they call it, sport. The men on the microphones are today's scops and minnesingers, who shape the legends of rodeo's supermen and often become authentic celebrities in their own right, as did Cy Taillon, who has been saluted by a rodeo historian as "one of the few educated men I know who talk educated without sounding unnatural."[5]

Rodeo generates purse money in the range of $3 million to $4 million annually for the dues-paying members of the Rodeo Cowboys Association. This is a kind of trade union interested in fees and percentages and fair judges; in ethics (pay your hotel bills before leaving town; always have a permanent address); in the elimination of conflicting dates, and in the bonding of officials who handle the money.[6] The association also keeps an eye on antirodeo legislation. Other ramifications include a national intercollegiate rodeo and a women's auxiliary called the Girls' Rodeo Association. The rodeo game even has its Little League: the members of the American Junior Rodeo are already in training for a cut of the prize money of the future, and with luck, a chance someday to be immortalized in rodeo's national shrine, which stands on Persimmon Hill in Oklahoma City and is known as the Cowboy Hall of Fame and Western Heritage Center. In fact, they don't have to wait. Missy Long, aged twelve, earned $9,782 in 1969 as a barrel racer and enjoyed the use of an Opel station wagon for a year.[7] Even the devotees of rodeo are organized. They are called the International Rodeo Fans. Card-carrying members yard up in units known as "corrals" or "chuck wagons."[8]

The cowpoke was long ago elevated to a unique position in American popular culture by Owen Wister's *The Virginian* and its imitators, by the western pulp magazines, by the movies, juke-boxes, shoot-'em-up television dramas and by the manufacturers of cap pistols.[9] Theodore Roosevelt and Mark Twain praised the manly qualities of the cowboy, and he continues to appear on the backs of the cereal boxes as, in the wry phrase of Professor David Brion Davis, "the hero of the preadolescent, either chronologically or mentally."[10] The sum of this idealization, despite its incongruities, has been skillfully appropriated by the propaganda arm of rodeo. Athletes who rodeo (in familiar usage the noun becomes a verb) are accepted as modern reincarnations of Wyatt Earp and James Butler ("Wild Bill") Hickok. These latter-day buckeroos in their denim pants of faded blue have been received by the highest officials, such as Robert F. Wagner, Jr., as mayor of New York, and President Eisenhower, at the White House.[11] Episodes of this sort give rodeo a spuriuos respectability and provide highly visible endorsement of the "heritage" angle.

Rodeo has a tenuous connection with the era of the trail herds, but it could easily be exaggerated, and usually is, in rodeo rhetoric. The voyageur is gone. The mountain men are gone. So are the Virginia City miners. The buffalo hunters, too, have ridden as one rodeo belletrist has written, "across the Great Sunset."[12] What we do have left are the arena shows and rodeo prose, a literary genre that owes much to the style of sports reporting passed on to us by the 1920s. It is elaborate, redundant, and loaded with clichés, circumlocutions, and euphuisms. Oklahoma becomes "the Sooner state." Clowning is "the baggy profession." Bulldogging is "toro twisting." The man who performs the act is "the leather-tough twister whose guts and wits are matched in the arena with the worst action outlaw stock has to offer. . . ."[13]

Sympathy is carefully directed away from the rodeo bronc. He is vicious and ornery, a "widow maker," or sometimes, "a scary explosion of animal energy" with "thrashing hooves splintering the chute boards"; while the bulldogger, as he makes his leap for the steer's head, "slams into sudden brute power."[14] There is also a more poetic but equally inflated style that associates the performance with an appreciation of the natural world: the coyote's howl, the starry heavens, clean air, clean living, the call of the wild, and "the immensity of God's sublime creation."[15]

The origins of rodeo (from the Spanish *rodear*, "to surround") may be discerned in the spring roundup of the range cattle before the long drive began to the northern cow towns. Trail-driving the longhorns actually lasted for only a very short generation, with the big years falling between 1870 and 1885. But some time shortly after the Civil War, the men who earned their living trailing cattle found amusement and relaxation in doing rope tricks and in competing in breaking wild horses, testing for themselves the legend of "the man who couldn't be thrown." It was homemade recreation, a work-play situation. No fanfare. No audience. No gate receipts.

According to one account, an intercamp broncobusting was held at Deer Trail, Colorado, on July 4, 1869, where "outlaw" ponies pitched, kicked, and seesawed to escape the spurs and rawhide whip. Another early source places the first rodeo at Point of Rocks, Arkansas, in 1872. Still another agrees as to the year but not the location: there was an exhibition of steer riding on the Fourth of July at Cheyenne, Wyoming.[16] Better documentation comes in a letter dated June 10, 1874, which mentions a gathering of cowboys at Sante Fe, where they had a "donnybrook fair" accompanied by generous infusions of whiskey and dancing in the streets.[17]

The free grass and the free rodeo came to an end at about the same time, because at Prescott, Arizona, in 1888, an admission was charged for the first time to see the "passion play of the West." Rodeo had become a spectator sport, and the concept changed in the direction of attracting an audience, winning points, and making money.[18] In the decade of the eighties William F. "(Buffalo Bill") Cody added cowboy acts to his wild west show. But the roping and the riding were incidental to the reenactment of such melodramas of the plains as an attack on a wagon train or Custer's Last Stand.[19]

It is safer to say that rodeo has no beginning that can be identified. By the 1890s, at any rate, when the trailing of cattle had been
terminated by the completion of the rail network, the arrival of the
granger and barbed wire, brisk rivalries had sprung up over the
staging of rodeos—Cheyenne versus Denver, Pendelton vis-à-vis
Walla Walla, each discovering in the go-arounds a tourist attraction and a stimulus for local business.[20]

"Up in the air and down with all four legs bunched stiff as an
antelope's, and back arched like a hostile wildcat's, went the animal," wrote the *Denver Republican*'s man on the spot at an 1887
tournament.

> But the rider was there, and deep into the rowels he sank the
> spurs, while he lashed shoulders and neck with keen stinging
> quirt. It was brute force against human nerve. Nerve won.
> ... The crowd cheered, and an admirer dropped a box of cigars
> into the hands of the perspiring but plucky victor.[21]

The newspaper concluded that the performance was "as exciting
as a bull fight . . . the kind of sport nine men in ten like."[22] With
such credentials, the man in the ten-gallon hat, leather-fringed
chaparajos, and bright fuschia shirt began to appear regularly at
fairs, expositions, jubilees, vigilante days, stock shows, and especially Fourth of July celebrations.

Modern rodeo consists of five standard acts, usually run off in
this order: saddle bronc riding; bareback riding; bull riding; steer
wrestling, a euphemism for bulldogging; and steer or calf roping.
These are de rigueur. There may also be team roping, novelty acts
such as working a bull with a cape, comedy style, and optional
events such as the wild cow milking competition, in which two
men try to catch a few drops of milk in a Coke bottle, a hilarious
number that adds "zest and a bit of robust humor. . . ."[23]

Rodeos open with a serpentine parade called the Grand Entry,
consisting of fifty to a hundred horsemen and horsewomen, richly
garbed in gabardine and satin, with silver-mounted equipment
glittering and jingling, a color guard, judges and officials in line,
sheriff's posses and Shriners' patrols, and the nubile queen of the
rodeo in her royal regalia and escorted by her court, all of whom
receive much attention, not because their duties are onerous, but

because their indubitable good looks make rodeo day one of those days when it pays to get up in the morning. The colors are posted, the national anthem played, and the fun begins.[24]

The 'dogging and bull riding are strictly show biz; they were never a part of the working hand's routine.[25] Steer and calf roping both trace their origins back to the working ranch, but steer roping has largely given place to the throwing of light, low-grade stock because, says Mary S. Robertson, in *Rodeo: Standard Guide to the Cowboy Sport,* "It got so a stockman would cringe every time he saw a man rope and slam down a full grown steer."[26] Under ranch conditions a calf is roped quietly in a corral to avoid injury, or restrained for doctoring in a "squeeze chute." The economics of rodeo call for something quite different. Rodeo is a show. Speed and drama are the essence of it. So the "dogie" bolts out of the gate at a furious gallop. The rider who drops the loop over the "vealer" is racing the clock to down the animal and make a fast tie.

The ranch calf gets roped once in his lifetime. The rodeo animal can be chased and roped as many as seven times a day in a large rodeo. If the beast flies head over heels it is said to have been "busted," which is prohibited but often unavoidable. In practice sessions the calf can be used over and over again, until he breaks a leg or the taut rope burns out an eye. When this happens in competition, the band strikes up a tune and a clown draws the attention of the customers away from the crippled animal. The dogie will soon be dog food. In fact, one packing house markets its dog food under the trademark "Rodeo."[27]

Complicated and minute rules govern all contests approved by the Rodeo Cowboys Association. The performers accumulate points that determine their scores and the prize money they receive. In bronc riding, for instance, the rules specify, not only the length of time the rider must be able to stay on the horse (ten seconds), but the kind of equipment he uses, how the rein is held, and how he must come out of the chutes—raking the animal from shoulder back to the rump with steel spurs to produce the desired bucking action.[28] As a further guarantee of frenzied reaction, just before the gate is opened, a bucking strap or flanking strap—a device that can be clearly seen in most photographs of rodeo action —is passed around the animal aft of the rib cage, in the area of the genitals and intestines, and cinched up tight. Every kick draws it tighter, and it leaves no mark.[29]

At the same time an electric prod, known back of the chutes as the "hot shot," is applied. It is most effective in the rectal area. Since the same animals are used over and over, knowledgeable horses often begin to fight the strap even before it is tightened, especially if a nail, tack, piece of barbed wire, or a device made of sharp metal and known as a "spider" has been placed under the bucking strap. "Rigging" the strap is a breach of the rules but hard to detect.[30]

The rodeo bull is also fitted with the flanking strap, and he, too, bucks to get rid of it.[31] Bull riding has "some of the atmosphere of the Mexican bullfight," according to one rodeo publicist. The appeal is spiced by the fact that a man *may* be gored.[32] But bull riding has nothing to do with life on the range. It is a made-up thriller.

Bulldogging, on the other hand, is so old that it is the subject of an epigram in the Greek Anthology, and in Greek sculpture Thessalian bullfighters are shown leaping from the backs of their horses to throw the bull to the ground by twisting his head. In American practice, the 'dogger springs from his horse at the target, grips the horns, and forces the head down and sideways until the glaring eyeballs stare straight up and a fall is achieved. In times past the 'dogger set his teeth in the bull's sensitive lip and held on like a bulldog—hence the colloquial name of the event—or he dug his fingers into the beast's eyes or nostrils.[33] According to the rule book, contestants may be disqualified for "mistreatment of stock." The regulation is applied with discretion. There is no penalty, for example, for breaking off a horn.

These unwilling performers, the livestock, actually consist of tame, domestic animals, which have to be activated in the ways described. The Texas longhorn is now a zoological novelty— lonely, unlovely, and unloved, a grotesque and pathetic beast, rarer than the buffalo, existing only for stock shows and the requirements of the rodeo arena.[34] But it says in rodeo propaganda that the steers are fierce and malevolent, and the crossbreed Brahma used in bull riding is a "loose-hided, hump-backed, droop-eared bundle of fury."[35] The horses are described as "outlaws," and they bear names chosen to deflect sympathy, such as Dynamite, Tombstone, Bad Whiskey, or Cyanide. The clowns, in their fright wigs and long red underwear, fill in the dull spots and gloss over delay at the chutes if an animal proves to be a "chute fighter." It is especially their job to distract the bull so that the bull rider can leave the arena without being trampled.[36] The ticket holders strongly hope that there will be no mischance. But if the worst occurs, they want to see it.

Cheyenne, Wyoming, elaborated the first of the big-time rodeos under the nostalgic name of "Frontier Days." On September 23, 1897, at twelve noon, Battery A of the 76th Field Artillery fired a salvo, bells rang, factories and locomotives blew their whistles, and the visitors who had arrived on a Union Pacific excursion from Denver ($2) and Greeley ($1) shot off their artillery, too. At the rodeo grounds there were, in addition to the usual contests, a pony express ride, a sham battle, and a "predominant Western mood."[37] Contributing to this atmosphere was the seizure of a "robber" by masked vigilantes, who hustled their captive to a high pole across from the race track. In the melee the victim was allowed to escape so that the figure that was hauled up the pole and riddled with bullets was merely a realistic dummy.[38]

The Frontier Days Rodeo has been innovative and imaginative in many other ways—in hiring operatives from the Burns Detective Agency to patrol the streets and in introducing the first rodeo clown, bucking chutes, and a baby-sitting service. William Jennings Bryan came to see the fun, Sally Rand brought her fan dance, and in 1931 an inspired committee presented the first Miss Frontier, which "made queen participation both popular and dignified." One spectator, making a sentimental return to the epoch of lassos and six-guns, has rhapsodized: "The slow, surging crowd, the roaring whoops and shreiking horns, the damp odor of hot humanity, the prancing horses, the bark of the fakir, the blare of bands, the hunted look in the eyes of steers, the tickling, stinging dust—each and in combination is Frontier Days."[39]

There were, of necessity, Indians present. One year when the local committee negotiated with the Indians directly, the red men refused to work unless they were issued beefsteaks and watermelon twice a day. After that the chiefs were hired through "a responsible Indian." Today, incidentally, the Indians are no longer able to clothe themselves in traditional apparel and such accessories of Indian culture as bear claws and elks' teeth. So the chamber of commerce supplies the costumes, the eagle feathers, beads, and authentic copies of tepees, including a big council tepee manufactured by a local awning company.[40]

Equally rich in tradition and prize money is the important Oregon rodeo that pays homage to the pioneers, the Pendleton Round-Up, where the boys who are "ridin' the shows" gather in September, when the nights are getting cooler and the goldenrod is turning to bronze. Since 1910, when the first Pendleton Round-Up was held on the banks of the Umatilla, Pendleton has been honoring "the qualities of the American West" by means of an annual rodeo. Visitors are entertained by simulated shoot-outs, ox teams and Mormon carts, travois-mounted Indian chiefs, a competitive "tribal ceremonial dance"—a total of eighteen crowd-pleasing happenings "run with clock-like precision."[41]

Rodeos come in all shapes and sizes. There are other big extravaganzas in addition to those domiciled at Cheyenne and Pendleton. Many are held in indoor sports ampitheaters, such as Houston's Astrodome, where in March of 1970 Elvis Presley worked the show with brilliant results, as reported by *Variety*, the trade journal of show business: "Elvis Ups Houston Rodeo/To New Attendance Peak."[42] Other big indoor arenas on the circuit are Denver, San Antonio, Omaha, San Francisco's Cow Palace, and Madison Square Garden in New York City. The importance of civic-group sponsorship is underlined in such names as the Annual Lions' Rodeo at Alexander, Louisiana, and the 4-H Benefit Rodeo at Saint Pierre, South Dakota. Some names aim for picturesqueness, such as the Heart O' Texas Fair and Rodeo at Waco; the Hellsapoppin' Rodeo at Benson, Arizona; or the Strawberry Festival Rodeo at Pleasant Grove, Utah, near Salt Lake City, where the committeemen wear glorious strawberry vests during glamorous rodeo days and nights.[43]

At least two unusual rodeos are exhibited in prisons. One is held to divert the convicts at the Texas State Penitentiary at Huntsville, where some of the toughest prisoners do battle with the broncs and the bulls. Another show is presented at the Oklahoma State Reformatory, McAlester, where professionals perform first and then the inmates flock en masse to the oval and try to remove a Bull Durham sack tied to the horn of "a fighting bull." At Huntsville, where only two convicts have escaped during a rodeo, the money collected is used in part for the purchase of Bibles and choir robes.[44]

Middle-sized rodeos include La Fiesta de los Vaqueros in "sun-drenched" Tucson, under the patronage of the chamber of commerce, which owns an original Butterfield stage coach and the carriage in which Maximilian and Carlota rode into Mexico City. Phoenix combines rodeo with resort atmosphere, while the Elks' Helldorado and Rodeo at Las Vegas, Nevada, offers the Strip, Hollywood stars, a plush gambling setting, girly shows, and the Twenty Mule Team from Death Valley. There are also small, folksy rodeos, affectionately called "punkin rollers," where the fans can get "dirt in the face and dung on the feet." They are held all over: at Grover, Colorado; Vernal, Utah; Hill City, Kansas. Boonville, California, offers a combined apple festival and rodeo, while at Angels Camp, California, the rodeo is run in tandem with a jumping frog contest. All provide "wild competition between man and man, and man and beast."[45]

American rodeo has been exported with varying results to Canada, England, Australia and New Zealand; to the 1958 World's Fair at Brussels, Belgium; to France, Italy, China, India, Venezuela, and the islands of the Pacific. The rodeo even followed the flag to Okinawa. When the United States government sent nearly a thousand head of horses to the island to improve the native pony, rodeo flourished, briefly. Japanese bulls and calves— quite appropriately, as enemy aliens—took the punishment. Unfortunately, many of the American horses succumbed to Oriental diseases and the task of grinding sugarcane. The Okinawans ate the rest.[46]

Several attempts were made by the late promoter, John Van ("Tex") Austin, to introduce rodeo in England. But the shock of the steer-roping event, requiring the pursuit and "busting" of tame animals in an area from which there was no escape, was too much for the British sense of fair play. Rodeo can, however, take a large part of the credit for the passage by Parliament of the Protection of Animals Act of 1934, which made it an offense to rope an untrained animal or to ride a horse or bull using a cruel appliance such as a strap cinched tight around its genitals. Watered-down versions of rodeos were tried in 1945 and 1947, but a performance that would pass the inspectors of the RSPCA turned out not to be rodeo at all and quietly folded.[47]

Canada's most spectacular venture in rodeo, and one of the largest spreads anywhere, is the Calgary Exhibition and Stampede. Today it is also a trade fair, agricultural show, and "the Mardi Gras of the prairies provinces." Canadians look with disfavor upon the "bite-'im-kid" school of bulldogging, and have substituted their own variation, called "steer decorating." The 'dogger makes his leap, but instead of applying the head twist, he attaches a band decorated with ribbons to the horns.

Whatever rodeo is or isn't, it is a genuine expression of the American booster spirit, for its sponsorship is provided by such socially potent organisms as the Elks, chambers of commerce, Shriners, Jaycees, American Legion, or volunteer firemen. Profits go into plant equipment or for worthy charities whose social values no one can argue about, like eye banks, orphanages, 4-H clubs, clinics for crippled children, and so on.[48] When profits are elusive, there still remain such benefits as a lift in business for local motels, gas stations, and eateries, and a sense of community pride in working together and of having competed for a slice of America's amusement dollar. A sincere tribute to the pulling power of rodeo was paid when the chamber of commerce of Eden Valley, Minnesota, scheduled a fox chase with snowmobiles to tell the world about Eden Valley and raise some money. Borrowing the glamour and prestige of rodeo, the promoters called their bizarre event the "Snowmobile Rodeo Fox Hunt," although the miniscule first prize would hardly have been regarded as walking-around money by a rodeo athlete. It was fifty dollars plus a small (one foot high) gold-plated trophy.

The future of this growth industry, rodeo, which is "as American as 'Old Glory' and apple pie," is clouded by one nagging problem which won't go away: adverse legislation. Rodeo is inherently cruel. As was demonstrated in England, when it isn't cruel it isn't rodeo, and the fans sit on their hands. Cruelty is defined by the animal protection laws in most American states as the infliction of pain and suffering. In the state of Washington, to take one example, it is a misdemeanor for any animal to "be chased, worried or injured by any man or animal" as an amusement, or even for a devotee of rodeo to "be present at such fighting, chasing, worrying or injuring of such animal as spectator."[49] Nevertheless, rodeos were recently held in Bremerton, Ellensburg, Kennewick,

Monroe, Moses Lake, Newport, Omak, Othello, and Puyallup. Nor should it be omitted that at Walla Walla and Yakima, too, one can witness saddle bronc riding, bareback riding, bull riding, calf roping, team roping, and what is jocosely called "longhorn grappling"—in short, the works. And New York law, which forbids baiting animals, makes a curious exception of "exhibitions of a kind comonly featured at rodeos."[50] This remarkable exception demonstrates the political power this industry can exert.

Why? Perhaps Max Lerner put his finger on the reason when he wrote in *America as Civilization:* "Every people . . . must have a chance to yell for blood."[51] Probing deeper, perhaps our urbanized society, having lost touch with its natural environment, finds in the hell-for-leather athlete in his distinctive costume a reassuring, if remarkably juvenile, symbol of man's ability to conquer the brute forces of nature. The package becomes all the more seductive if presented as Americana. Leaders in the humane movement describe rodeo as "phony romanticism," and rodeo apologists dismiss their critics as radicals, agitators, fanatics, and probably vegetarians. But Texas and New Mexico have outlawed steer busting, and the state of Ohio and the city of Baltimore have ruled out the flanking strap and electric prod. Bills directed to the same purpose have been pressed in recent times in California, Connecticut, Illinois, Massachusetts, Michigan, Pennsylvania, Rhode Island, West Virginia, and Wisconsin.[52]

To many observers no worthwhile purpose is served by rodeo. The animals consumed in this fun industry don't feed us, clothe us, or promote the general welfare. They are simply props in a theatrical production, something to shout at. Considerable skepticism exists as to how rigorously the cowboy "sport" polices itself. And there is the moral problem of how much pain and abuse the animals should have to endure for such a shallow purpose, or whether they should have to endure any. Pro-rodeo witnesses are not especially sensitive to the issues involved, judging by the lighthearted answers they gave during the hearings conducted on the Baltimore anticruelty bill. They testified that the use of the bucking strap is just like fastening a girdle for a couple of minutes on a South Seas maiden. As for the "hot shot" prods: "They just tickle, like your wife sticking you with a pin."[53]

Proceedings against rodeo performances could be initiated in most states under general anticruelty laws. But for the most part this doesn't happen—not because of any defect in the laws, but because of lack of enforcement. The police are overoccupied, and tend to relegate cruelty cases to the local animal welfare societies. But these brigades are chronically short of funds and staff, frequently depending on untrained volunteer help, and have their attention focused on stray dogs and cats. Society, it appears, is not yet ready to put down rodeo cruelty, our modern recreational equivalent of the public hanging.

17

Hard Noses
and Bleeding Hearts

W hile rodeo, America's own distinctive contribution to the harassment of large, domestic animals, is the fastest-growing form of recreational animal abuse in the United States, many of the older pleasures that arise from torment-ing animals still retain their appeal. State anticruelty laws gener-ally prohibit combat between animals, yet there are two magazines published in this country at the present time devoted to what is affectionately called "chicken fighting." The existence of these publications is well-known to the U.S. Postal Service. They enjoy the advertising support of breeders of game cocks, announce dates of future tournaments, and function as a buying guide to cockfight-ing equipment and supplies. Both magazines—their names are *Grit and Steel* and *The Gamecock*—are edited, oddly enough, by women, one of whom, Mrs. Ruth DeCamp McMillan, is a certified Bible teacher who declares she has seen very little blood in the pits, certainly not enough to make her "scringe." Furthermore, *Grit and Steel* points out, the cadavers are often given to a charitable institution and they make delicious eating. "The sport is a controversial one," Mrs. McMillan mourns, adding that "most of the criticism comes from humane societies. . . ."[1]

Although cockfight derbies are clearly illegal, local politicians are cooperative, provided the chicken fighters observe reasonable discretion. Announcements of coming events do not mention exact locations, but the word is passed along and white muslin strips tacked to trees show the route to the pit. While tournaments occur in many states, the sport thrives with particular vigor in the Old Confederacy and in the Southwest. Arizona's pits have seen some classical fights. People know how to enjoy themselves in the Copper State, according to *Grit and Steel*. They follow the philosophy of "live and let live," though "live and let die" might be a more accurate appraisal. March is a good time for visiting Louisiana, too, to see the cockfights and visit Opelousas, "Yam Capital of the World."[2]

Probably no animal is the victim of more ingenious forms of cruelty than the friendly raccoon. It is hunted with dogs in every state where it ranges, and raccoons have been baited in the southern states since colonial times, in what are known as "coon on a log" tournaments. An animal is chained to a log and anchored in a pond, and as many as twenty to thirty dogs compete to drag the desperate beast off its log. Other variations on the same idea are "coon in a hole" and "coon in a keg." In these diversions the dogs haul the coon out of a hole or a swinging barrel. There is also a water race, in which a raccoon floats confined in a cage while dogs torment it. Sometimes both coon and dogs drown.[3] These boisterous amusements are referred to euphemistically as "special events," but the crowd, which brings chairs, a picnic lunch, and iced beer for the day's outing, knows what is coming.

In Alabama, state law exempts raccoons from the general protection of animals. And coon on a log contests are considered to be good, clean fun in Mississippi, where the sport may be seen every Saturday. The Fourth of July, 1970, was celebrated in Raleigh with a double bill—a coon baiting and a tobacco-spitting contest.[4]

When Mrs. Ann Gough Hunter, of Dallas, Texas, who is dedicated to the concept of "adding compassion to conservation," learned that coon on a log affrays were common diversions in Texas, she said to Judge Robert Hughes, then a representative in the state legislature, "Mr. Hughes, there oughta be a law. . . ." "Mrs. Hunter, there *is* a law," replied the judge, and he quoted from the Texas Penal Code, Art. 613.1510. The defect was not in the law but in the mayors, sheriffs, and county attorneys charged with the duty of enforcement. Some, Mrs. Hunter has recalled, "were members of the cooners' gang." Not until the Texas Rangers took a hand did coon baiting come under control, and today it has all but disappeared from the Texas scene.[5]

The howls of elation that greeted the gutting of captive Gauls in the arenas of Rome still echo in the modern bullring, a survival of the old triumphal games. This combat also provides the titillation of watching a man who, for applause and money, risks being wounded or killed. The bullfight, Spanish style, is opposed by all humane societies, including those representing the Spanish humanitarians who have formed their own Association for the Prevention of Cruelty in Public Spectacles and who appeal to tourists not to visit the bullrings.[6]

Although some Roman Catholic writers defend bullfighting on the ground that it is an art and bulls are just things, there is a new sensibility about this in Catholic thought that rejects all such apologies and equivocations. This view emerges in the writings of Professor Justus George Lawler, of St. Xavier's College, Chicago, and the English priests, the Reverend Ambrose Agius and the Reverend Basil Wrighton. Father Agius, chairman of the Catholic Study Circle for Animal Welfare (London), member of the council of the RSPCA, and vice-president of the National Catholic Society for Animal Welfare in New York, sees the bullfight as "an appeal to the lowest emotions of human nature." Father Agius rejects the idea that bullfighting is the national sport in Spain: "Spanish correspondents write to the English press to deny it. And the persons most concerned, the *toreadors*, do not think of it as a sport at all." To them it is a lucrative branch of the butcher business.[7] It must be a particular source of anguish to Father Agius or any Roman Catholic priest who is also sensitized to man's inhumanity to animals, to know that, not only are the bullfights held on feast days of the Church, but that one of the stylized "passes" with the cape is called the "veronica" because the cloth is held in the same way St. Veronica is represented as having held her kerchief when she wiped the drops of agony from the face of Jesus.[8]

What keeps the corrida alive is not the Latin passion for gore but the eager tourists, mostly from the northern European countries and America, who must go "even if only once," and so participate by proxy in the violence and the kill. The tourist industry understands how the matter lies. "Run with the bulls" in Pamplona, invites Pan American World Airways. Braniff International Airways, when the line was awarded additional routes to South America, urged "socialites, secretaries and starlets and gold diggers" to "bellow at the bullfights" and to get their kicks from "the best, the *scariest* matadors." Travelers who have humane feelings toward animal life may wish to take note that Braniff is an old hand at this sort of thing. The line also offers duck hunters "a chance to literally burn up more ammunition in one day than most hunters fire in five seasons" at "exotic Southern Hemisphere species." The hint that there is no bag limit will not be lost upon those who are attracted by the idea. Braniff has also proposed, "You can go out with powerful searchlights and shoot a crocodile between its glowing red eyes. Or you can stay on board with an icy martini and dance." After this, it seems almost tame that the El Panamá Hotel in the Republic of Panama works bullfights into its appeal, along with native girls and such homey touches as a "cheeseburger with coke."[9]

Bullfighting is also promoted by the French Government Tourist Office, which points out that the spectacles are a part of the tradition and culture of Languedoc, the lower Rhône region, and Provence, where the small black bulls of La Camargue perform in the Roman ampitheater at Arles while trumpets blow flourishes and the band strikes up Bizet's toreador music. The French version of the bullfight, the *course aux cocardes,* represents an improvement over the Spanish in that no horses are used and the bull is harried but not killed. So bullfighting has a lot going for it; the fashion industry, tourism, Hemingway novels, the Jet Set and a vast corpus of sedulous writings that romanticize the spectacle and slide past the squalid rackets, the eviscerated horses, and the tormented bovines.[10]

Real bullfights are unlawful in every state in the American union. But the promoters of such affairs are crowding the law with what are called "bloodless" fights, stressing the "pageantry" angle and the fact that the animal survives, and actual bullfights staged in Mexico have been televised in the United States. Both are foot-in-the-door efforts to introduce the "real thing" into this country. Florida and Colorado recently legalized the mock bullfight, but Florida reversed itself and repealed the permissive legislation shortly after a bloodless bullfight held in Manatee County resulted in a bull being killed when it broke out of a pen and had to be shot.[11]

A vigorous effort to turn back the picadors and matadors is being mounted by the animal protection societies generally. They may be successful, too, because who is this galloping hell for leather out of the West to help repel the invaders? None other than the hard-ridin' Rodeo Cowboys of America and their entourage of stock contractors, press agents, and clowns, indignant at the thought of bulls being tormented in an arena, *Mexican* style.

Gambling and cruelty to animals are inseparable. Betting is the essential feature of cockfighting and dog and horse racing. The greyhounds are trained, incidentally, on live rabbits in preparation for their life work of chasing a mechanical rabbit.[12]

When Dr. Samuel Johnson remarked that he was vividly impressed with the paucity of human enjoyments by the fact that thousands of men and women could find no more interesting occupation than to determine which of two horses could run faster, he directed his wit at the wrong target. Horse racing isn't merely a jejune amusement. It is all about money, gambling money, which leads to the unsavory conditions found at the tracks and the scandals that predictably recur. Today the shadow of the Mafia is present, and so is evidence of large wagers sent from the paddock to the pari-mutuel windows just before a race. Persons of humane feelings deplore the racing of two-year-olds before they have made their growth and the doctoring of unsound horses so they can make one more race. Instances are endemic in the United States and Canada of horses turning strangely lethargic, with eyes dilated and lumps on their necks. If the needle wasn't used, at any rate the animal had had his pill. Owners, jockeys, trainers, and handlers can take care of themselves. The horses, highest strung of all animals, are, it seems, on their own.[13]

"Some are wealthy enough to deny it," Mel Morse, a respected voice in the humanitarian field, concludes, "but all those associated with horse racing are in it for the money, and the thoroughbreds are a necessary means to that end."[14]

On the dog show circuit the aristocrats of dogdom lead a life of restricted movement, and if they are poodles or boxers they lose their tails. Boxers also have their ears cropped, a painful operation requiring a long period of healing. But boxer fanciers want the ears to stand erect and nature does not provide that effect without surgical assistance. Several states have laws against ear cropping, but veterinarians licensed by those same states find it profitable to dock and crop.[15]

Another handsome animal that has suffered much at the hands of cruelists is the Tennessee Walking Horse, a breed developed from the southern plantation horse. It can be taught to prance delicately, lifting its front feet high in an odd but spectacularly attractive gait. Since, however, training is a slow, costly process, human ingenuity found a cost-saving shortcut. The method employed is called "soring." Trainers apply blistering agents such as "creeping cream" (oxide of mercury) or a chemical called "scootin' juice" (oil of mustard), which blister the pastern area. Toxic substances are also injected under the hoof to act as an irritant, and chains are arranged so as to rub up and down at each step the animal takes, or decorative boots, worn in the show ring, accomplish the same purpose.

The horse, trying to carry his weight on his back feet to avoid the pain, achieves the reaching stride with the forelegs, which is admired as the "big lick." Several states have laws aimed at soring. But exhibitors are influential people—doctors, lawyers, chiefs— and it is unlikely that a local jury would convict. At this point comes some good news. Congress has passed legislation protecting the Walking Horse, and in December 1970 President Nixon signed the bill into law. The statute prohibits interstate shipment of sored horses, and the U.S. Department of Agriculture, which participated in drafting the provisions of the act, is charged with its enforcement.[16] But more protection is urgently needed.

With regard to one form of animal exploitation, and possibly only one, the United States has a better record than England's. The pursuit of the native red fox with horses, hounds, and pageantry, is not a major diversion in America. Society—the Beautiful People, *tout-Paris*, whatever the reigning phrase may be—adores horses, dogs, and dressing up in the style of English country life as portrayed in the sporting novels of R. S. Surtees.[17] There have been small enclaves of fox hunters in New York, Pennsylvania, Maryland, and Virginia since the eighteenth century, dedicated to pink coats and Briticisms: the hounds are "in covert," the fox, or "Reynard," is "viewed away."[18]

Apologists for fox hunting have argued that "old red" *likes* being pursued, perhaps for a whole day, covering in some instances up to thirty to fifty miles in its desperate effort to save its life. If the small, weary animal loses this macabre ballet with death, the inedible little carcass is "broken up" for its valued parts, the mask, brush, and pads, by the gentlemen and ladies in white stocks and red coats. Young riders witnessing their first kill are initiated by a blooding ceremony in which the Master dips into the gore to make the sign of the cross on the forehead of the neophyte. The rite indicates that the child shares both the honor and the guilt of the death. This recidivistic ceremony, well known to all followers of the hounds, is for some reason seldom mentioned in the copious literature of fox hunting.[19] An optional practice is the blessing of the hounds by a hard-riding parson, who afterwards exchanges his vestments for the garb of the hunting field.[20]

But what of the animal who gives the party? In England the public attitude has now shifted in favor of the fox. The extent of this change may be gauged from the fact that the Joint-Master of the Heythrop Fox Hounds has found it necessary to place in the hands of little fox-hunting trainees a syllabus with the engaging title, *How to Win Arguments About Fox Hunting.*

Well, we have at least the security of knowing that fox hunting insures our having a small but well-trained cavalry corps, and that fox hunters do join with humanitarians in opposing the squalid activities of the predator-control bureaucrats and the game butchers who use airplanes and electronic calls. Fortunately, the fox adapts well to barbed-wire fencing, housing developments, and shopping centers—better, indeed, than its pursuers do. In one hilarious incident, the Potomac, Maryland, Hunt landed in a backyard swimming pool. In another, the "field" of the Fairfax, Virginia, Hunt found themselves chasing their prey down a main street in Reston, Virginia.[21] Perhaps we can best conclude this short treatment of neolithic sportsmen by recalling the satiric remark of England's poet, William Shenstone: "The world may be divided into people that read, that write, people that think, and fox hunters."[22]

But for savage and witless destruction of wildlife resources, nothing equals the big business of hunting as the term is understood in America. Primitive man hunted in order to survive, but he also demonstrated a reverence for life and understood perhaps better than we do his connection with the natural world. Today's hunter, by contrast, just to pass the time, slays "those pathetic, kindred lower creatures we no longer fear as enemies, hate as rivals, or need as slaves."[23] Something in the range of half a billion birds and mammals fall before the guns of American hunters every year, producing more than a million tons of carcass.[24] And it has been estimated that for every clean kill two maimed animals escape to die later of gangrene, fever, starvation, or predation. In that outlandish and atavistic recreation, bow-and-arrow hunting, one authority asserts that as many as ten deer are wounded for every one that is killed outright. How does this cruel and messy attack square with the concept of the "game harvest," which the game management functionaries never tire of telling us is carried on solely for the good of the deer herd? Critics of this clumsy bloodbath think otherwise. The object in view, they believe, is the license-fee dollar.[25]

For his fellow creatures man, it seems, has been the most colossal of all disasters. We have some 30 million hunters in the field today, backed by the National Wildlife Federation, a front for gunners, the National Rifle Association, the local sportsman's clubs, the conservation bureaus of government agencies, and the manufacturers of guns, ammunition, clothing, and other hunting accessories. The sports hunters are, in the words of Bil Gilbert, naturalist and author, "the most pampered, privileged, subsidized recreational group in existence."[26] By contrast, those who would like to enjoy our native wild game animals as an aesthetic and spiritual experience are ignored, except for one ironical aspect of the matter. Those who do not hunt at all are tapped to pay the major portion of the bill for keeping some kind of order among the pleasure killers when they march out into our woodlands and fields.

Many social theorists have speculated about why civilized men kill for fun: to collect trophies, bolster a wavering ego, or assert their virility. Dr. Karl Menninger considers the sexual symbolism of the impulse to kill to be too obvious for extended discussion. He recalls a patient, a great duck hunter, who learned through being psychoanalyzed that his compulsion to shoot ducks derived from the fact that every time he blazed away at a mallard or pintail he was killing his mother.[27]

The hunting brotherhood are rich in sophistries. The animals must be killed for their own good. The species being hunted is bloodthirsty, a danger to livestock and human life. Coyotes are "mean and tough." Eagles carry off little babies. Wolves pursue people in sleighs. And killer-bear stories are staple fare of the sporting magazines.[28] The entrenched game bureaucracies devote themselves with dedication to the about thirty shootable species (out of approximately one thousand) of North American birds and mammals. Representative John P. Saylor of Pennsylvania agrees that the career employees in the wildlife service are dedicated. He declared in a hearing on hunting from airplanes: "They are dedicated to self-preservation. That is what they are dedicated to. They are dedicated to preserving their own jobs, and getting a promotion."[29]

It is an unpalatable fact, but "free" hunting and fishing is a political matter. Every politician feels the pressure from the hunter of modest means who makes himself heard because he has bought his hunting license or duck stamp, which "entitles him to stand in line at the outdoor meat market and receive his allotment." Money, unlike animals, can talk. "The U.S. Department of the Interior, according to *National Parks Magazine*," Roger Caras wrote, "has estimated that every polar bear harvested in Alaska adds at least fifteen hundred dollars to the economy of the state."

Greed and betrayal still coexist in this ecological decade. In California, where the bighorn sheep has been protected since 1872, a charter member of the Bighorn Sheep Council and director of the Society for the Conservation of Bighorn Sheep was arrested, charged, and convicted of a felony for conducting secret poaching expeditions. Wealthy trophy hunters paid up to $3,000 for a ram's head, satisfaction guaranteed. If the client failed to bag his own ram a guide would shoot one for him. The enterprising leader of the ring even operated a taxidermy shop as an adjunct of his secret safari business, integrating vertically from raw material to finished product.[30]

Concern over cruelty to wild animals is of fairly recent origin, but the point of view is gaining as a new, less favorable conception of today's hunter emerges. Environmentalists are drawing attention to the tax-coddling of the hunting interests, and to such scandals as the so-called game preserves, where the hunter can select his own bear or whatever animal is available as one might choose a lobster at a lobster pound. Until recently one "preserve" in Maine offered even better service. The bear was kept in a cage and the nimrod could shoot his animal through the bars without the bother of a tramp through the woods.[31]

Slowly society discards its anything-goes attitude toward game species and fun shooting. But don't look for miracles. It will be a long, slow turnaround before our attitude toward the larger fauna of the forests will be determined by ecological rather than political considerations. The great majority of hunters are not vicious. They often respond to the natural world, and may even feel an emotional attachment to the animals they destroy, through that dark impulse which impels man to kill what he loves. Meanwhile the hunters are manipulated by the "outdoor" magazines and commercial propaganda that skillfully play upon the male ego, all of which is quite easy to do. "Man is indeed ingenious when he wants an excuse for blood-letting," Robert and Leona Train Rienow note in their eloquent report, *Moment in the Sun.*[32]

Many hunters scorn the idea of practicing deliberate inefficiency and therefore use all the means of tracking and killing that technology can provide. So wild horses roaming on government land were shot from planes and trucks until the Eighty-sixth Congress stopped the practice. This result was due largely to the national publicity generated in behalf of the animals by one woman, Mrs. Velma Johnston, known as "Wild Horse Annie," of Reno, Nevada. Another Wild Horse Annie is now urgently needed by the grizzly and polar bear populations of Alaska, which are being rapidly decimated.[33]

A new gadget has recently increased the pressure upon our wild areas: enter—the snowmobile. This nerve-shattering motorized sled is a catastrophe for such islands of serenity as remain in our forests and public lands. The manufacture of engine-powered, off-highway vehicles is now a $1.2 billion industry. The smelly scooters, roaring like outboard motors, with air horns and imitation leopard-skin upholstery, promise to accomplish what one dis-enchanted New Hampshire skier calls the "slobinization of the wilds." Once thought to be a passing fad, the "snowmos" or "cats," with mascot trade names like Panther and Scorpion, have made possible the mechanized invasion of our remaining wilderness areas and brought forth a new kind of "sporting event," the pas-time of chasing wild creatures in their native habitat.

An incident will suggest the dimensions of this new menace. Snowmobilers drove a small brush wolf across Lake Simcoe in Ontario for ninety minutes, striking it with their machines some twenty times before the exhausted beast was finally trapped be-hind a snowdrift. The operators then jumped their machines on the wolf, breaking its back. The lucky fellow who finished off the animal applied for and received a twenty-five-dollar wolf bounty.[34]

More serious because it was a mass assassination, was a vicious crime that occurred in Minnesota: A game warden found sixteen deer "sadistically run down by snowmobile machines. . . ."[35] Most of the snow-belt states have passed laws that prohibit the harass-ment of game species, but not wildlife in general. Enforcement is an enormous task, and proof of wrongdoing that would stand up in court is difficult to obtain. Meanwhile, scooter clubs flourish and motels offer package trips into wild lands that include rental of one's machine for the weekend. There are even miniscooters for the kiddies—one is called a "Kitty-Cat"—and merchandising lures include a snowmobile suit with every machine purchased.[36]

Several states have moved to stop the abuse of wild animals by this all-terrain nonnecessity. Michigan uses around ninety ma-chines in patrol work; apparently it takes a snowmobiler to catch a snowmobiler. New York registers the machines and requires that firearms be unloaded and broken down when carried on the scoot-ers. "Avoid disturbing wildlife," cautions Randolph E. Kerr, New York's assistant general manager of Forest Preserve Parks, a neat trick if you can do it.[37] When the deer season is over in Vermont most of the fellows in the Green Mountain Coon and Cat Club turn their attention to bobcat hunting. "Coon hunting got me started on cat and bear," reminisces James A. Harris, "and today there just isn't anything I'd rather do." But Pfc. Harris isn't going to get any more fine toms with the aid of a snowmobile—not legally, that is. Vermont has banned the snowmobile as a vehicle to be used in hunting and plans to bar the machines absolutely from a number of wild areas—"not because of any environmental problems," says Ben Huffman of the state's Forests and Parks Department, "but so we can provide some place on God's green earth for man to spend some time without hearing a damned motor."[38]

Further hazards lie ahead. The present snowmo is only the first generation of a variety of off-road vehicles known as ATVs (all-terrain vehicles) that will be able to traverse sand, mud, and swamp. Control is going to be the critical point, since snowmobilers are numerous, aggressive, and articulate. When the deputy commissioner of the New York State Conservation Department testified in 1969 (the department has a fancier name now) about snowmobiles and the new problem they presented, he said that he felt that licensing should be handled by the Motor Vehicle Bureau because it had had more "experience in the field." His statement was greeted with hearty laughter in the hearing room. The spectators understood that a sticky problem was being bucked over into another part of the forest.[39]

In the late 1970s, when the mechanized caveman of our time mounts his high-octane ATV, will the only tracks on the trail be his own, the only spoor a stream of nonreturnable bottles, discarded fuel containers, and similar debris? The prospect is for a decade of struggle between the hard-nosed mentality and those whom the despoilers categorize as "bleeding hearts." "There is one name we are called which we admit is accurate: 'bleeding hearts,' " Mrs. Ann Gough Hunter told the City Council of Dallas, Texas, in protesting against its policy of killing all wild animals that strayed into the city limits. "Our hearts bleed for those who can see nothing in the beautiful outdoors . . . but something to kill."[40]

Perhaps the slaughter in our overhunted forests and private woodlands will end within the present century for one of two rather disparate reasons: either mankind will at last come to believe that animals are "worthy of preservation for their own sake" or because there are no more living targets to shoot at.[41]

M. Claude Lévi-Strauss, a world figure in the field of social anthropology, who deplores and fears the arrogance of twentieth-century man, has observed in primitive societies that "people who live entirely by hunting have all sorts of beliefs and institutions that keep them from exterminating natural species." The American Indians, for example, held "that the capital of life existing in the universe is constant, and every share taken from the animal kingdom must be compensated by a shortening of the life of man."[42] What a monstrous joke it would be on the white demigods if it turned out that the Indians were right.

18

Fashion Fads and Fun Furs

From the pastoral and hunting stages of civilization down to the present time, women have decorated themselves with a tooth, a feather, or a piece of animal skin, and we haven't yet put aside the life style of a skin-working economy. Just which wild animal fragments confer distinction has varied from time to time, according to obscure and shifting ideals. Though the need for furs is today as obsolete as the human tail, rare skins remain a symbol of conspicuous leisure and expensive adornment. A considerable number of Venuses in furs experience sexual excitement from contact with the skins of beasts, a phenomenon upon which Dr. von Krafft-Ebing makes some interesting observations under the title *Zoophilia Erotica* in his classical study of perversions. If fashion can determine which animal shall be petted, it can also enforce its dictates as to which one shall be assassinated for the values discerned in its pelt. Thus some women snuggle in minks and sables, while feline females, swathed in spotted skins, "feel fleet, mysterious, beautiful and lethal. Ocelot, jaguar and tiger

—such furs express their personalities"; or so it is held.[1]

A bit of social history illuminates the irrationality of our stylish folkways. When bird plumage became high fashion in the third quarter of the last century, the ladies of the period bowed submissively to the vogue for bird feathers supplied by professional plume hunters. The market hunter was an elemental, rather unlovable character who farmed the sea shore and raided the heronries of Florida as matter-of-factly as he would have harvested potatoes, peaches, or cotton.

The millinery trade fought off critics with arguments that have a familiar ring. Wild bird feathers supported a legitimate business. They provided the livelihood of hard-working Americans. And the birds did do a lot of damage. The feathers of the snowy egret and the American great white egret, the trade insisted, were not procured by the death of the mothers and their broods during the breeding season: they were just picked up off the ground. Moreover, those who raised questions were clearly cranks, busybodies, and probably socialists.[2] If the woman who was tempted by the nuptial plume of the egret voiced a scruple, her milliner had a story ready to satisfy her qualms. The plumes had been molted. They were obtained from game birds only. And so on.

Reform came through organized action of humane societies, the Audubon Society, the federated women's clubs, and the dedication of scientific leaders, notably Dr. Henry Fairfield Osborn.[3] Many groups joined to seek remedies in legislation and finally got them.

The situation with regard to furs today is about where the plumage trade was in the early 1900s. Whether it will be possible to make fur fashions unfashionable, as conservationists and humanitarians are trying to do, will probably depend upon how American women respond as they acquire a more detailed knowledge than they previously had of the barbarities of the leg-hold trap.

Millions of fur-bearers are caught each year in North America by the jaws of the steel trap, to die of thirst, starvation, freezing, or the attack of a predator, unless the trapper arrives first to end the misery of his catch. About twenty-five percent of the animals gnaw their legs off in the struggle to escape. Efforts have been made to introduce a humane trap (more difficult to operate), or to enforce standards of inspection of trap lines, but they have not been productive.[4] There is clearly an information gap between the wild animal that dies in agony and the glistening fur in the salon, so far as the woman who turns to the skin trade for her security blanket is concerned. Trapping is carried on without spectators, and trappers are not loquacious about the details of their trade. Furthermore, magazines and newspapers that derive revenue from furriers' advertisements prefer to romanticize trapping rather than dwell upon the crunch of steel teeth on a furry leg, or on desperate animal mothers trying to drag their pain-racked bodies and a trap back to hungry kits or cubs.[5]

The body count is high. It takes forty raccoon skins to make one coat for a human, and an unknown number of miscellaneous animals die in the traps—turtles, groundhogs, porcupines, dogs, cats, even eagles—before the forty pelts are collected. For each mink coat about a hundred animals are sacrificed.[6] The fur-manufacturing union, rather aptly named the Amalgamated Meat Cutters and Butcher Workmen of North America, are understandably against any tightening up of trapping laws. The fur manufacturers display the outlook of a "nihilistic industry," while the news media prattle brightly about the new dripping-with-furs look, the grave question of coat length and "other dashing developments."[7]

Yet there are signs of some slight movement. Abercrombie & Fitch, the swank New York specialty store, has discontinued the sale of any product that uses the fur or skin of an endangered species. *The New Yorker* magazine no longer accepts the advertisements of clothing or accessories made from threatened species like leopards, tigers, harp seals, or alligators. *Vogue*, the special journal of the high fashion world, which has close associations with the New York fur industry, has expressed concern about the endangered species and has promised to make every effort not to print pictures of the skins of such beasts. "You won't see in the pages of *Vogue*," the editors have vowed, "any fur you can't wear and enjoy with a clear conscience."[8]

One New York furrier, doing business under the name of Georges Kaplan, has hired expensive advertising space to associate himself with Dr. Albert Schweitzer's philosophy of reverence for all life. This fur salon places "decency and reason," the text of one announcement says, "over monetary profit."[9] Kaplan's competitors responded to this ringing statement with deep suspicion. "It's just a publicity stunt," said a spokesman at The Tailored Woman,

who preferred to change the subject to leopards (coats from
$4,500), which he said are highly dangerous animals that kill little
children.[10]

The self-denying announcements of the various corporations
mentioned above are not quite as generous or idealistic as they
appear to be. They are based on the definition of endangered
species in the *Red Data Book*, published in Switzerland by the
Union for the Conservation of Nature and Natural Resources.
First of all, the list is incomplete. It presents only those mammals
for which irrefutable scientific evidence exists. It omits regional
problems. A species or race may be exterminated in one habitat but
still hang on in another, an aspect of animal destruction on which
the *Red Data Book* does not report.[11]

It would be premature, then, to conclude that the American
furrier himself is about to become endangered. Yet there is some
evidence that the trade may lose control of events, as did the
Eastern Millinery Association and the Feather Importers Association some six or seven decades ago. Today the belief that unendur-
able pressure on hunted fur species lowers the quality of human
life itself is winning new supporters. This is not straight
humanitarianism but part of the total ecological issue. Yet the
practical effect is the same. The fur coat as a social symbol is in
trouble.

Socially prominent San Francisco men and women have signed
a pledge not to buy fur coats or accessories if they are made from
the skins of wild animals. Conservationists and animal friends
have developed guerrilla tactics. They have demonstrated in front
of the business establishments that sell furs. They have organized
telephone barrages to department stores and to Air Canada, as a
carrier of tourists, in behalf of the harp seal pups, in the latter
instance following the Machiavellian tactic "Be *brave* and *persistent*
. . . if one word will do—use thirty!" Letters to the editors of
newspapers, opposing seal clubbing and trapping and deploring
the think-mink propaganda, appear frequently. Not all of this is
organized. Freelances have scored solid successes. When a woman
living in Falls Village, Connecticut, protested against the advertising of a sale of polar bear rugs by G. Fox & Company, the Hartford, Connecticut, department store, the store replied that it
would dispose of the stock on hand and buy no more.[12]

As is usual with issues concerned with animal misery and human ethics, there are gradations of opinion and commitment. Mrs. George Plimpton, wife of the writer and exhibitionist, has expressed deep concern about the consumption in the fashion industry of beasts that are in peril of extinction, but was herself a cause célèbre at a fashion show when she made a few quotable but injudicious remarks about her skirt, which was made of alley-cat fur. Cleveland Amory is against extinction, plus cruelty plus killing. "Life is indivisible," as he puts it. "Furs have as little appeal to me," says Alice Herrington, president of Friends of Animals, "as lampshades made of human skin."[13]

The hesitations of some fur-wearers are overcome if their fur garments are supplied by domestic animals. Others make their personal adjustment by wearing only farmed furs. But many people with humane feelings reject the ranch-grown skins as well as the wild, because the ranched animal has lived unnaturally for all of its short life in a small cage, and its violent death revolts them. Mink kits at seven months get the needle, enter the gas chamber, or their necks are broken by machine, whereas the free, wild animal at least lives with its natural joy and vivacity until caught.

One might suppose that humanitarians would applaud the current trend toward imitation or "conservationist" furs. But not always. If the synthetic or "fake" fur looks marvelously like animal fragments, if it cannot be distinguished from "a concourse of funerals," the very success of the artifice compromises the lady swathed in the furs, according to this way of thinking.

The United States government is in the fur business. About 50,000 northern fur seals are clubbed to death by government employees each summer in the Pribilof Islands off the coast of Alaska, where the fur seal has its breeding rookeries. The clubbers, stickers, rippers, and strippers are Aleutian Indians, a friendly enough people who detest their brief—the season is six to nine weeks—and brutal employment.

The island natives are descendants of Russian serfs, now living under the paternal eye of the U.S. Department of Commerce. About one hundred and twenty families are maintained in the islands by the department, at a cost in 1970 of over a million dollars, while forty-two full-time bureaucrats supervise the affairs of the Aleuts and the seals. Skins are shipped at government expense to far-away Greenville, South Carolina, where a concern known as the Fouke Fur Company, operating under a monopoly contract, does the processing and auctions off the skins in the presence of milling pickets ("Let a Seal Wear Your Skin"), grinding TV cameras, and an embarrassing amount of unwanted publicity.[14]

As more information about the fur seal hunt becomes available to the general public, including the failure on the part of the government to put into effect humane measures it has already agreed to, the issue of how this bloody business is conducted heats up. And beyond that question lies another: whether the slaughter of these sea mammals should occur at all. The National Audubon Society is satisfied with existing conditions because the fur seal, it claims, is not rare. The animal welfare societies, holding to their historic mission—the elimination of cruelty and suffering—emphasize the moral revulsion against men crushing the fragile skulls of inoffensive animals with multiple blows of a club. They maintain a simple thesis: the seals should not be killed. "The ultimate solution," says the International Society for the Protection of Animals, " lies in the abolition of the hunts," and it shares the expectation of the Humane Society of the United States that we shall see a change of heart on the part of the women who buy and wear wild animal furs.[15] To help make furs unpopular, the Friends of Animals offers a receipt for the market value of contributed furs that permits the donor to deduct the amount from income taxes.

Often confused with the seal hunt conducted by the United States government in the Bering Sea islands is the killing of newborn harp seal pups on the rafting ice off the coasts of Labrador, Newfoundland, and in the gulf of the St. Lawrence River. For over two hundred years, and to many Canadians the time period seems to validate the practice, the sealers have been clubbing the baby seals, known as "white coats," and skinning them, often while still alive, as the mothers watch helplessly.[16] The tiny creatures, among the most appealing in the world, have no defense against their executioners. The "hunt," in reality, is a massacre; it is, in the homely phrase, about like shooting fish in a barrel. The men who do the gaffing, kicking, and live skinning are not especially sadistic. They are in a hurry. The season is short. They have paid their license fee. The wind is bitter. The pay is by the skin. Fast work inevitably raises the level of violence.

Humane societies and conservationists cooperate in opposing the slaughter of the seal puppies because both ethical and biological issues are involved. The cruelty is real and extinction of the species is imminent. Worldwide pressure on Canada's Department of Fisheries has steadily increased since a film of the hunt was shot and exhibited in 1964. The government of Canada, concerned about the effects of adverse publicity on pleasure travel in Canada, announced that it would prohibit the taking of "white coats" in 1970 and gave the move the widest possible self-congratulatory publicity. Actually, this maneuver was a simple ruse to reduce the pressure of public opinion. The baby seals were again clubbed in 1970, and in 1971 the method was still defended in soothing press releases as "the most humane." But early in 1972 the Canadian government shifted its position and cancelled the seal hunt in the Gulf of St. Lawrence. This does not yet represent a permanent policy change at Ottawa, though the pressure of public, indeed of world opinion, remains heavy. The government is still meditating on an advisory committee's recommendation that the seal hunt should be phased out entirely by 1974.[17]

Seal products are consumed in the fur and leather trades, and in the manufacture of margarine and beauty oils. The animals are also esteemed for their edible flippers, and the sex organs of the males are highly thought of in Hong Kong as an aphrodisiac. The question of when it is right and when it is wrong to take life, and whether fashion and cosmetic oils constitute a sufficient reason, remains unresolved. But by the time a clear, ethical point of view emerges in commercial sealing or on the Ottawa scene, the harp seal may have followed the Labrador duck into extinction.

The demand for the skins of lizards, snakes, and alligators is a reminder of the special coldness that humans reserve for cold-blooded animals. Many snake skins come from undeveloped countries. Snakes eat rodents. Rodents are one of the chief threats to the food supplies of those countries. But the snakes continue to die anyway for the cause of fashion. So, too, do the alligators of the Florida Everglades, which contribute to ecological balance by maintaining water holes useful to other forms of wildlife. The poaching of alligators for their hides, known humorously as "frog hunting," has been described by a conservationist magazine as "the dirtiest business in America since the slaughter of egrets for women's hats," but the shiny, costly symbols of affluence remain objects of feminine desire despite the racket's sordid background.[18]

Killing alligators has been illegal in Florida since 1961, but arrests have been few and penalties light. Hide hunters coolly accept the possibility of getting caught; it is an entrepreneurial risk. But the outlook has brightened for the saurians. An amendment to the federal Endangered Species Act prohibiting the interstate shipment of skins went into effect in 1970, and both New York City and New York State have outlawed the sale of alligator products.[19]

Cecil Clemens of Palmdale, Florida, who owns a tourist attraction known as a "Gatorama," has successfully bred both native alligators and Jamaican crocodiles in his sixteen-acre compound and thinks that there may be a future in alligator farming, which would be something like ranching mink. This would be a perfectly legal business and might preserve the market for handbags, pocketbooks, shoes, and belts, while taking the pressure off the wild animals. But there are difficulties. The necessary permits would be hard to get, the conservationists would square away for a rough fight, and Clemens has confessed to an unusual personal reason why he is not really enthusiastic about butchering his reptiles. "You get attached to the bloomin' things," he explained.[20]

If it continues to be chic to wear alligator fragments, however, there are still various possible maneuvers for keeping the customers outfitted with their matching ensembles. The state of Louisiana would like to get the alligator off the endangered species list so it could sell hunting licenses. There has been a suspicious increase in the collecting of live animals in Florida for "display" purposes, under a license that is quite easily obtained. Another possibility is that American hides may end up in American hands after making a long journey, possibly to France, returning home ticketed as a foreign species. Close relatives do exist abroad. One importer has asserted that there are "10,000 to 100,000 alligators in Africa and South America," adding, "No one wants to keep that many alligators any place. It makes the rivers unsafe."[21]

Psychologists and neurologists have concluded that furs, feathers, and all animal substances used as personal adornment represent a survival of primitive fetishism. They explain it this way: the animal tissues are essentially mascots, which symbolize the wearer and bring luck through tactile sensations that also act as erotic stimulants. This is particularly true of furs and leathers, although shoe fetishism is also a widely recognized phenomenon. And further study is needed on such animalesque delights as kangaroo-paw bottle openers, trophy horns for the sportsman's den, and such elegances as elephant-foot wastebaskets made from "a genuine elephant's foot."[22]

A French writer of the period of Louis XV, Jean François Marmontel, in his *Contes moraux* draws a biting portrait of a self-styled philosopher who at a dinner party condemns man for slaughtering and eating innocent animals but concludes that since the feast has been prepared it might as well be eaten.[23] Human nature hasn't changed noticeably in the two hundred years since Marmontel began to publish his moral tales. For example, when the posh Mark Cross store on New York's Fifth Avenue decided to discontinue stocking "croc" items in June 1970, the premises were mobbed by well-dressed women after the clearance sale was announced. Their general point of view was expressed by one of the early birds, a silver-haired matron from Rochester, New York, who told Judy Klemesrud of *The New York Times:* "As long as they're here, I don't feel guilty. After all, I didn't go out and shoot the crocodile myself."[24]

It is interesting to note that the Mark Cross salespeople approved the step management took to help preserve the world's ecosystem. "I think crocodiles should lead a happy life just like we do," said Stephanie Bonventre, nineteen, warmly if ungramatically. A summer employee and a political science major at St. John's University, Stephanie added, "how would people feel if they had their skins peeled off like that?"[25]

It's a good question.

19

Animal Experiments:
Trying It on the Dog

Vivisection has been practiced upon both animals and men from time immemorial, and in the early centuries of our era the burden of sacrifice may have pressed even more heavily upon human than subhuman creatures. Though graphic representations exist of Galen, the great physician of classical times, dissecting a pig, both he and Celsus, encyclopedist of the time of Tiberius, mention the ready availability of human material in the form of those who were "rightless"—slaves, gladiators, condemned criminals, or members of the inferior races. Few members of the general community who are not closely in touch with physicians or clinical investigators (the new name for human experimenters) understand that human experimentation flourishes today on a grand scale—promoted by agencies of the United States government, showered with grants, and condoned by the courts. That moral values often get lost is strongly underlined by the fact that it is not uncommon for a new drug to be given simultaneously with the last rites. And not long ago a doctor in Portland, Oregon,

192

was quoted as "acidly" suggesting that it would be a splendid idea to use antivivisectionists and their children as experimental subjects.[1]

If ethical considerations became blurred in human experiments, a situation where valid consent is supposed to be obtained and the legal threat exists, at least in theory, of prosecution for common assault, what measure of compassion can be expected of the experimenters for creatures who can neither protest, consent, or sue? Meanwhile the order of the day is relentless expansion. The veterinary-oriented National Institutes of Health say that facilities for using laboratory animals must be doubled by 1978 for what may be termed "trying it on the dog." Exact figures do not exist on the annual consumption of animals in biomedical research in the United States at the present time, but estimates are in the range of 100 million or more vertebrate animals, and the mega-deaths continue to rise steeply.[2]

There are three general attitudes that people take toward experimenting on animals. Careerist researchers want no discussion or surveillance. Like all social organisms whose first concern is self-preservation, the trade bodies that speak for the vivisectionist point of view react angrily and defensively when outsiders suggest the possibility of wrongs, abuses, or improvements, their spokesmen reciting as a kind of litany the long list of the contributions to public health made by investigations performed on living beings. But students of human nature contend that many of the experiments are designed not for the public good but to enhance the prestige of the researcher.

In opposition are the antis, who demand the total abolition of all animal experimentation, which they view as being an absolute evil, not to be condoned because it may produce results profitable to the human race or even to the animals themselves. A third view is that of the animal protection organizations. Most of them, but not all, somewhat uncomfortably accept in principle the necessity for biological experiments. But they advocate strict regulation. Investigations, they say, should be undertaken only to find new truth. No painful experiments should be permitted by unskilled persons working in unsuitable premises, none simply to improve operative dexterity, none merely to illustrate a law or fact already known. And the zoophiles insist that the inquiring physiologists, clad in their white robes of office, should not be the sole judges of their own actions, any more than any other group with a vested interest.

In this often-bitter clash of irreconcilable goals the moderate animalitarians have been roundly abused by both factions. The former consider them to be "animal cranks" for even bringing up the question of vivisection, the latter, because they are willing to yield something to win something, charge them hotly with being false to humanitarian ideals. After years of strife, the careerists of science are clearly ahead, largely because they are adept in arousing fearful and self-regarding thoughts among the lay public by threatening a new Dark Age for medicine if there is any curtailment of their absolute freedom.

Central to the problem is the most thorny philosophical issue man has ever faced, the problem of evil. This mysterious and harsh dilemma arises when one contemplates the undeserved sufferings of blameless animals.[3] Is the pursuit of knowledge the highest good? If so, what knowledge? Should animals suffer misery, stress, pain, and slow death for trivial human purposes? To test a hair dye? To advance the interests of cigarette manufacturers? Should the beasts die in experiments that have already been performed countless times? Is mutilation, torment, and death a price our animal companions on this planet should be required to pay so that a high school biology student may win a science-fair prize and be interviewed on television?

These questions, which are not rhetorical but reflect what goes on, pinpoint frivolous purposes and a contemporary blunting of moral perceptions. A reporter touring the Jackson Laboratory at Bar Harbor, Maine, saw a little lady in a white coat drop a handful of white mice into a jar. There was a hissing sound. Soon the rodents were still. "We don't think of them in an emotional context," a senior scientist explained. "They're laboratory tools. I suppose I've killed ten thousand mice . . . and never thought twice about it."[4]

The figure of the mad scientist, though overdrawn and often invoked by antivivisectionist propaganda, cannot be entirely disregarded when the investigator's mind is narrowed by an order of priorities that leaves no room for compassion. And when life is cheap and money plentiful, it may be easier to repeat the experiment than to make a tedious search of the literature to see if it hasn't already been performed, described, and abstracted. Laboratory animals are abundantly available. In fact, they are sold by the pound, and the scientific community can afford a great deal of nonsense. Konrad Lorenz has proposed an interesting test to determine the humanity scale of biologists. Let a researcher, he says, try in imagination to kill in succession a lettuce leaf, a fly, a frog, a guinea pig, a cat, a dog, and a chimpanzee. He concluded, "To any man who finds it equally easy to chop up a live dog and a live lettuce, I would recommend suicide at his earliest convenience!"[5]

A landmark attempt to arbitrate between the claims of science and the claims of mercy came in England in the early 1870s upon the initiative of leading men of science, including such illustrious figures as Charles Darwin, T. H. Huxley, Sir William Jenner, Sir Richard Owen, and other leaders of British biology. There was also a powerful lay movement that called attention to the subject, supported by, among others, J. A. Froude and William E. H. Lecky, the historians, and eminent literary personalities such as Harriet Martineau, Thomas Carlyle and Lord Tennyson, the poet laureate, as well as the lord chamberlain and the Queen herself. The result was the passage in 1876 of the Cruelty to Animals Act, "badly drafted and difficult to understand," as C. W. Hume has noted, which some said went too far and others not far enough. But it did at least establish three principles: the licensing of researchers, adequate inspection of laboratory premises, and the Pain Rule. This last standard "sets the limit to the amount of suffering which may be caused in any circumstances." Because of restraints imposed upon themselves by both the Research Defence Society and the English humane organizations, their debate has been carried on in recent years with good temper. An atmosphere has thus been established, Hume concludes, "in which it is now possible to discuss vivisection without provoking a breach of the peace."[6]

In America, where the man of science enjoys an almost sacerdotal character, and it sometimes seems as though we have transferred our faith from God to the National Society for Medical Research, a considerable number of compassionate people have concluded that the fight for total elimination of animal experimentation is a counterproductive policy. Many anticruelty societies, therefore, confine their efforts to supporting legislation that regulates the life and care of the animal before and after operative procedures. This position, it should be noted, does not place any limitation upon the experiments themselves, yet it has brought the humane movement into violent collision with the formidable American Medical Association.

However, despite massive opposition, a Laboratory Animal Welfare Act became law in 1966 and was amended in December 1970. It was designed to protect all species of warm-blooded animals during their stay in research laboratories, and safeguards were extended to animals in circuses, zoos, and the pet trade. Congress, however, having apparently exhausted its feelings of solicitude for the beast kingdom, has subsequently shown itself to be extremely parsimonious in appropriating funds for enforcing the law.[7]

As for regulating the design, model, or performance of actual experiments, it appears highly unlikely that any law could be passed in the United States in this century that would touch this area. Public opinion still sanctions the infliction of pain because of "the almost universally held credo of Western civilization that advancement of medicine is desirable."[8] Meanwhile those sensible of the torments visited upon animals in the laboratories of American educational institutions have to live with the knowledge that millions of creatures are being scalded, burned, beaten, crushed, poisoned, given cancers, and skinned alive. Sometimes they come out of anesthesia, as the result of technical virtuosity, with two heads instead of one. And anticruelty laws cannot be invoked. Most states specifically exempt research laboratories in their statutes dealing with animal protection.

Since the universities, government agencies, and research staffs of commercial enterprises who do biological testing enjoy extraordinary freedom from social restraints, it seems reasonable to inquire what purposes are served by the suffering and destruction. The National Society for Medical Research reiterates the contributions to medicine made by animal experimentation, and Dr. Selman A. Waksman, the microbiologist and winner of the Nobel Prize for medicine, has called attention to the fact, or rather the conjecture, that had an antibiotic existed it could have saved Mimi from dying of tuberculosis in *La Bohème.*[9] In that case, of course, we shouldn't have had *La Bohème.*

It must also be acknowledged that scientific experiment has its roll of human martyrs, such as Dr. Jesse William Lazear, who died of yellow fever, while engaged in the study of its transmission by the mosquito later identified as *Aëdes aegypti*. The memory of Dr. Walter Reed, who headed the United States Army Yellow Fever Commission, is preserved in the name of the great military hospital at Washington, and the Johns Hopkins University displays a memorial tablet to Dr. Lazear. But there is no eternal flame anywhere, so far as I know, honoring "The Unknown Animal," who, moreover, was not a consenting participant in the arrangements that terminated its brief existence.

Today painful procedures are carried out routinely in fields of inquiry that have nothing to do with the conquest of disease. Many of them raise, or should raise, questions of conscience. Permanent-wave lotions are injected into the eyes of rabbits held rigid in stocks, and at the Ohio State University, as this is written, rabbits are wearing contact lenses in search for softer materials, although softness can be measured mechanically in other ways than by punishing rabbits. The Ford Motor Company used baboons, strapped in sleds, as high-speed crash victims, because for precise data on impact and stress there is, apparently, nothing like a baboon. The Air Force has conducted experiments on pregnant monkeys in crash tests. Results are encouraging, but as is so often the case, the findings are only "preliminary" and will have to be repeated over and over. How many pregnant women are expected to fly military aircraft has not yet been disclosed.[10]

The Tobacco Institute and the American Cancer Society are locked in a titanic struggle, but the only casualties so far are beagles. The tobacco men want to prove that dogs, who don't really like to smoke, will not get lung cancer when hooked up to a machine that forces them to inhale smoke every time they draw a breath. The cancer men, led by the pathologist, Dr. Oscar Auerbach, of the Veterans Hospital at East Orange, New Jersey, supported by an epidemiologist and large infusions of tax money, has slit the throats of his dogs and inserted smoking tubes for precisely the opposite purpose. Auerbach's "thing" is to produce emphysema and malignant tumors. As these lines are written Auerbach seems to be out in front. He has produced splendid examples of lung damage in an interminable experiment that has been going on since May 1967. If the unfortunate animals don't die from the forced inhalation of cigarette smoke, they are killed anyway, so that lung sections can be examined microscopically.

Those who look on with wonderment at this scramble for "facts" to shore up a predetermined position can only hope that the beagles of the future will give up their lives in experiments designed with greater precision. Lincoln Pierson Brower, professor of biology at Amherst College and who owns no tobacco stocks —has described the three-and-a-half-year Auerbach adventure in search of a tumor as unsound and unacceptable, and he has spoken with frankness of "the misuse of so-called scientific results by one group with vested interests to attack another."[11]

One's thoughts upon man's arrogant exploitation of the other animals may well begin with an examination of purpose. Does the benefit in view justify the suffering and the taking of life? Research that illustrates once more that tobacco irritates is simply a demonstration of a fact already thoroughly documented. So it is with automobile collisions. They are very unhealthy. In reviewing research work of the sort just discussed, it is hard to avoid the conclusion that guidelines developed outside the laboratory world are needed to arbitrate between the activities of researchers and the minimal rights of animals about to die.

Various societies have tried to push this idea. But the plain fact is that the United States government departments and agencies keep the humane constituency so busy they scarcely have time to look into commercial abuses. The National Institutes of Health dispense more than $1 billion a year, largely for programs requiring animal sacrifice. Included in NIH budgets have been such items as $1 million for a study on "the mating call of the mosquito" and a few paltry thousands, hardly worth mentioning, for looking into the question, "Does a romantic rat keep his interest longer when he has a change of females?" This may be science but it sounds more like salable pornography. The Department of Defense unrolled a three-year $600,000 scheme called Project Themis, which was assigned to the psychology department of the University of Mississippi, whose turn it was to get a grant because the science program at Ole Miss needed beefing up. The job was to determine if birds can be trained for dangerous combat work. Purpose: to learn how to kill human beings more efficiently. Mercifully, this brainstorm was terminated "as a result of Congressional action."[12]

Federal employees working at St. Elizabeth's Hospital in Washington, a mental institution, have also tried to make alcoholics out of cats, rats, mice, and monkeys. The monkeys are placed in restraining chairs, where they cannot even blow their noses. If they refuse the booze they get an electric shock. Despite the ingenuity of the scinetist-bartenders engaged in this exhilarating endeavor, no test animal has become an addict, and many display an active aversion to spiritous liquor.[13] Meanwhile, nongovernment agencies also collect funds from the public in the name of science for all sorts of investigations, which include beating animals, starving and freezing them, forcing them to swim or run until they die, conditioning them à la Pavlov and spinning them in the Noble-Collip drum, a torture device that would have won the admiration of the Spanish Inquisition. Biological experiments for rocketry have worked up the chain of life from spores, fruit flies, bees, frogs, mice, hamsters, cats, dogs, hogs, and bears to the chimpanzee which is one of the ten most intelligent of the lower animals and is able to perform assigned tasks under stress in a space capsule in flight. In one test, made of course on the ground, a monkey performed better than a congressman. The chimpanzee is, moreover, a social animal, gregarious, outgoing, likeable. The chimp can be prepared for his lonely ordeal among the cold stars since he is easily taught to trust man. The animal is not asked to volunteer. A Pentagon general, speaking of an ape that took part in a particular experiment, put it this way: "He's not like a man, you know. A man could have turned the assignment down."

When they are not streaking into the stratosphere, the animals caught up in the space program live, if we can rely upon a reassuring little book, *Animal Astronauts*, written by two Air Force public relations majors, in an atmosphere of love and solicitude, especially the chimpanzee, whom the majors call "the pampered pet of America's space people." Furthermore, the human trainers who fit the beasts to their tight-fitting nylon jackets or restraining couches, and implant electrodes in their skulls, are selected "because they are naturally fond of animals in the first place."[14]

Test animals have names assigned to them. This rather pretty conceit is carried out "to provide more dramatic interest in the press coverage. . . ." Thus, early in the space program, there were two monkeys known for dramatic interest as Pat and Mike. They were lofted thirty-six miles above the earth trapped in a crude capsule accompanied by two mice, unnamed. It was a rough trip and ended in death for all aboard. Albert I, also, in another try, quietly perished, probably before the liftoff. No one really knows. But he was a gone rhesus monkey in any case, since the parachute arranged for him failed to function. Albert II was another casualty. Parachute trouble again. In centrifuge tests, five chimpanzees survived centrifugation but were dissected anyway to determine the damage they had sustained in hearts and other internal organs. The chimps didn't suffer, the authors go on to say, because they were handled according to standards set by the American Medical Association, a body whose name cannot be found, however, in a directory of humanitarian societies.

Many Americans remember unhappily the misery and despair shown on the countenance of Bonny, the young male monkey who was photographed before he was sent upon an earth-orbiting flight elaborately instrumented with wires imbedded at ten points in his head and a catheter sticking out of every orifice of his body. The little fourteen-pound primate was supposed to last thirty days, but Bonny died on the ninth day. Many elaborate theories were kicked around among the Monday-morning quarterbacks about this inopportune conclusion to the experiment, but a satisfactory answer, as was so often the case, was never found. Perhaps the little beast died of fright or because he no longer wanted to live. The bill for this excursion was $92 million. "I suppose it's easy for scientists," mused Paul Harvey in his syndicated column, "accustomed since medical school to laboratory experimentation with animals, to accept casually the painful death of one of them. I can't."[15]

Our worship of *Homo technologicus* has brought upon us the teenage scientist who adds glamour and interest to his homemade rocket by enclosing a mouse in it. And there is a definite loss in reverence for all life when youngsters are encouraged to dress up in surgical masks, caps, and rubber gloves, and sacrifice animals to demonstrate facts of no significance to win a prize, a trip, and attention in the press. Some do it for prestige, just like a grown-up scientist, some for kicks, but whatever the motivation, high school biology students are implanting cancers, inducing grotesque abnormalities in small beasts, whirling them in centrifuges, and bathing goldfish in detergents. Thalidomide experiments are reported to be popular in Huntington, West Virginia, heart transplants in Columbus, Ohio.[16]

One little sorcerer's apprentice gouged out the eyeballs of house sparrows, punished them with electric shocks when they failed to respond to light, and won a prize of $250. It is gratifying to add that such sadistic and imbecilic experiments are no longer accepted as projects for the nationally known Westinghouse Science Talent Search. Westinghouse has considered the question of purpose, and sensationalism in high school-level biology has failed to pass the test.[17] Unfortunately, ambitious children are still carrying out atrocities under pompous titles. At the International Science Fair held in Baltimore in May 1970, a sixteen-year-old exhibitor had performed crude surgery on a monkey and implanted electrodes in the animal's brain. His experiment was grandiloquently described as "Dissipation of Traumatic Neurosis by Subcortical Stimulation." The conclusion drawn: "The monkey is very sensitive to pain."[18] The present fad for children to perform radical experiments that hurt or destroy animals decreases our common stock of human decency and suggests that we have not yet advanced significantly beyond the exploit of a fifteen-year-old Brooklyn girl, which was headlined in a New York newspaper in 1956: GIRL CUTS ANIMALS INTO TALENT MELON.[19]

"There is no justification," says W. W. Armistead, dean of the College of Veterinary Medicine at Michigan State University, "for conducting in the secondary school an experiment which would cause pain to an animal." Doctor F. Barbara Orlans, the physiologist, is equally clear about this. "In my opinion, experiments involving pain to animals have no rightful place outside of research institutions," she says. "High school experimental work should conform to the 'painless' rule which states that: 'no vertebrate animal used for primary or secondary school teaching may be subjected to any experiment or procedures which interferes with its normal health or causes it pain or distress.'"[20]

Since it is now possible in Great Britain to discuss animal experimentation without starting a riot, perhaps we can in the years ahead cultivate the same temper here in America, searching always for facts before arriving at judgments. Conflicting objectives make adjustments difficult. The lay public would prefer that there be no animal pain, but accepts the pain to the extent it knows about it in the belief that medical progress is at stake. The issue has been on dead center for a century. The antivivisectionists are hostile to any suggestion of accommodation. On the other hand, it seems unlikely that the we-know-best response from the vivisectionist camp will continue to satisfy the questions that are being asked today as to whether materialistic science is to be exempted forever from the moral law.

There are encouraging possibilities of replacing the orthodox "veterinary" research methods with cell and tissue-culture techniques, mathematical models, and computer-controlled robots, which report almost instantly and can even bleed, breathe, cough, react to anesthesia, and say "ouch." Perhaps there are limitations on the use of nonsentient biological models. But the broad public has heard little as yet about this subject. Fuller disclosure, such as is being undertaken by United Action for Animals, Inc., is needed, as is wider understanding of the humanistic importance of a more compassionate philosophy. As for those medicobiologists who doggedly oppose the idea of any protective arrangements for the animals in their hands, why, one wonders, do they reject social controls so summarily if there is no abuse?[21] And why do they cling so compulsively to old-fashioned methods.?

20

The Most Dangerous Animal in the World

Man, the most numerous, aggressive, and adaptable large mammal on earth, is not less capricious and unpredictable in the exercise of his powers than were the pagan deities. It is with good reason that New York's Bronx Zoo has placed a large mirror in the Great Apes House. When a visitor looks at the mirror—through the realistic bars of a cage—he sees this legend: "You are looking at the most dangerous animal in the world. It alone of all the animals that ever lived can exterminate (and *has*) entire species of animals. Now it has achieved the power to wipe out all life on earth."[1] Somewhat in the same vein, in one of his characteristic epigrams Mark Twain declared: "Man is the only animal that blushes. Or needs to."[2]

As to our relations with the animal world, the human community has an unspecific but comforting impression that animals today are surrounded with safeguards against cruelty. But there are many shadings and degrees of mistreatment, and much cruelty is invisible or at least unseen. The tormenting of domestic animals in the rodeo arena is an example of a permissive attitude toward animal exploitation: the spectators are conditioned to see some things and not others. The same is true of the unfortunate beasts that appear in televised bullfight programs or in motion pictures that unroll scenes of animal torment despite the existence of an industry code of ethics that reads like the Ten Commandments.[3]

Nothing illustrates more clearly the primitive attitudes lying just below the surface of twentieth-century man's psyche than the use of goldfish, canaries, baby turtles, and even poisonous snakes by quick-sell merchants, discount houses, and variety and department stores as promotional gimmicks. "I have found out," wrote one observant child to the ubiquitous columnist, Ann Landers, "that the people who sell turtles in dime stores and pet stores don't know much about them."[4] Listen to the spieler at the grand opening of a shopping center on the subject of budgerigars: "For ten minutes only, parakeets are yours for only ninety-nine cents . . . see these amazing birds in our pet department. . . . Speak to them in Polish and they'll answer you in French. Now don't all rush over at once. . . ." Cages are stacked up like shoe boxes under blinding fluorescent lights. The anguished merchandise goes into the shopping cart along with the canned goods and the hair spray.[5]

A related mindless cruelty is the Easter chick trade. Other varieties of Easter merchandise are bunnies, ducklings, and other fowl, sometimes dyed in rainbow colors. The sale of living creatures as toys is widely condemned by humane societies, who know that responsible care is not provided, and that a fluffy baby chick grows up to be a chicken and a cunning baby rabbit all too soon becomes a full-grown he or she. If they live, that is. What is more probable is that the animals will die or become one more charge on the resources of the nearest SPCA. Few creatures are less likely to survive in the home atmosphere than tiny, fragile chickens whose legs are easily broken or wings crushed by an enthusiastic tot. Furthermore, close contact with baby Easter animals may introduce salmonellosis, a severe form of gastrointestinal illness, into the home.[6] If an animal is essential to your celebration of the great festival commemorating the Resurrection, the *National Humane Review* begs its readers, make it a chocolate bunny!

Come-ons of the sort described above confront enforcement

agencies with a dilemma, because cruelty is difficult to prove at the time the animal changes hands. The state of Connecticut has a better-than-average statute covering the use of animals, reptiles, or birds as prizes or awards or to attract trade. Penalties range up to one hundred dollars or thirty days in jail. But the law exempts, unfortunately, "any theatrical exhibition or circus."[7] There is always a "but" in animal protection legislation. The exemptions in this instance probably represent the price that had to be paid for getting any law at all.

Large merchandisers with prestigious names have also been unable to resist the attractions of live animals as promotional aids. Gimbel Brothers in New York has given away "a real live pony" to a winner who didn't even have to be present at the drawing but was required, the advertisement said, to provide a home for the pony, who came from "Cowtown" at Woodstown, New Jersey, "Home of the Eastern Rodeo."[8] One can imagine the rigor with which this last regulation was enforced. Some zoos quietly hire out animals, but understandably do not publicize this activity. One such arrangement backfired when Woodward & Lothrop, the Washington, D.C., department store, rented a baby Indian elephant, just off the boat from Bangkok. The small beast was displayed in the swank store's F Street window, highly visible, yet in a very real sense not seen at all. Eighteen months old, thirty-eight inches high, weighing 175 pounds, the little elephant occupied its glassed-in niche "so that children could get a close-up look," the store's display director said, or as another and more perceptive commentator on the incident expressed it, "People want to touch mystery." There was no mystery about what happened. The wretched small herd animal died right there in the window, to the considerable embarrassment of "Woodie's" and the cooperative zoo that was to receive the little beast after it had served its purpose on F Street. The elephant never acquired a name. But it was insured. The replacement was three African cranes. 'We wouldn't want to go through this again," said Julia Lee, vice-president for advertising of the high-fashion store.[9]

Less imposing retailers also turn an honest penny out of live-animal jewelry, such as sea horses and snails imprisoned in a bubble containing a nutrient solution and worn as pendants. One direct-mail pitch reads "See Miracle of Birth," which means that the C.Q.F. Manufacturing Company of Savannah, Georgia, sells six quail eggs in a plastic dome accompanied by an "Egg Hatcher's Guide Book." "This necklace is Alive!" exclaims another advertiser in this shady category, " high fashion in this age of groovy necklaces . . . ." And in San Antonio, Texas, U.S. customs agents seized more than 500 black, inch-long beetles with varicolored rhinestones glued to their backs, and little chains attached. These grotesque "living jewels," as they are touted to be, are smuggled into the United States from Mexico and are sold in boutiques, jewelry stores, and discount houses. American women wear them as lapel ornaments and men sport them as tie clips. The tiny animals eat scraps of beetlewood and can survive for a year or so.[10]

One passenger on a 747 flight from JFK International Airport to Europe and the Near East received one of these insects, wearing patriotic red, white, and blue sequins, as a going-away present from his daughter. "The chance to bug the old man was too great," chuckled the father in recalling the occasion. The small animal of the class *Insecta*, whose owner called it a "jeweled creep," created a sensation wherever it was displayed. However, the fatigues of foreign travel, an unscheduled dunking in aquavit, the heat of photoflash bulbs, and frequent climatic changes were too much for the little conversation piece. It expired in Athens. But the last resting place of the beetle was one of many splendors—a hole in the facade of the Parthenon.[11]

Probably the most highly visible of all contemporary forms of pressure upon animal life is what is known in state police circles as the "highway kill," a linguistic creation that deserves a place beside the "body count" of Vietnam fame. Every traveler on American highways has seen the heap of bird feathers, the squashed skeleton of the land turtle or reptile on the roadway, the bundle of fur which was lately one of our native small mammals —opossum, rabbit, muskrat, raccoon, squirrel, or skunk. Foxes and deer are struck down, too, but the highway crews bury the deer, and the foxes don't often show up in the statistics, at least in the states where fox or coyote is bountied, because the remains are quickly scooped up and presented for the bounty payment, sometimes two or three times if the location makes a trip into another jurisdiction worthwhile. Fraudulent? Yes. But who can prove how the fox was killed, or where? Occasionally an unalert clerk pays off on a "wolf" scalp, which in fact came from a German shepherd or coydog.[12]

The scale of this slaughter boggles the mind. A forest zoologist traveling between State College, Pennsylvania, and Syracuse, New York, a trip of 223 miles, according to the road map, counted 205 dead squirrels along the way, about one animal per mile. And red squirrels were included only for the last half of the journey. The American Automobile Association says we destroy about a million animals each day on our highways. For just one state—Pennsylvania—the recorded figure for the year 1967 was 22,610 deer and thirty-seven bears. These statistics represent only verified kills. The animals who made it into the surrounding cover with a broken leg or internal injuries are believed to double the figure for this sacrifice to the gods of the highway. Many of the kills, says John R. Paul, curator of zoology at the Illinois State Museum, are "the results of indifferent or willfully negligent acts." He attributes much of this waste to "our societal and cultural values which enhance the automobile to the detriment of our wild life".[13]

Some drivers even head deliberately for the animals, with the intention of running them down, and go into reverse to hit them again. They are said to get a honk out of the sound of the thump as the tires strike the creature's body. This grisly recreation at least benefits the turkey buzzards.[14] They, as a consequence of the highway body count, enjoy many an unexpected banquet. In the West, too, the coyote dines upon traffic-killed rabbits, and the turkey vulture is ranging north into New York State, where it finds the pickings good.[15]

Pathological cruelty, by which sadists redirect their aggressions and frustrations toward animals—sometimes called the office-boy-kicked-the-cat syndrome—remains a permanent element in the human-animal equation. The familiar plastic bag, for example, represents a new refinement in callousness, often becoming the instrument of execution for a puppy dropped off near an SPCA shelter. The psychology of the ghetto and teen-age alienation also triggers many incidents of animal torture.[16]

Like man himself, animals feel the impact of modern technical developments. Birds die because of tall buildings and high-voltage power lines. They get swallowed up by the compressor inlets of jet aircraft. On one especially bad night in Georgia about 50,000 birds of 53 different species crashed into the ground around an Air Force base ceilometer. The sonic boom has had disastrous effects upon the mortality rates of pregnant and young animals. Cattle have charged wildly into barbed wire, and a steep-banking jet has produced hysteria in poultry flocks.[17] Plastics again: the six-pack rig for carrying beer and soft drinks, carelessly discarded by litterbugs on a lake or pond, floats just below the surface, so that surface-feeding birds become entangled in the loop. Thus the birds can neither feed nor fly.[18]

Our animal companions share the consequences of urban blight. New York dogs and cats wheeze and cough along with their human masters. When two leopards at the Staten Island Zoo became paralyzed, and one died, automobile exhaust fumes from leaded gasoline were suspected as the cause. Animals share our economic dislocations as well. When the Brooklyn Navy Yard closed, 1,500 cats were out of work. And animals feel the havoc when there is civil disorder, reports the Michigan Humane Society, which has had experience with riots in Detroit.[19]

During the last twenty-five years the concept of assembly-line manufacture has been applied increasingly to the production of food and fiber animals, resulting in the machine-fed fowl, the conveyor-belt egg from the robot hen, and broiler houses in which disease-prone chickens are sustained by massive doses of antibiotics. Their psychoses, the result of crowding and alienation from their natural world, which includes man, are controlled by de-beaking, de-winging, and the use of tranquilizing drugs. Everything is under control except the natural instincts. The fact that we generally regard the idea of psychological security of a food animal as a joking matter demonstrates how lightly we take our trusteeship of the natural environment we manipulate. Meanwhile, the yields from fordized fowls are high, the meat tender and cheap although insipid. The long-range effects upon those who eat the flesh are simply unknown.

In the mind of the pragmatic factory farmer the living creature is already a carcass. So if pigs produced by the "sweatbox" method develop stomach ulcers and bite off each other's tails because they are not allowed to act like pigs, the response is to de-tail the pigs. The line has disappeared between what is profitable and what is permissible, and special pleading is reworded to justify strange new forms of exploitation and stress. The moral question is ignored. But it is still there and remains unanswered: Is there no limit at all to what man may do to the other forms of sentient life? The American humane movement has not so far addressed itself seriously to the animal abuses incident to factory farming, and the educative process will be no easy assignment. The public knows little of the conditions that exist, and its demand for more information is not insistent. It will be extremely difficult to prove to the satisfaction of a judge or jury that cruelty to calves, chickens, and hogs is a matter of real urgency.[20] The same is true of the methods of slaughter used for the larger food animals. The public is ignorant of the subject, and the industry is stubbornly resistant to change. The situation is complicated by the Jewish method of slaughter.

"It is generally agreed," writes Emily Stewart Leavitt, "that kosher killing. . .is humane. . . . However, the preslaughter handling of animals in kosher slaughter is definitely inhumane." Economics and cruelty mingle again: the technique used, not because it is kosher but because it is fast, is to shackle and hoist the animal by a chain wrapped around a hind leg. Dangling, struggling and screaming, the beast is positioned for the knife, often with an iron clamp in the nostrils or human fingers rammed into the eyes to insure control. Humane alternatives exist—holding pens, captive-bolt pistols, electrical stunning and the use of carbon dioxide gas. Progress has been obstructed by a small group of ultra-Orthodox rabbis who easily raise the cry of anti-Semitism and have been able year after year to convince legislators that they speak for the Jewish community as a whole. What is greatly needed to clear up this issue is for mainstream organizations in Jewish life to speak out clearly in favor of humane procedures in the slaughter houses. This, regrettably, they have not done. Among the consequences, quite apart from the cruelties still visited upon conscious animals, are that urban consumers pay for kosher meat whether they want the service or not, and that the laws which support this situation are at present under challenge in the Federal Court in New York as a violation of the First and Fourteenth Amendments to the Constitution which guarantee separation of church and state.[21]

When human conscripts fight and die, animals are usually part of the slaughter, too. Asiatics introduced the war elephant to the

West, and Hannibal employed the huge beasts, covered with heavy metal plates, as the "ultimate weapon" against Rome in the second century of our era. And ever since, untold millions of horses, mules, camels, bullocks, water buffalo, dogs, and other innocents have perished as a sacrifice to human aggressions. The animal participants in the First World War are memorialized in a touching plaque erected by the RSPCA, which says they suffered "knowing nothing of the cause, looking forward to no final victory. Filled only with love, faith and loyalty, they endured much and died for us. . . ."[22]

An apocalyptic note was struck in the cheerful announcement made by our own Atomic Energy Commission in connection with the detonating of the five-megaton H-bomb on the island of Amchitka that the sea otter can take 300 pounds of overpressure. The AEC acknowledged that a few pregnant females and pups might be killed, but probably not many because the otters had been pretested by "bombarding them," writes William Zinsser, "in a sealed tank of water with shock waves created by cannon shells. That's where it learned about the overpressure." After the event and the issuance of a number of conflicting and misleading reports playing down the after-effects of the $200 million Cannikin bang, the Atomic Energy Commission finally conceded that an estimated 900 to 1,100 otters died of massive hemorrhages as a result of the explosion, which many Americans regard as an offense "against life itself."[23]

Even rabbits fit into our war-making plans. At the sprawling Rocky Mountain Arsenal northeast of Denver, where mustard and nerve gases are stored, a technician carries a rabbit in a wire cage as he makes his rounds to check the deadly cylinders. Leaks have been infrequent and minor, the Army says, and there have been no fatalities in seventeen years. Whether this statistic includes the rabbits is unknown, and not the sort of thing an army likes to talk about. Rabbits again served patriotically when the Army shipped two trainloads of nerve gas to Sunny Point, North Carolina, to be dumped in the Atlantic Ocean. The small, long-eared, gas-sensitive beasts monitored each train. "If the rabbits start twitching and die, we will know that leaks have developed," an Army spokesman explained when the story of the gas disposal was released to the press. The rabbits survived, but less fortunate were the 5,000 or so sheep that died when gas was being tested at Dugway Proving Grounds in Utah. Well, accidents will happen in the best of Pentagons.[24]

There is an untold story of animal suffering and destruction in the Vietnam war. Here are just a few fragments of the evidence. In the early days of the war it was an accepted recreation for American military personnel to shoot, *pour le sport*, the large quadrupeds native to the country—rhinos, tigers, and elephants—from helicopters. Now years of destruction have made of South Vietnam a land as cratered and naked as the moonscape. Along the Ho Chi Minh Trail, according to a dispatch distributed by Agence France-Presse, fires set by the planes "burn for entire months" and "nothing lives . . . not even crickets." One of our herbicides, 2-4-5 T, known in military jargon as "Orange," is reported as being more potent than thalidomide in producing anatomical abnormalities in unborn animals. In free-fire zones everything that moves is attacked. The land doesn't heal. The forests are rotting. Along the waterway between Saigon and the sea, bird life has virtually disappeared.[25] Leaves wither. Insects die. Small animals have fled, following the monkeys, the deer, the remnants of the tiger population, and the wild boar. "Soldiers," says a dispatch from Saigon, "cannot be conservationists." While elephants and water buffalo "suspected" of helping carry supplies for the Viet Cong have been machine-gunned and shelled by American artillery, the United States Department of Defense, on its part, developed plans to parachute tranquilized elephants into the combat zone. This action showed a spirit of great kindness toward animals, the military attaché at the American Embassy in London assured angry British animal friends, because the airlift would spare the elephants the fatigue of a long walk in the woods.[26]

Those who scoff at the military mind and cite the canard that generals always fight the last war might be surprised to know how imaginative the Pentagon has been in trying to get animals to fight for us in Vietnam, although inciting animals to fight is a crime in every state of the Union. But that is, presumably, a different ball game. A scheme for recruiting wild birds for war purposes has been referred to in Chapter 19. Geese have also been considered as a possible early warning system for guarding Saigon bridges. They would honk, or that was the idea, when unauthorized persons approached. We have used dogs on a considerable scale for scouting, tracking, sentry duty, and exploring tunnels. And that is not all. Now that addiction to narcotics has been recognized as a pullulating problem in the American Army, pot-sniffing dogs are being used to interdict GI smuggling of dangerous drugs. The tickets of the war dogs, incidentally, read one-way. When their service is ended, the faithful animals are turned over to the Vietnamese, many of whom regard roast dog as a gourmet feast.[27] All of these ideas and brainstorms, bizarre though they are, constitute just a small part of the fallout of war, in which men have shown contempt for animal life, for the earth itself, and for human life. Other nightmarish possibilities lie ahead. It has been suggested that dolphins may yet reach the threshold of humanness and be trainable in such naval operations as submarine detection, underwater demolition, rescue of missile cones, and the performance of hazardous nocturnal harbor work.[28] A fear: What if the dolphin community did not share our political views? A hope: Maybe they would turn out to be pacifists.

American social attitudes still show a persistence of the fur trader mentality, so succinctly expressed by the atavistic ex-governor of Idaho, Don Samuelson. "The good Lord," said Samuelson, "never intended us to lock up our resources."[29] On the more hopeful side, protest is rising against the massive and indiscriminate poisoning programs against ecologically-important wildlife in the sheep-ranching states and which has recently been ordered stopped by presidential order so far as the Public Lands are concerned. More individuals are pondering the delicate relationships of man and animal, and more are appreciating the enormous contribution of animals to human culture. More find repugnant man's historic assault upon other forms of life. With encouraging frequency we hear of compassionate acts of individuals, even government organs, acts that refresh one's faith in the decent impulses of mankind and lend support to the faith that man at his best is truly a loving animal.

It is pleasant to know, for example, that the Board of Public Works of the City of Los Angeles has a helicopter that makes an "animal run" once a week. Its purpose is to conduct native denizens of the wild that stray into the city back to their natural homes. A California veterinarian treats injured wild animals (no charge) because there are no state facilities for rendering such help, and because "he figures mankind owes something to the living non-human things injured by today's technology." And not long ago Whitney North Seymour, Jr., United States Attorney for the Southern District of New York, reached back for a long-unused federal law to obtain criminal indictments against five firms for barbarous mistreatment of a cargo of wild animals on the voyage to America from their home in Kenya.[30]

When the animal cause seems to go into reverse, the fault is not in the stars, but in ourselves. There is, first of all, the lethargy of the human mind, which dislikes above all else to rethink its philosophical position. We have to overcome an ancient arrogance toward the earth's community that causes us to throw our weight around like gods, finding nothing criminal in, say, the destruction of the ocean's last whales to provide cosmetics and mink food. Progress is slowed by differences of opinion that greatly divide the humane movement as to what acceptable standards for our animal stewardship actually are. Although humanitarianism is not a religious movement, it does have a teleological basis, for it is concerned with the marvelous evidences of design or purpose in nature. Active humanitarians are romantics and perfectionists at heart because they believe, they *must* believe, that they can modify human behavior and produce a peaceable kingdom where man and beast can dwell amiably together.

Ironies, anomalies, hypocrisies, and conflicts abound. Cruelties can hardly ever be stopped without interfering with the privileges or financial interests of someone—furriers, manufacturers of steel gaffs for cockfighters, wildlife bureaucrats, and so forth. Thus the animal friends are assured of a swarm of enemies. There are some 3,000 terms of contempt and abuse in the English language. Most have been applied to the defenders of animals at one time or another by hostile critics, some of whom, unfortunately, have been humanitarians themselves.

Dr. Fernand Méry, the brilliant French leader of Les Amis des Bêtes (The Friends of Animals), thinks less should be said about the rights of animals and the duties of men and more emphasis placed upon how animal protection work serves the dignity, morals, and deepest interests of the human community; and that animal welfare associations should approach the problem from the inside out—that is, work toward new groupings for common action drawn from diverse disciplines—conservationists, biologists, animalitarians, clean environmentalists—all of whom share concern over animal pain and have a common respect for the mysteries of the natural world.[31] If the active humanitarians are still in the minority they are also in the right, for they sense that the treatment we as individuals accord animals reveals our true character and as a people the character of our civilization.

"Nature is a part of our humanity," Henry Beston wrote in his nature classic, *The Outermost House*, and without an awareness of that fact man becomes "a kind of cosmic outlaw, having neither the completeness and integrity of the animal nor the birthright of a true humanity." As he reflected upon the human-animal predicament during his year of life and thought on the great outer beach of Cape Cod, Beston added:

> We need another and a wiser and perhaps a more mystical concept of animals. Remote from universal nature, and living by complicated artifice, man in civilization surveys the creature through the glass of his knowledge and sees thereby a feather magnified and the whole image in distortion. We patronize them for . . . their tragic fate of having taken form so far below ourselves. And therein we err, and greatly err. For the animal shall not be measured by man. In a world older and more complete than ours they move finished and complete, gifted with extensions of the senses we have lost or never attained, living by voices we shall never hear. They are not brethren, they are not underlings; they are other nations, caught with ourselves in the net of life and time, fellow prisoners of the splendour and travail of the earth.[32]

Dr. Méry and eloquent Henry Beston point the way to a more sensitive appreciation of those often charming creatures that occupy a different position than we do on the evolutionary scale. Man is not a god, nor is he in any imminent danger of becoming one. But he is plastic, still unfinished, and able to modify his social code if he wishes to. Let us remember with humility the loneliness of being man in a universe we do not understand and the vulnerability of the human condition. The animals could do very well without us, but we cannot do without them.

Abbreviations and Notes

T he abbreviations that appear below are used in the notes that follow and occasionally in the text. The notes are numbered and arranged by chapters, and correspond to superior numbers found in the text. When several citations are grouped in one note, they are either alphabetized or appear in sequence as they relate to the text. The first citation of a reference in each chapter gives bibliographical details; subsequent appearances are in shortened form.

ABBREVIATIONS

American Heritage	*AH*
American Humane Association	AHA
American Society for the Prevention of Cruely to Animals	ASPCA
Animal Welfare Institute	AWI
Defenders of Wildlife	Defenders
Dictionary of American Biography	*DAB*

NOTES

Part I: 100,000 Years of Living Together

Preface

1. Charles Darwin called weeping a "special expression" in man. See *The Expression of the Emotions in Man and Animals* (New York, 1897), p. 146; John Anderson, director of the Research and Sanctuaries Division, National Audubon Society, points out that the elephant and sea turtle shed tears, the latter when laying eggs. But it is a physiological reaction without the emotional implications of human weeping.

2. Quoted in Joseph Wood Krutch, *Biology and Humanism: A Lecture* (n.p., 1960), p. 4.

1. Men, Beasts, and Gods

1. Marston Bates, *Man in Nature* (Englewood Cliffs, N.J., 1961), p. 1.

2. René Dubos, *So Human an Animal* (New York, 1968), pp. 158–59; Heini Hediger, *Studies of the Psychology and Behaviour of Captive Animals in Zoos and Circuses* (New York, 1955), p. 136.

3. John Grahame Douglas Clark, *World Prehistory* (Cambridge, 1961), pp. 16, 25, 33; Desmond Morris, *The Biology of Art* (New York, 1962), pp. 143, 146; C. Loring Brace, "The Origin of Man," *Natural History* 79 (January 1970): 46–49.

4. Konrad Lorenz, *On Aggression* (New York, 1963), pp. 241–42.

5. Hediger, *Studies*, p. 39.

6. Frederick E. Zeuner, *A History of Domestic Animals* (London, 1963), pp. 9, 36, 39, 41.

7. Hediger, *Studies*, p. 49.

8. Marston Bates, *Animal Worlds* (New York, 1963), p. 272; idem, *Man in Nature*, pp. 63–64; Hediger, *Studies*, p. 104.

9. James Fisher, *Zoos of the World* (Garden City, N.Y., 1967), p. 21.

10. Weston La Barre, *The Human Animal* (Chicago, 1954), pp. 48, 220.

11. Karl A. Menninger, "Totemic Aspects of Contemporary Attitudes Toward Animals," in *Psychoanalysis and Culture*, ed. George B. Wilbur and Werner Muensterberger (New York, 1951), p. 59.

12. George Jennison, *Animals for Show and Pleasure in Ancient Rome* (Manchester, England, 1937), p. 1.

13. Fisher, *Zoos of the World*, pp. 22, 24–25.

14. Jacques Boudet, *Man & Beast: A Visual History*, trans. Anne Carter (London, 1964), p. 146.

15. Ibid., p. 20; Peter Lum, *Fabulous Beasts* (New York, 1951), pp. 1–17, 22.

16. Boudet, *Man & Beast*, p. 14; *Universal Jewish Encyclopedia*, s.v. "Animal Worship."

17. William Graham Sumner, *Folkways: A Study of the Sociological Importance of Usages, Manners, Customs, Mores and Morals* (Boston, 1940), pp. 26, 336, 339.

18. Michael Lamm, "When Birds & Beasts Went Motoring," *Audubon* 72 (January 1970): 36–39.

19. Bates, *Animal Worlds*, p. 274; Menninger, "Totemic Aspects," p. 56.

20. Clark, *World Prehistory*, p. 56; V-H. Debidour, *Le bestiaire sculpté du moyen age en France* (Paris, 1961), p. 9; George Gaylord Simpson, "How Dost Thou Portray the Simurgh?" *Natural History* 47 (February 1941): 87.

21. Boudet, *Man & Beast*, p. 149; *Encyclopedia of Philosophy*, s.v. "Reincarnation"; Arthur W. Moss, *Valiant Crusade: The History of the R.S.P.C.A.* (London, 1961), p. 5; A. Lytton Sells, *Animal Poetry in French & English Literature & the Greek Tradition* (Bloomington, Ind., 1955), p. xiv.

22. Menninger, "Totemic Aspects," pp. 72, 49–50; *Encyclopedia of Philosophy*, s.v. "Jainism."

23. *New Catholic Encyclopedia* (1967), s.v. "Egypt, Ancient"; Moss, *Valiant Crusade*, p. 2.

24. *New Catholic Encyclopedia*, s.v. "Egypt, Ancient."

25. *Essays of Montaigne*, trans. E. J. Trenchmann (New York, n.d.), 1: 426–27; *Universal Jewish Encyclopedia*, s.v. "Bull Worship."

26. John Hunt, *A World Full of Animals* (New York, 1969), p. 34; Kathleen Szasz, *Petishism: Pets and Their People in the Western World* (New York, 1968), p. 8.

27. Hunt, *World Full of Animals*, pp. 342, 345–46; Jennison, *Animals for Show*, p. 9.

28. *Montaigne*, 1:427–28.

29. Homer, *Odyssey*. 17:245–97.

30. Menninger, "Totemic Aspects," p. 64; Havelock Ellis, *Studies in the Psychology of Sex* (Philadelphia, 1928), 5:46.

31. Quoted in Edward P. Buffet, *The Animal's Magna Charta* (Boston, 1925), pp. 5–6.

32. Boudet, *Man & Beast*, pp. 48–49; Fisher, *Zoos of the World*, p. 28.

33. Hester Hastings, *Man and Beast in French Thought of the Eighteenth Century*, The Johns Hopkins Studies in Romance Literature and Languages (Baltimore, 1936), p. 10.

34. Jennison, *Animals for Show*, pp. 1, 5, 7, 99.

35. Ibid., p. 58.

36. Ernest Ingersoll, *Birds in Legend, Fable and Folklore* (New York, 1923), pp. 5, 212–14.

37. Boudet, *Man & Beast*, pp. 66–67; Jennison, *Animals for Show*, pp. 44, 72; Sumner, *Folkways*, pp. 569–70.

38. Jennison, *Animals for Show*, p. 522; Charles D. Niven, *History of the Humane Movement* (New York, 1967), pp. 156–57.

39. *Montaigne*, 1:425; Hunt, *World Full of Animals*, p. 348.

2. No Hope of Heaven

1. Joseph Wood Krutch, comp., *The World of Animals: A Treasury of Lore, Legend and Literature by the Great Writers and Naturalists, from the 5th Century B.C. to the Present* (New York, 1961), p. 21.

2. Lynn White, Jr., "The Historical Roots of our Ecological Crisis," *Science*, 10 March 1967, p. 1205.

3. The sentence above is a paraphrase of Cicero, *De Natura Deorum*, trans. H. Rackham (London, 1933), pp. 156, 159–60.

4. *Universal Jewish Encyclopedia*, s.v. "Animals, Protection of."

5. William Edward Hartpole Lecky, *History of European Morals from Augustus to Charlemagne*, 3rd ed. (New York, 1894), 2:167.

6. Hugo Hartnack, *202 Common Household Pests of North America* (Chicago, 1939), p. 16.

7. *Catholic Encyclopedia* (1907), s.v. "Animals in the Bible"; C. W. Hume, *The Status of Animals in the Christian Religion* (London, 1957), pp. 4–5, 51; idem, *Man and Beast* (London,1962), p. 160.

8. Henry Stephens Salt, *Company I Have Kept* (London, 1930), p. 159.

9. Hume, *Status*, p. 1; *Encyclopedia of the Social Sciences*, s.v. "Humanitarianism"; Francis H. Rowley, *The Humane Idea: A Brief History of Man's Attitude Toward the Other Animals* . . . (Boston, 1912), p. 23.

10. *Bulletin of the Theological Section of UFAW*. No. 1 (March 1961), pp. 8, 4.

11. *Catholic Encyclopedia*, s.v. "Cruelty to Animals."

12. *New Catholic Encyclopedia* (1967), s.v. "Cruelty to Animals."

13. Ambrose Agius, *God's Animals* (n.p., 1970), p. 56; Robert Chambers, ed., *The Book of Days* . . . (Philadelphia, 1899), 1:126; "Il Folklore," *Conosci l' Italia* (n.p.: Touring Club Italiano, 1967), pp. 30–31; "Bénédiction des troupeaux sur le plateau d'Emparis," *Le Figaro* (Paris), 3 September 1970; Pierre Courtines to author, 26 April 1970; Jesús Ezquerra to author, 21

April 1970; Lynn Setford, "Blessing the Mule," *Our Dumb Animals* 102 (June 1969): 6–7.

14. Jean-Hervé Donnard to author, 17 April 1970; Hume, *Status*, p. 54, footnote.

15. Evelyn Hazeldine (Carrington), Contessa Martinengo-Cesaresco, *The Place of Animals in Human Thought* (London, 1909), pp. 346–47.

16. "Pets," *Saturday Review*, n.d., quoted in the *Arcadian*, 25 December 1875, p. 7; Lecky, *European Morals*, 2:172.

17. G. C. Coulton, *Social Life in Britain* (Cambridge, 1918), p. 397, quoted in Dix Harwood, *Love for Animals and How It Developed in Great Britain* (New York, 1928), p. 23.

18. The quotation is from Dr. Alfred G. Etter, in a memorial to his dog, poisoned with strychnine bait set out by a state fish and game agent, quoted in Robert Reinow and Leona Train Reinow, *Moment in the Sun* (New York, 1967), p. 52.

19. Havelock Ellis, *Studies in the Psychology of Sex* (Philadelphia, 1928), 5:87.

20. White, "Historical Roots of Our Ecological Crisis," pp. 1206–1207.

21. *New Catholic Encyclopedia*, s.v. "Animals in Christian Art"; Agius, *God's Animals*, p. 58; *New Catholic Encyclopedia*, s.v. "Animals, Symbolism of "; Ernest Ingersoll, *Birds in Legend, Fable and Folklore* (New York, 1923), pp. 109, 149.

22. V.-H. Debidour, *Le bestiaire sculpté du moyen age en France* (Paris, 1961), pp. 247, 249, 261, 274 and plate no. 425; Françoise Olivier-Michel and Claude Gisler, *Guide to the Art Treasures of France*, trans. Raymond Rudorff (New York, 1966), pp. 336–37.

23. Debidour, *Bestiaire*, p. 187; Olivier-Michel and Gisler, *Guide*, p. 20.

24. Ellis, *Studies*, 5:80.

25. Hermann Dembeck, *Animals and Men*, trans. Richard Winston and Clara Winston (Garden City, N.Y., 1965), p. 365.

26. Beatrice White, "Medieval Beasts," in *English Association, Essays and Studies Collected for the English Association by Sybil Rosenfeld*, comp. Sybil Rosenfeld, n.s. (New York, 1965), 18:40. This useful study was called to my attention by Marianne (Mrs. Alden) Briscoe.

27. Ibid., p. 41.

28. Mrs. Alden Briscoe to author, 18 February 1970; Hume, *Status*, p. 26; Harwood, *Love for Animals*, pp. 29–31; Arthur W. Moss, *Valiant Crusade: The History of the R.S.P.C.A.* (London, 1961), p. 8.

29. T. H. White, trans. and ed., *The Book of Beasts, Being a Translation from a Latin Bestiary of the Twelfth Century Made and Edited by T. H. White* (New York, 1954), pp. 49–51, 125–27.

30. Dembeck, *Animals*, p. 159; Adolf Zeckel, "The Totemistic Significance of the Unicorn," in *Psychoanalysis and Culture*, ed. George B. Wilbur and Warner Muensterberg (New York, 1951), pp. 344–60.

31. Laurence Wylie, *Village in the Vaucluse* (New York, 1964), pp. 52–53.

32. Rosalind Hill, *Both Small and Great Beasts* (London: UFAW, 1964),

pp. 3–8 and *passim;* E. S. Turner, *All Heaven in a Rage* (London, 1964), p. 25; *Beasts and Saints,* trans. Helen Waddell (New York, 1934), pp. xi, xiii, 17–18, 122.

33. Hume, *Status,* p. 37 and footnote 3.

34. Debidour, *Bestiaire,* p. 179; Dembeck, *Animals,* pp. 262–63.

35. Jacques Boudet, *Man & Beast,* trans. Anne Carter (London, 1964), pp. 84–85.

36. Debidour, *Bestiaire,* pp. 179, 181; James Fisher, *Zoos of the World: The Story of Animals in Captivity* (Garden City, N.Y.,1967), p. 47.

37. Johan Huizinga, *Waning of the Middle Ages* (London, 1924), p. 17; Kathleen Szasz, *Petishism: Pets and Their People in the Western World* (New York, 1968), p. 14.

38. Dembeck, *Animals,* pp. 300–303; Beatrice White, "Medieval Beasts," p. 38.

39. H. S. Bennett, *Life on the English Manor: A Study of Peasant Conditions, 1150–1400* (London, 1960), pp. 259–67, quoted in *The History of Popular Culture to 1815,* ed. Norman F. Cantor and Michael S. Werthman (New York, 1968), p. 158.

40. Ingeborg Flugel, "Some Psychological Aspects of a Fox-hunting Rite," *Int. J. Psa.,* 12 (1931): 485.

41. Richard Lewinsohn, *Animals, Men and Myths* (New York, 1954), p. 207.

42. Harwood, *Love for Animals,* pp. 13–14, footnote; Desmond Morris, *The Human Zoo* (New York, 1969), p. 76.

3. Bugs and Beasts Before the Law

1. Walker Woodburn Hyde, "The Prosecution and Punishment of Animals and Lifeless Things in the Middle Ages and Modern Times," *University of Pennsylvania Law Review,* 64:709.

2. E. Cobham Brewer, *A Dictionary of Miracles* (Philadelphia, n.d.), p. 170.

3. Ibid., pp. xiv, 342.

4. Ibid., p. 128.

5. Robert Chambers, ed., *The Book of Days* . . . (Philadelphia, 1899), 1:126–27; Hyde, "Prosecution and Punishment of Animals," p. 704.

6. Chambers, *The Book of Days* . . . , 1:126–27.

7. Rosalind Hill, *Both Small and Great Beasts* (London: UFAW, 1964), p. 10; Hyde, "Prosecution and Punishment of Animal," p. 705.

8. E. P. Evans, *The Criminal Prosecution and Capital Punishment of Animals* (New York, 1906), pp. 3–5; Elbridge Thomas Gerry, "The Law of Cruelty to Animals . . . ," typescript (New York: New-York Historical Society, n.d.) p. 7.

9. Emile Agnel, *Curiosités judiciaires et historiques du moyen âge: Procès contre les animaux* . . . (Paris, 1858), pp. 35–36, quoted in "Animals as Offenders and as Victims," *Albany Law Journal,* 21:265; Berriat-Saint-

Prix, "Prosecution Against Animals," *American Jurist* 1 (April 1829):225.

10. Edward G. Fairholme and Wellesley Pain, *A Century of Work for Animals: The History of the R.S.P.C.A. 1824–1924* (London, 1924), p. 139.

11. Hyde, "Prosecution and Punishment of Animals," pp. 696–98, 700 and footnote 17, 701, 703; E. P. Evans, "Bugs and Beasts Before the Law," *Atlantic Monthly* 55 (August 1884): 241.

12. Evans, *Criminal Prosecution,* pp. 165–66.

13. Fairholme and Pain, *Century of Work for Animals,* p. 141.

14. Hyde, "Prosecution and Punishment of Animals," pp. 708–709.

15. Chambers, *The Book of Days . . .* , p. 129.

16. Evans, *Criminal Prosecution,* pp. 138–39, 156–57; Hyde, "Prosecution and Punishment of Animals," p. 709.

17. Evans, *Criminal Prosecution,* pp. 10–11, 157.

18. Hampton L. Carson, "The Trial of Animals and Insects: A Little Known Chapter of Medieval Jurisprudence," *American Philosophical Society Proceedings,* 56:410.

19. Evans, "Bugs and Beasts Before the Law," p. 241.

20. Hyde, "Prosecution and Punishment of Animals," pp. 709, 712.

21. Carson, "Trial of Animals and Insects", pp. 410–11; Berriat-Saint-Prix, "Prosecutions Against Animals," pp. 123–24.

22. Evans, *Criminal Prosecution,* pp. 18–21; Dix Harwood, *Love for Animals and How it Developed in Great Britain* (New York 1928), pp. 5–6; Edmund Collins, "Animals Tried in Court," *Our Animal Friends* 19 (December 1891):85.

23. Collins, "Animals Tried in Court," p. 86.

24. William Morton Wheeler, *Foibles of Insects and Men* (New York, 1928), pp. xxiii–xxiv.

25. Evans, *Criminal Prosecution,* pp. 148–49.

26. John Winthrop, *The History of New England 1630–1649,* ed. James Savage (Boston, 1853), 2:49.

27. "Dillio's Monkey," *New York Herald,* 29 November 1877; "A Monkey in Court," *New York Sun,* 29 November 1877.

28. *Baltimore Sun,* 21 February 1888, reprinted in *NYT,* 23 February 1888, quoted in William Wells Newell, "Conjuring Rat," *Journal of American Folklore* 5 (January–March 1892):24–25.

29. Ibid., pp. 23–24.

4. The Animal-Machine Theory

1. Tennessee Williams, *Cat on a Tin Roof* (New York, 1955), p. 85, quoted in Dan Isaac, "Big Daddy's Dramatic Word Strings," *American Speech* 40 (December 1965):272–73.

2. William Morton Wheeler, *Foibles of Insects and Men* (New York, 1928), pp. xix–xx.

3. A. C. Crombie, *Medieval and Early Modern Science* (Garden City, N.Y., 1959), 2:270, 282.

4. René Descartes, *Discourse on the Method of Rightly Conducting the Reason, and Seeking Truth in the Sciences,* trans. John Veitch (Chicago, 1920), p. iv.

5. E. P. Evans, *The Criminal Prosecution and Capital Punishment of Animals* (New York, 1906), p. 67.

6. George Boas, *The Happy Beast in French Thought of the Seventeenth Century* (New York, 1966), pp. 111–15.

7. *The Encyclopedia of Philosophy,* s.v. "Animal Soul"; *New Catholic Encyclopedia* (1967), s.v. "Interactionism, Psychological."

8. Descartes, *Discourse,* Part 5.

9. Joseph Wood Krutch, *Biology and Humanism: A Lecture* (n.p., 1960), p. 8; Jean de La Fontaine, *Mémoires pour servir à l'histoire de Port-Royal* (Paris, 1758), 2:52–53, quoted in Leonora D. Rosenfield, *From Beast-Machine to Man-Machine: Animal Soul in French Letters from Descartes to La Mettrie* (New York, 1941), p. 54.

10. Dix Harwood, *Love for Animals and How it Developed in Great Britain* (New York, 1928), pp. 99–111; E. S. Turner, *All Heaven in a Rage* (London, 1964), p. 46.

11. Weston La Barre, *The Human Animal* (Chicago, 1954), p. 235.

12. J. Howard Moore, *The Universal Kinship* (Chicago, 1908), pp. 146–47; Ernest P. Walker, *Studying Our Fellow Mammals* (n.p.: AWI, n.d.), p. 17; William Morton Wheeler, *Essays in Philosophical Biology* (Cambridge, Mass., 1939), pp. 244–45.

13. John Locke, *The Works of John Locke* (London, 1801), 10: 283, quoted in Dagobert de Levie, *The Modern Idea of the Prevention of Cruelty to Animals and Its Reflection in English Poetry* (New York, 1947), p. 35.

14. Rosenfield, *From Beast-Machine to Man-Machine,* p. 192; Robert Shackleton, "Free Inquiry and the World of Ideas," in Alfred Cobban et al., *The Eighteenth Century: Europe in the Age of the Enlightenment* (New York, 1969), p. 273; Richard Lewinsohn, *Animals, Men and Myths* (New York, 1954), pp. 174–76; Peter Gay, *The Enlightenment: An Interpretation* (New York, 1967), pp. 8–9.

15. A. Lytton Sells, *Animal Poetry in French & English Literature & the Greek Tradition* (Bloomington, Ind., 1955), p. xxv.

16. Voltaire, "Commentaire sur Malebranche," *Oeuvres complètes de Voltaire* (Paris, 1878), 28:94, quoted in De Levie, *The Modern Idea,* p. 34; Lewinsohn, *Animals, Men and Myths,* p. 177.

17. Paris, 1858, p. 5.

18. Pierre Tielhard de Chardin, *The Phenomenon of Man* (New York, 1959), p. 168.

19. Charles Darwin, *The Expression of the Emotions in Man and Animals* (New York, 1897), p. 144.

20. Hester Hasting, *Man and Beast in French Thought of the Eighteenth Century,* The Johns Hopkins Studies in Romance Literatures and Languages (Baltimore, 1936), p. 207; Sells, *Animal Poetry,* pp. 127–31.

21. Krutch, *Biology and Humanism,* p. 13.

22. James J. Quinn, "A Proper Respect for Men and Animals," *U.S. Catholic* (June 1965), quoted in Justus George Lawler, "Do Animals Have Rights?" *Jubilee* 12 (November 1965): 37.

23. Leslie Stephen, *History of English Thought in the Eighteenth Century* (New York, 1881), 2:447; Harwood, *Love for Animals*, pp. 145–46.

24. Carl L. Becker, *The Heavenly City of the Eighteenth-Century Philosophers* (New Haven, 1932), p. 41; Jack Rochford Vrooman, *René Descartes: A Biography.* (New York, 1970), p. 194.

25. De Levie, *The Modern Idea*, p. 41.

5. A New Idea: Rights for Animals

1. John Barr, "Nation of Pet-Keepers," *New Society*, 15 July 1965, p. 6.

2. Arthur W. Moss, *Valiant Crusade: The History of the R.S.P.C.A.* (London, 1961), p. 9.

3. R.S.R. Fitter, *London's Natural History* (London, 1946), pp. 41–42.

4. Jacques Boudet, *Man & Beast: A Visual History*, trans. Anne Carter (London, 1964), pp. 286–87.

5. Patrick Moore, ed., *Against Hunting* (London, 1965), p. 147.

6. Dagobert de Levie, *The Modern Idea of the Prevention of Cruelty to Animals and its Reflection in English Poetry* (New York, 1947), pp. 13–14; C. W. Hume, *Man and Beast* (London, 1962), pp. 18–20; Basil Wrighton, "Justice and the Animals," *The Ark*, April 1952, reprinted by NCSAW (Washington, n.d.), p. 1.

7. Edward Chamberlayne, *Angliae Notitiae, or the Present State of England* (1669), quoted in Carl Bridenbaugh, *Vexed and Troubled Englishmen 1590–1642* (New York, 1968), p. 154; Dix Harwood, *Kindness to Animals in Great Britain* (New York, 1928), p. 59; Ernest Ingersoll, *Birds in Legend, Fable and Folklore* (New York, 1923), pp. 122–23; Joseph Strutt, *The Sports and Pastimes of the People of England . . .* (London, 1831), p. 283.

8. E. S. Turner, *All Heaven in a Rage* (London, 1964), p. 61.

9. John Ashton, *Social Life in the Reign of Queen Anne* (New York, 1925), p. 186; Harwood, *Kindness to Animals*, pp. 225–27.

10. Holinshed, *Chronicles of England*, vol. 3, folio 1552, quoted in Strutt, *Sports and Pastimes*, p. 257.

11. Chamberlayne, *Angliae Notitiae*, pp. 46–47, quoted in Bridenbaugh, *Vexed and Troubled Englishmen*, p. 155.

12. Sumner Chilton Powell, *Puritan Village: The Formation of a New England Town* (Garden City, N.Y., 1965), pp. 51, 53, 55.

13. Moss, *Valiant Crusade*, pp. 130–33; Strutt, *Sports and Pastimes*, pp. 277–78.

14. J. Leslie Hotson, "Bear Gardens and Bear-Baiting During the Commonwealth," *PMLA* 40 (June 1925):276–88.

15. Edward G. Fairholme and Wellesley Pain, *A Century of Work for Animals: The History of the R.S.P.C.A. 1824–1924* (London, 1924), p. 15.

16. Ibid., p. 15; Strutt, *Sports and Pastimes*, p. 239; Turner, *All Heaven in a Rage*, p. 42.

17. Laurence Sterne, *The Life & Opinions of Tristram Shandy* (New York, 1950), p. 115; Harwood, *Kindness to Animals*, p. 64.

18. Arthur O. Lovejoy, *The Great Chain of Being* (Cambridge, Mass., 1948), pp. 14, 184, 189.

19. *Encyclopedia of the Social Sciences*, s.v. "Humanitarianism"; Joseph Wood Krutch, comp., *The World of Animals* (New York, 1961), p. 23; Justus George Lawler, *The Range of Commitment: Essays of a Conservative Liberal* (Milwaukee, 1969), pp. 8, 144; Frank J. Klingberg, "The Evolution of the Humanitarian Spirit in Eighteenth-Century England," *Pennsylvania Magazine of History* 66 (July 1942):264–65.

20. Francis H. Rowley, *The Humane Idea: A Brief History of Man's Attitude Toward the Other Animals* . . . (Boston, 1912), p. 31; Henry S. Salt, *Animals' Rights Considered in Relation to Social Progress* (New York, 1894), p. 5.

21. Thomas Chalmers, "Cruelty to Animals," *Methodist Magazine* 9 (July 1826):265.

22. [James Boswell], *Boswell's Life of Johnson* (London, 1957), pp. 1216–17; Harwood, *Kindness to Animals*, pp. 168, 214, 217–18.

23. Fairholme and Pain, *Century of Work*, pp. 7–10; Moss, *Valiant Crusade*, p. 9.

24. Sydney H. Coleman, *Humane Society Leaders in America, with a Sketch of the Early History of the Humane Movement in England* (Albany, N.Y., 1924), pp. 20–21.

25. Fairholme and Pain, *Century of Work*, pp. 13–14.

26. *Encyclopedia of the Social Sciences*, s.v. "Humanitarianism."

27. *DNB*, s.v. "Thomas, Lord Erskine."

28. Fairholme and Pain, *Century of Work*, pp. 142–43.

29. John H. Ingham, *The Law of Animals* (Philadelphia, 1900), p. 526.

30. *DNB*, s.v. "Martin, Richard"; Roswell C. McCrea, *The Humane Movement: A Descriptive Survey* (New York, 1910), pp. 30–31; Moss, *Valiant Crusade*, pp. 15–19.

31. Fairholme and Pain, *Century of Work*, pp. 142–53.

32. Ibid., pp. 32–33.

33. Ibid., p. 31.

34. I am indebted to C. W. Hume for sharply defining these areas. See his *Man and Beast* (London, 1962), pp. 159–60, 202.

35. Harwood, *Kindness to Animals*, pp. 304–305.

36. Wrighton, "Justice and the Animals," p. 3.

37. Boudet, *Man & Beast*, p. 243; Leonora D. Rosenfield, *From Beast-Machine to Man-Machine: Animal Soul in French Letters from Descartes to La Mettrie* (New York, 1941), p. 236; Emily Stewart Leavitt, *Animals and Their Legal Rights: A Survey of American Laws from 1641 to 1968* (n.p.: AWI, 1968), pp. 9–10.

6. The Beginning of Animal Protection

1. Roswell C. McCrea, "The Humane Movement," in *Legislation for the Protection of Animals and Children*, ed. Samuel McCune Lindsay. Bulletin of Social Legislation on the Henry Bergh Foundation for the Promotion of Humane Education, no. 2 (New York, 1914), p. 7; idem, *The Humane Movement: A Descriptive Survey, Prepared on the Henry Bergh Foundation for the Promotion of Humane Education in Columbia University* (New York: Columbia University, Henry Bergh Foundation Publications, 1910), p. 7.

2. Edward G. Fairholme and Wellesley Pain, *A Century of Work for Animals: The History of the R.S.P.C.A. 1824–1924* (London, 1924), pp. 54, 277; Arthur W. Moss, *Valiant Crusade: The History of the R.S.P.C.A.* (London, 1961), pp. 20–22.

3. Moss, *Century of Work*, p. 25.

4. Ibid., p. 28.

5. Ibid., p. 29; Fairholme and Pain, *Century of Work*, pp. 89, 94; T. Richardson, "The Heart of a City," *The Hub* (London), Summer 1963, p. 7.

6. Moss, *Century of Work*, p. 31; *The A.B.C. of the R.S.P.C.A.* (London, n.d.), p. 7.

7. Moss, *Century of Work*, pp. 61–64, 34.

8. Ibid., pp. 110–11.

9. "La photo du jour," *La Parisien*, 8 July 1970; "Heroic Dog Saves Cat," *NYT*, 22 September 1970; Moss, *Valiant Crusade*, p. 55.

10. *The Royal Society for the Preservation of Cruelty to Animals. The Society's Policy on Fox-Hunting* (n.p., n.d.), pp. 1–2.

11. Patrick Moore, ed., *Against Hunting* (London, 1965), pp. 70–79; "r.s.p.c.a. meeting Ends in Uproar," *Guardian* (London) 15 June 1961; "Police Are Called to R.S.P.C.A. Meeting," *Scotsman* (London), 15 June 1961.

12. "Field Sports," *Royal Society for the Prevention of Cruelty to Animals. One Hundred and Forty-Sixth Annual Report, 1969* (London, 1970), pp. 34–35.

13. Glynn Mapes, "Yoicks! Fox-Hunting Territory Is Overrun By Suburbia's Sprawl," *Wall Street Journal*, 9 January 1969.

14. "Otter Hunt is Utter Chaos," *Poughkeepsie Journal*, 17 May 1970.

15. Moore, *Against Hunting*, pp. 33–35.

16. Helen Trevelyan, *Laugh, Clown, Laugh!* (London, 1936), pp. 49–51.

17. E. S. Turner, *All Heaven in a Rage* (London, 1964), pp. 286–88.

18. Moore, *Against Hunting*, pp. 125–26, 139.

19. C. W. Hume, *The Status of Animals in the Christian Religion* (London, 1957), p. 1.

20. "Thanksgiving and Prayer," *Animal World* (February 1964), typed extract, no pagination.

21. Adapted from a news account, "A Section of the Young People Who Attended . . . ,", *Macclesfield Express* (Cheshire, England), 10 July 1969.

22. Moss, *Century of Work*, pp. 166–69; "Pony and Steer 'Rodeos,' " *Royal Society for the Prevention of Cruelty to Animals Annual Report 1966*

(London, 1967), pp. 46–47; "Pony and Steer 'Rodeos,'" and "Ritual Slaughter," *Royal Society for the Prevention of Cruelty to Animals. One Hundred and Forty-Fifth Annual Report, 1968* (London, 1969), pp. 40, 50–51.

23. "Beauty Without Cruelty," *Animal World* 60 (November 1965):176.

24. "Specimen Court Cases," *Royal Society for the Prevention of Cruelty to Animals Annual Report 1966* (London, 1967), pp. 16–17.

25. Ibid., "Performing Animals," p.49.

26. "Export of Food Animals," "Sale of Pet Animals," "Performing Animals," *Royal Society for the Prevention of Cruelty to Animals. One Hundred and Forty-Fifth Annual Report, 1968* (London, 1969), pp. 34–35, 37–39, 44–45.

27. "The Work of the Society Overseas," *The A.B.C. of the R.S.P.C.A.* (London, n.d.), p. 7; *International Society for the Protection of Animals. Review for Period May 1967–April 1969* (London and Boston, n.d.), pp. 1–16.

28. April Hersey, "Gangster Dies; Leaves Brothels to Charity," *Mexico City News*, 10 June 1968.

29. "Annual Report of the Council, 1969," and "Intensive Systems of Animal Husbandry," *Royal Society for the Prevention of Cruelty to Animals. One Hundred and Forty-Sixth Annual Report, 1969* (London, 1970), pp. 3, 23–28; also, for a general survey of "intensivism" in farming operations, see Ruth Harrison, *Animal Machines: The New Factory Farming Industry* (New York, 1966).

Part II: Kindness and Cruelty in the United States

7. *Animals in Early America*

1. Jennie Holliman, *American Sports 1785–1835* (Durham, N.C., 1931), pp. 3–4,7.

2. Foster Rhea Dulles, *America Learns to Play: A History of Popular Recreation 1607–1940* (New York, 1940), p. 71; Holliman, *American Sports*, pp. 37–38.

3. Peter Matthiessen, *Wildlife in America* (New York, 1959), p. 76.

4. Holliman, *American Sports*, pp. 21–23; "Shooting for Gobblers," *New York Clipper*, 5 December 1869; Everett Dick, *The Dixie Frontier: A Social History of the Southern Frontier from the First Transmontane Beginnings to the Civil War* (New York, 1948), p. 144.

5. Dulles, *America Learns*, p. 71.

6. "Kiwanis Turkey Shoot," *NCSAW Report* (November 1969); "Kiwanis Club Drops Live Turkey Shoot," *Milwaukee Journal*, 3 November 1970; "Let's Put End to This Cruelty," *Madison* (Wis.) *Capital Times*, 19 March 1971. A bill prohibiting this amusement was signed into law by the Governor of Wisconsin on 28 October, 1971.

7. Dick, *Dixie Frontier*, p. 142.

8. Thomas Gilbert Pearson, *Adventures in Bird Protection: An Autobiography* (New York, 1937), p. 7.

9. *The Boston Gazette* 23–30 May 1726, advertised a bear baiting, the announcement quoted in George Francis Dow, *Everyday Life in the Massachusetts Bay Colony* (Boston, 1935), p. 114.

10. Soeren Stewart Brynn, "Some Sports in Pittsburgh During the National Period, 1775–1860," *Western Pennsylvania Historical Magazine* 51 (October 1968): 347, 351–52, 356, 361.

11. "To the Printer," *Virginia Gazette*, 2 January 1752; Louis B. Wright, *First Gentlemen of Virginia* (San Marino, Calif., 1940), p. 12. I am indebted to Professor James Harvey Young for the *Virginia Gazette* reference, one of many valuable suggestions from him which are here gratefully acknowledged.

12. Charles M. Andrews, *Colonial Folkways* (New Haven, 1919), p. 114; Joseph J. Shomon, "Vanished and Vanishing Virginia Animals," *Virginia Cavalcade* 3:(Winter 1959),25.

13. Shomon, "Vanished and Vanishing Animals," pp. 26–29; Charles E. Clark, *The Eastern Frontier: The Settlement of Northern New England 1610–1763* (New York, 1970), pp. 117, 343.

14. Dick, *Dixie Frontier*, p. 146.

15. *Spirit of the Times*, 28 June 1851, quoted in Walter Blair, *Native American Humor* (San Francisco, 1960), p. 69.

16. Friedrich Gerstächer, *Wild Sports in the Far West: The Narrative of a German Wanderer Beyond the Mississippi, 1837–1843* (Durham, N.C., 1968), pp. xi–xii, 85.

17. James F. Rusling, *Across America, or the Great West and the Pacific Coast* (New York, 1874), quoted in *Mirror for Americans*, ed. Warren S. Tryon (Chicago, 1952), 3:769–70; Dulles, *America Learns*, pp. 176–77; Wells Drury, *An Editor on the Comstock Lode* (New York, 1936), pp. 90–91, 106, 111, 299.

18. John Ross Browne, *Adventures in the Apache Country: A Tour Through Arizona and Sonora* (New York, 1869), pp. 421–25.

19. Carl Bridenbaugh, *Cities in the Wilderness: The First Century of Urban Life in America 1625–1742* (New York, 1938), pp. 118, 278, 435, 441.

20. *New York Clipper*, 13 March 1869; *Spirit of the Times*, 5 and 12 January 1867.

21. R. W. G. Vail, "Random Notes on the History of the Early American Circus," *Proceedings of the American Antiquarian Society*, vol. 43, n.s., Part 1 (April 1933):135.

22. 21 July 1827.

23. I owe this felicitous phrase to Robert B. Downs' "Apocryphal Biology: A Chapter in American Folklore," in Mody C. Boatright, Robert B. Downs, and John T. Flanagan, *The Family Saga and Other Phases of American Folklore* (Urbana, Ill., 1958), pp. 20–46. My discussion of mythical animals draws generally upon Dr. Downs' essay.

24. Peter N. Carroll, *Puritanism and the Wilderness: The Intellectual Significance of the New England Frontier 1629–1700* (New York, 1969), p. 137; Clark, *Eastern Frontier*, p. 33.

25. Harold W. Thompson, *Body, Boots and Britches* (Philadelphia, 1940), p. 128, quoted in Downs, "Apocryphal Biology," p. 22.

26. Royal Society of London, *Philosophical Transactions* 29 (April–June 1714):68, quoted in Downs, "Apocryphal Biology," p. 23.

27. Dixon Ryan Fox, *Ideas in Motion* (New York, 1935), pp. 100–101; Richard M. Dorson, *American Folklore* (Chicago, 1965), p. 14.

28. Ben C. Clough, *The American Imagination at Work: Tall Tales and Folk Tales* (New York, 1947), pp. 133–222.

29. Downs, "Apocryphal Biology," pp. 38–39; Vance Randolph, *We Always Lie to Strangers* (New York, 1951), pp. 61–62.

30. Downs, "Apocryphal Biology," p. 42.

31. Gordon W. Wilson, "Some Calloway County Animal Lore," *Kentucky Folklore Record* 3 (January-March 1957):9–10.

32. Francis H. Rowley, *The Humane Idea: A Brief History of Man's Attitude Toward the Other Animals . . .* (Boston, 1912), p. 40; Samuel Eliot Morison, *Builders of the Bay Colony* (Boston, 1930), pp. 229–32; *DAB*, s.v. "Ward, Nathaniel."

33. "The Body of Liberties: The Liberties of the Massachusetts Colonie in New England, 1641," *Old South Leaflets*, no. 164 (Boston, n.d.).

34. David Levin, ed., *What Happened in Salem? Documents Pertaining to the 17th-Century Witchcraft Trials* (New York, 1952), p. 7.

35. My account of show animals relies generally upon Vail, "Random Notes." See also Robert McClung and Gale McClung, "Captain Crowninshield Brings Home an Elephant," *American Neptune* 18:137–41; Andrews, *Colonial Folkways*, pp. 126–27; *Boston News-Letter*, various dates in 1719, 1726, 1737, 1741; Bridenbaugh, *Cities in the Wilderness*, pp. 278, 434–38; Dick, *Dixie Frontier*, p. 158; Dulles, *America Learns*, pp. 131–33; Richardson Wright, *Hawkers & Walkers in Early America* (Philadelphia, 1927), pp. 189–97.

36. Louis Agassiz, *An Introduction to the Study of Natural History, in a Series of Lectures Delivered in the Hall of the College of Physicians and Surgeons* (New York, 1847), pp. 5–8, quoted in Carl Bode, *American Life in the 1840s* (Garden City, N.Y., 1967), pp. 127–28.

37. Pearson, *Adventures in Bird Protection*, p. 51.

8. The Trek to the Cities

1. Carl Bridenbaugh, *Cities in the Wilderness: The First Century of Urban Life in America 1625–1742* (New York, 1938), pp. 167–68, 323; E. B. O'Callaghan, ed., *Register of New Netherland: 1620 to 1674* (Albany, 1865), p. 124, quoted in John Duffy, *A History of Public Health in New York City 1625–1866* (New York, 1968), pp. 10–12; see also Duffy, pp. 30, 47.

2. Duffy, *History of Public Health*, pp. 190–91, 195, 198, 357, 385.

3. Charles Dickens, *American Notes* (Boston, n.d.), p. 83.

4. Duffy, *History of Public Health*, p. 386.

5. *Manual for the Use of the Legislature of the State of New York* (Albany,

1866), p. 92. The census figure for New York for 1870 was 942,292; *World Almanac* (New York, 1960), p. 240. Shortly after 1870 the estimated total passed the million mark. For the discussion of the housing of the "dangerous classes," I drew upon Matthew Hale Smith, *Sunshine and Shadow in New York* (Hartford, 1869), p. 207; Stephen Smith, *The City That Was* (New York, 1911), pp. 81, 90, 93–94, 97; George Rogers Taylor, "The Beginnings of Mass Transportation in Urban America: Part I," *Smithsonian Journal of History* 1(Summer 1966):39.

6. Edward Winslow Martin (pseud.), James Dabney McCabe, *The Secrets of the Great City: A Work Descriptive of the Virtues and the Vices, the Mysteries, Miseries and Crimes of New York City* (Philadelphia, 1868), pp. 117, 45–47; James Miller, publisher, *Miller's New York As It Is; or Stranger's Guidebook to the Cities of New York, Brooklyn and Adjacent Places* . . . (New York, 1872), p. 101.

7. "Nuisances of Streets of New York," *Leslie's*, 28 December 1867; "Summer Noises," *NYT*, 28 July 1889; Charles Loring Brace, *The Dangerous Classes of New York, and Twenty Years' Work Among Them* (New York, 1872), p. 332; "Michael Kane, a Dealer in Manure. . . ," *NYT*, 27 March 1886; "Moving Manure," *New York Herald*, 23 May 1872.

8. Stephen Smith, *City That Was*, pp. 62, 80–81; Melusina F. Pierce, Director, Ladies' Health Protective Association, "The East Side Odors," *NYT*, 12 August 1887; *Report of the Council of Hygiene and Public Health of the Citizens' Association of New York Upon the Sanitary Condition of the City. Published, with an Introductory Statement, by Order of the Council of the Citizens' Association* (New York, 1865), pp. 262, 310.

9. Marston Bates, "A Naturalist At Large: Natural History in Cities," *Natural History* 77 (November 1968):26, 28.

10. *Report of the Council of Hygiene*, pp. 309–10; George Templeton Strong, *The Diary of George Templeton Strong*, ed. Allan Nevins and Milton Halsey Thomas (New York, 1952), 4:155.

11. James Miller, *Miller's New York As It Is* . . . (New York, 1866), p. 31; Henry Hope Reed and Sophia Duckworth, *Central Park, a History and a Guide* (New York, 1967), pp. 19, 122.

12. McCabe, *Lights and Shadows*, p. 337.

13. Strong, *Diaries*, 4:251.

14. Ibid., 4:492.

15. Frederick Van Wyck, *Recollections of an Old New Yorker* (New York, 1932), p. 130; James Julius Chambers, *The Book of New York: Forty Years' Recollections of the American Metropolis* (New York, 1912), p. 28.

16. Zulma Steele, *Angel in Top Hat* (New York, 1942), p. 141; "Fight Between Two Game Fowls for $50," *Leslie's*, 22 December 1866.

17. "A Man Rat Killer," *New York Herald*, 27 November 1866; "General Telegraph News," *NYT*, 25 December 1879; Denis Tilden Lynch, *The Wild Seventies* (New York, 1941), pp. 301–103, 307.

18. P. 114.

19. Peter J. Schmidt, *Back to Nature: The Arcadian Myth in America*,

Urban Life in America Series (New York, 1969), pp. 38–39; George Laycock, *The Alien Animals* (Garden City, N.Y., 1966), pp. 75–80; Strong,
Diaries, 4:296.

20. "Monkeys Are 'Noxious,' " *NYT*, 14 August 1887.

21. Marston Bates, *Animal Worlds* (New York, 1963), pp. 300, 306–307,
310.

22. Junius Henri Brown, *The Great Metropolis: A Mirror of New York*
(Hartford, 1869), pp. 92, 97–98; Martin (pseud.), McCabe, *Secrets of the
Great City*, pp. 510–11; "Cruelty to Animals," *Chicago Times*, 10 November
1870.

23. "Cattle Driving in the Streets," *Leslie's*, 28 April 1866.

24. "Knocked Down by a Cow," *NYT*, 10 December 1889; "Chased an
Ox for Blocks," *NYT*, 14 October 1889.

25. *Dickson v. McCoy* 39 N.Y. 400, quoted in John H. Ingham, *The Law
of Animals* (Philadelphia, 1900), p. 339.

26. Constance Mayfield Rourke, *Trumpets of Jubilee* (New York, 1927),
p. 307; "Mr. Fuller Fulminates," *NYT*, 24 July 1887.

27. New York, 1915, pp. 313–17.

28. Bates, *Animal Worlds*, p. 309; Hugo Hartnack, *202 Common Household
Pests of North America* (Chicago, 1939), pp. 23, 27; Martin Tolchin, "City
Officials Say Rats Thrive Here," *NYT*, 1 August 1967.

29. Lynch, *Wild Seventies*, pp. 303, 306.

30. "Mr. Whitman, Deputy Commissioner of Internal Revenue. . . ,"
NYT, 11 March 1866; Horatio Newton Parker, *City Milk Supply* (New
York, 1917), pp. 182, 184.

31. Parker, *City Milk*, pp. 182–83; Steele, *Angel in Top Hat*, pp. 110–11
ff.

32. "Frank Leslie's Illustrated Newspaper," *AH*, 14 (June 1962):98–99;
Alvin Fay Harlow, *Henry Bergh: Founder of the A.S.P.C.A.* (New York,
1957), p. 87.

33. Robert E. Riegel, *Young America 1830–1840* (Norman, Okla.), pp.
34–37, quoted in *The History of Popular Culture Since 1815*, ed. Norman D.
Cantor and Michael S. Werthman (New York, 1968), 28; Duffy, *History
of Public Health*, pp. 386–87; "Where the Dogs Go," *Leslie's*, 14 August
1858; "Method of Decoying Dogs for the Pound by Vagrant Boys in New
York City;" ibid., 24 August 1867; "Opening of the Dog Trade," *NYT*, 9
June 1874.

34. "Dog Catchers Defeated," *NYT*, 15 July 1886.

9. Horses Are Cheaper Than Oats

1. Samuel Carter, III, *Cyrus Field: Man of Two Worlds* (New York, 1968),
p. 308; "Cruelties to Horses and Passengers," *Leslie's*, 16 March 1867;
George Rogers Taylor, "The Beginnings of Mass Transportation in Urban America: Part I," *Smithsonian Journal of History* 1 (Summer 1966):
35–39.

2. "Caring for the Streets," *NYT*, 22 April 1887.

3. George Rogers Taylor, "The Beginnings of Mass Tranpsortation . . . Part I," p. 40; idem, "Beginnings . . . Part II," ibid., 1, no. 3 (1966):34.

4. Raymond S. Tompkins, "Horse-Car Days," *American Mercury* 16 (April 1929): 446–47; Benson J. Lossing, *History of New York City . . . to 1884* (New York, 1884), 1:99; Taylor, "Beginnings of Mass Transportation . . . Part I," pp. 40–44. For a detailed account of how it felt to ride in a New York omnibus, see James D. McCabe, *New York by Sunlight and Gaslight* (Philadelphia, 1881), pp. 158–59, 163.

5. [Isabella Bird], *The Englishwoman in America* (London, 1856), quoted in Bayard Still, *Mirror for Gotham* (New York, 1956), p. 154; Philip M. Stimson, "A Poetic Souvenir: The Crossing of Pathways in Memorable Lives," *Yale University Library Gazette* 43 (October 1968):85.

6. "The Departing Omnibus," *NYT*, 13 November 1881.

7. Taylor, "Beginnings of Mass Transportation . . . Part II," pp.39, 47.

8. Tompkins, "Horse-Car Days," pp. 445–47.

9. Alexander B. Callow, Jr., *The Tweed Ring* (New York, 1966), p. 49.

10. "Around the City's Edges," *NYT*, 29 February 1880; Tompkins, "Horse-Car Days," p. 448; McCabe, *New York by Sunlight*, p. 239.

11. Tompkins, "Horse-Car Days," p. 450.

12. Ibid., p. 448; "The One-Horse or 'Bob-Tail' Street Car . . . ," *NYT*, 12 October 1881; "Not a Bob-Tail Left," *NYT*, 2 December 1888.

13. *A.S.P.C.A. Second Annual Report* (New York, 1868), p. 14.

14. Zulma Steele, *Angel in Top Hat* (New York, 1942), p. 61.

15. Dawne Hulett, "He Did Most for the Horse," *Cattleman* 38 (September 1951):173; Henry Bergh, "The Cost of Cruelty," *North American Review* 83 (July 1881):76–77.

16. *A.S.P.C.A. Eighth Annual Report* (New York, 1874), p. 27.

17. "Lot of the Car Horse," *NYT*, 18 March 1883.

18. Bergh, "Cost of Cruelty," p. 76.

19. "A California Paper Relates . . . ," *NYT*, 9 September 1882.

20. "Defending New-York," *NYT*, 20 November 1886.

21. "A California Paper Relates . . ."

22. *A.S.P.C.A. Fifteenth Annual Report* (New York, 1881), pp. 7–8.

23. "The Streets and the Cars," *NYT*, 21 June 1888.

24. Hulett, "He Did Most for the Horse," p. 174.

25. *A.S.P.C.A. Eighteenth Annual Report* (New York, 1885), p. 7; Henry Bergh, *The Horse: His Comfort, Discomfort, and Torture* (n.p., 1875), pp. 1–12; Bergh, "Cost of Cruelty," p. 76.

26. William Fullerton Reeves, "Rapid Transit Elevated Lines in New York City," *New-York Historical Society Quarterly Bulletin* 18 (January 1935):59–82; idem, "Rapid Transit Elevated Lines . . . ," ibid. 19 (April 1935):3–17.

27. "Elevated Railroad Travel," *NYT*, 30 March 1882.

28. William Alan Swallow, *Quality of Mercy: History of the Humane Movement in the United States* (Boston, 1963), p. 25.

10. Don Quixote of Manhattan

1. Henry Collins Brown, *Brownstone Fronts and Saratoga Trunks* (New York, 1935), p. 198.
2. "Humanity in New-York," *New York Tribune*, 16 March 1878.
3. "Hon. Henry Bergh. His Lecture on 'Our Speechless Slave,'" *Cincinnati Commercial*, 12 December 1873; Henry Bergh, "The Cost of Cruelty," *North American Review* 133 (July 1881):75–81.
4. Roswell C. McCrea, "The Humane Movement," in *Legislation for the Protection of Animals and Children*, ed. Samuel McCune Lindsay. Bulletin of Social Legislation on the Henry Bergh Foundation for the Promotion of Humane Education, no. 2 (New York, 1914), p. 8; idem., *The Humane Movement: A Descriptive Survey* (New York, 1910), pp. 33–34; William J. Schultz, "The Humane Movement in the United States, 1910–1922," *Bulletin of Social Legislation*, ed. Samuel McCune Lindsay, no. 6 (New York, 1924), pp. 12–13.
5. McCrea, *Humane Movement*, 1910, pp. 16–17.
6. Henry Bergh to Henry W. Bellows, 2 March 1867, quoted in Edward P. Buffet, "Bergh's War on Vested Cruelty," typescript (Stony Brook, N.Y., n.d.), 8: no pagination. ASPCA Archives. The author gratefully acknowledges the courtesy of the ASPCA officials in making available unique archival materials relating to Bergh and the Society's early history.
7. George M. McCarthy, *The Evolution of a Sentiment* (Jersey City, N.J., 1905), p. 13.
8. McCrea, *Humane Movement*, 1910, p. 155; Zulma Steele, *Angel in Top Hat* (New York, 1942), pp. 2–3.
9. Beverley R. Betts, "The Berghs of New York," *New York Genealogical and Biographical Record* 19 (July 1888):122–25; Joseph H. Tooker, "Christian Bergh's Son," *NYT*, 18 March 1888; "Henry Bergh Dead," *New-York Daily Tribune*, 13 March 1888.
10. "Married," *New York Herald*, 11 September 1839.
11. "Our Speechless Slaves: Lecture by Henry Berg,", *Cincinnati Gazette*, 12 December 1873; H. B. (Henry Bergh), "Correspondence of the Mirror," *New York Evening Mirror*, 16 June 1848.
12. Henry Bergh, "Russian Diary," 31 May 1864. Bergh Papers, ASPCA Archives; David L. Smiley, *Lion of White Hall: The Life of Cassius M. Clay* (Madison, Wis,. 1962), p. 210.
13. Sydney H. Coleman, *Humane Society Leaders in America, with a Sketch of the Early History of the Humane Movement in England* (Albany, N.Y., 1924), p. 35; *DAB*, s.v. "Bergh, Henry."
14. Clara Morris, "Riddle of the Nineetenth Century: Mr. Henry Bergh," *McClure's Magazine* 18 (March 1902):418.
15. Henry Bergh, "Our Speechless Slaves," *Cincinnati Gazette*; "Henry Bergh's Story," *Philadelphia Press*, 22 September 1884.
16. Steele, *Angel in Top Hat*, p. 35.

17. Bergh to Earl of Harrowby, 12 June 1866, Bergh Papers, ASPCA Archives; Coleman, *Humane Movement*, p. 37; *DAB*, s.v. "Bergh, Henry."

18. Coleman, *Humane Movement*, p. 37; "Local News," *NYT*, 9 February 1866; Steele, *Angel in Top Hat*, p. 37.

19. *ASPCA First Annual Report* (New York, 1867), pp. 62–66; "Henry Bergh Dead," *New York Herald*, 13 March 1888.

20. F. Morse Hubbard, "Prevention of Cruelty to Animals in New York State," *Bulletin of Social Legislation*, ed. Samuel McCune Lindsay, no. 3 (New York, 1915), pp. iii, 1–3.

21. Buffet, "Bergh's War," 8: no pagination; "Our Dumb Animals," *Christian Weekly*, 27 May 1871.

22. Alexander B. Callow, Jr., *The Tweed Ring* (New York, 1966), pp. 58, 144; Denis Tilden Lynch, *The Wild Seventies* (New York, 1941), p. 303; Steele, *Angel in Top Hat*, pp. 142–43.

23. Buffet, "Bergh's War," 8: no pagination.

24. "A Friend of the Helpless," unidentified, undated newspaper clipping. Miscellaneous Papers, Henry Bergh folder, Manuscript Division, New York Public Library.

25. Retained copies of letters dated 3 May, 12 June and 15 November, all 1866. Letterbooks, ASPCA Archives.

26. "Henry Bergh's Story," *Philadelphia Press*, 22 September 1884; *ASPCA First Annual Report* (New York, 1867), pp. 5–8; Coleman, *Humane Society Leaders*, pp. 42–43.

27. "More Cruelty to Animals—a Queer Gastronomic Revolution," *New York Herald*, 1 June 1866.

28. Buffet, "Bergh's War," 8: no pagination; M. R. Werner, *Barnum* (New York, 1923), p. 327.

29. Werner, *Barnum*, pp. 330–32. The three-way correspondence on what was called "The Great Snake Question . . . How Should the Boa Constrictor Be Fed, etc., etc." was printed in full under the heading "Cruelty to Animals," in the *New York World*, 19 March 1867.

30. Werner, *Barnum*, p. 330; Steele, *Angel in Top Hat*, pp. 242–44.

31. J. K. Asoliko, Bridgeport (Conn.) Public Library, to author, 31 January 1967.

32. *ASPCA Third Annual Report* (New York, 1869); "Mr. Bergh Cries Halt," *Buffalo Daily Courier*, 12 September 1886; "Death of Henry Bergh," *New York World*, 13 March 1888.

33. *New York Society for the Prevention of Cruelty to Children. First Annual Report* (New York, 1876), pp. 6–8; Jacob A. Riis, *Children of the Poor* (New York, 1905), pp. 142–44; William Alan Swallow, *Quality of Mercy: History of the Humane Movement in the United States* (Boston, 1963), pp. 158–60.

34. William H. Van Benschoten, *Concerning the Van Bunschoten or Van Benschoten Family in America* (New York, 1907), p. 674; Morris, "Riddle of the Nineteenth Century," p. 421.

35. 26 December 1869.

36. 17 March 1875.

37. "Men of the Hour. IX. Henry Bergh," *Arcadian*, 31 December 1874, p. 9.

38. Coleman, *Humane Society Leaders*, p. 49.

39. Ibid., p. 59; *A.S.P.C.A. Nineteenth Annual Report for 1884* (New York, 1885), p. 5.

40. John Friend Noble, "Christian and Henry Bergh," typescript (New York: New-York Historical Society, 1933), p. 47; "Henry Bergh Dead," *New-York Daily Tribune*, 13 March 1888. The author makes general acknowledgment of courteous, skillful assistance received from The New-York Historical Society, New York Public Library and New York State Library in the reconstruction of urban life and Henry Bergh's activities in Chapters 8, 9 and 10.

41. "Henry Bergh Dead," *New York Herald*, 13 March 1888; "Henry Bergh," *New York Citizen*, 13 March 1888.

42. "Statue of Henry Bergh," *Lore* 10 (1960): 119; "Bergh's Statue Has Great Day," *Milwaukee Journal*, 28 April 1941.

43. Henry Bergh to Lester Wallack, 7 November 1881.

11. How Mercy Came to Massachusetts

1. "Sporting Intelligence. Long Race—Death of the Winning Horse," *Boston Daily Advertiser*, 24 February 1868.

2. George T. Angell, "Cruelty to Animals," *Boston Daily Advertiser*, 25 February 1868.

3. "Massachusetts Society for the Prevention of Cruelty to Animals," *Boston Daily Advertiser*, 31 March 1869.

4. George T. Angell, *Autobiographical Sketches and Personal Recollections* (Boston, n.d.), p. 43.

5. Ibid., pp. 9–11; *ASPCA Thirteenth Annual Report for 1879* (New York, 1880).

6. "Cruelty to Animals," *Chicago Times*, 10 November 1870. The article gives a good general account of the formation of the MSPCA. It was signed by a committee of local citizens, but prepared by Angell.

7. George Rogers Taylor, "The Beginning of Mass Transportation in Urban America: Part I," *Smithsonian Journal of History* 1 (Summer 1966): 41, 43.

8. Angell, *Autobiographical Sketches*, Appendix, p. 4.

9. Ibid., p. 20.

10. Ibid., pp. 62–63.

11. Ibid., pp. 7–8.

12. "Recent Deaths. Friend of 'Dumb' Animals Dead," *Boston Evening Transcript*, 16 March 1909; *DAB*, s.v. "Angell, George Thorndike."

13. Christine Stevens, "Befriending Animals," *Childhood Education* 38 (May 1962):426.

14. "The Humane Educator," *National Humane Review* 5:13–14.

15. Frank Luther Mott, *Golden Multitudes: The Story of Best Sellers in the*

United States (New York, 1947), pp. 163–63, 311; Angell, *Autobiographical Sketches*, p. 94.

16. Mott, pp. 165, 311.

17. Angell, pp. 37–38, 48, 66, 86.

18. Guy Richardson, "Apostle of Peace and Justice to Animals—Centenary of George T. Angell," *Zion's Herald*, 6 June 1923, p. 732; "Thirty-eight Horses Lead the Sad Procession," *Our Dumb Animals* 41 (April 1909):172–74, *passim*.

19. Angell, *Autobiographical Sketches*, p. 64.

20. *DAB*, s.v. "Angell, George Thorndike."

21. Angell to Henry Wadsworth Longfellow, 24 March 1880. Houghton Library, Harvard University, Cambridge, Massachusetts.

22. "Not Doctor," *Our Dumb Animals* 19 (February 1887) :84.

23. "Thirty-eight Horses Lead the Sad Procession," p. 170.

24. The drawing appeared in the *Boston Traveler*, 20 March 1909 and was reproduced in *Our Dumb Animals* 41 (April 1909) :169.

25. Hereafter called ISPA. Offices are maintained in London and Boston.

26. Carlton E. Buttrick to author, 27 July 1970; David S. Claflin to author, 21 July 1970; John C. Walsh to author, 16 March 1970.

12. *Kindness Gains a New Dimension*

1. William J. Schultz, "The Humane Movement in the United States 1910–1922," *Bulletin of Social Legislation*, ed. Samuel McCune Lindsay (New York, 1924), no. 6, p. 64; Roswell C. McCrea, *The Humane Movement: A Descriptive Survey* (New York, 1910), pp. 66–74, 83, 87, 89; William Alan Swallow, *Quality of Mercy: History of the Human Movement in the United States* (Boston, 1963), pp. 10, 30–33, 118.

2. Schultz, "Humane Movement," pp. 66–67; for animal abandonment on Cape Cod see *Our Fourfooted Friends* 46 (September 1949): 8. The Animal Rescue League of Boston reports progress with regard to deserted pets: " . . . the number today is far, far fewer than thirty to forty years ago." Carlton E. Buttrick to author, 25 August 1970.

3. "Green Leaves," *Our Animals*, April 1943 pp. 23–24; McCrea, *Humane Movement*, p. 75.

4. "What Is AHA?" *Our Animals* 62 (September–October 1968): 7, 10–12; Swallow, *Quality of Mercy*, pp. 161–62.

5. Oliver Evans to author, 7 August 1967.

6. Karl A. Menninger, "Totemic Aspects of Contemporary Attitudes Toward Animals," in *Psychoanalysis and Culture*, ed. George B. Wilbur and Werner Muensterberger (New York, 1951), pp. 58–59; Pierre Courtines to author, 14 September 1970.

7. "Work Horses Parade Makes Fine Showing," *Boston Globe*, 31 May 1903; *Boston Work-Horse Relief Association Annual Report*, 31 May 1926; Schultz, "Humane Movement in the United States," pp. 72–73, 40.

8. "Proceedings of the Executive Committee," *Humane Quarterly* 1 (July 1930):5; "Letters to Newspapers," Ibid. 2 (February 1931): 3.

9. Janice Paprin, "The Food Animal—Someone Cared!" *National Humane Review* 55 (September–October 1967): 8–9.

10. Richard O. Cummings, *The American Ice Harvests: A Historical Study in Technology, 1800–1918* (Berkeley and Los Angeles, 1949), p. 66; "A New Service in an Old Tradition," typescript (Illinois Humane Society, 1966). Chicago Historical Society; "What Is AHA?" *Our Animals*, p. 13.

11. *Encyclopedia of the Social Sciences*, s.v. "Animal Protection."

12. Martin Kaufman, "The American Anti-Vaccinationists and Their Arguments," *Bulletin of the History of Medicine* 41 (September–October 1967): 422–73 Morris Fishbein, *Fads and Quackery in Healing* (New York, 1932), pp. 118–19.

13. Zulma Steele, *Angel in Top Hat* (New York, 1942), pp. 277–78; Charles H. Callison to author, 1 May 1970.

14. "Review for 1967," *ISPA* (London, 1969), no pagination; "The Seal Club," *Women's Wear Daily*, 29 April 1970.

15. John P. Heap, "History of the Washington Humane Society" (Paper delivered before the Society, Washington, D.C., 15 March 1921), *Columbia Historical Society Records* 25:57–59, 66.

16. George M. McCarthy, *The Evolution of a Sentiment* (Jersey City, 1905), pp. 7, 13, 16, 19.

17. *ASPCA Twentieth Annual Report for 1885* (New York, 1886), p. 6.

18. "Texas Tom—Miami Beach, Fla . . . ," *Hudson* (N.Y.) *Register-Star*, 23 July 1970.

19. "Dog that Attends Class Gets a Report Card, Too," *NYT*, 9 July 1968; Lillian McLaughlin, "Ralph's a College Canine," *National Humane Review* 58 (March–April 1970): 20; " Ralphine . . . " *Poughkeepsie Journal*, 19 July 1970; " 'Flower Ape' Freshly Scrubbed . . . Bride and Groom say 'I Do' at Zoo," *Omaha World-Herald*, 11 July 1969.

20. Christine Stevens, "Befriending Animals," *Childhood Education* 38 (May 1962):426.

21. *Boy Scout Handbook* (New Brunswick, N.J., 1959), p. 84; *Girl Scout Handbook* (New York, 1953), page opp. title page; Stevens, "Befriending Animals," p. 427; *You . . . and the Kindness Club* (Fredericton, New Brunswick, n.d.).

22. "That Special Week," *National Humane Review* 50 (January–February 1962):48–50; "Tribute Accorded Henry F. Lewith," *Charleston* (S.C.) *News and Courier*, 28 April 1941; Swallow, *Quality of Mercy*, pp. 173–74.

23. "Mrs. Fiske as Friend of Animals," *NYT*, 18 May 1919; Minnie Maddern Fiske, "Cruelty to Animals in Arkansas," *NYT*, 30 May 1926; *The Whims of Fashion* (Washington: HSUS, n.d.), p. 3.

24. Irving Drutman, "The Grand Manner," *Playbill* (New York [?], 1967 [?]) ,p. 15.

25. Edward Wagenknecht, *Mark Twain: The Man and His Work* (Norman, Okla., 1961), pp. 36, 134.

26. "Irene Castle, Dancer, Dies at 75; Was Toast of World War I Era," *NYT*, 26 January 1969. Her Orphans of the Storm shelter is still operating.

27. Henry Knepler, *The Gilded Stage: The Years of the Great International Actresses* (New York, 1968), pp. 147, 156, 181; Kathleen Szasz, *Petishism: Pets and Their People in the Western World* (New York, 1968), p. 176; Henri Garel, "Le courrier de Paris . . . Paris à l'aube de 1970," *France-Amérique*, 8 January 1970.

28. "The Seal Club," *Women's Wear Daily*, 29 April 1970.

29. Richard Brautigam, "Humane Takeover Detailed," *Madison* (Wis.) *Capital Times*, 25 January 1967.

30. F. Morse Hubbard, "Prevention of Cruelty to Animals in the States of Illinois, Colorado and California," *Bulletin of Social Legislation*, ed. Samuel McCune Lindsay (New York, 1916), no. 4, pp. 16–18, 11; J.J. Shaffer to author, 30 July 1970; Deidre Carmody, "Critics Assert A.S.P.C.A. Here Is Guilty of Cruelty to Animals," *NYT*, 21 June 1971; "Coalition Acting on the A.S.P.C.A.," 23 July 1971.

13. Going the Whole Way: Vegetarianism

1. "Mrs. Fiske as Friend of Animals," *NYT*, 18 May 1919.

2. Edith Efron, "Heydays for the Vegetarians," *NYT*, 8 April 1945.

3. Dr. Jesse Mercer Gehman to author, 27 September 1968.

4. Brigid Brophy, *Don't Never Forget* (New York, 1966), p. 21.

5. Statement of A.F. Bloese, long-time secretary to Dr. John Harvey Kellogg; quoted in Marie Duesenberg to author, 9 July 1968.

6. Gerald Carson, *Cornflake Crusade* (New York, 1957), p. 240.

7. Voltaire, *Dictionnaire philosophique*, s.v. "Viande défendue, viande dangereuse." Hester Hastings casts some doubt in *Man and Beast in French Thought of the Eighteenth Century* (Baltimore, 1936) on whether Voltaire was firmly on the side of the zoophilists. Her discussion appears on pp. 257–58.

8. Carson, *Cornflake Crusade*, p. 109.

9. Mel Morse, *Ordeal of the Animals* (Englewood Cliffs, N.J., 1968), p. 67.

10. "Views of a Vegetarian," *NYT*, 15 September 1895.

11. Bronson Alcott, *The Journals of Bronson Alcott*, ed. Odell Shepard (Boston, 1938), p. 115; William Henry Harrison to author, 24 September 1968.

12. "World Vegetarians Gather in London; Their First Theme and Food is 'Nuts,'" *NYT*, 27 May 1926.

13. Annie Besant, *Vegetarianism in the Light of Theosophy* (Madras, India, 1932), pp. 10–11, 14.

14. Carson, *Cornflake Crusade*, pp. 43–60; idem, "Graham: The Man Who Made the Cracker Famous," *New-England Galaxy* 10 (Spring 1969): 3–8.

15. Roland Case Ross, "The Nature and Role of the Grizzly Bear," *Defenders* 44 (Winter 1969):413; Desmond Morris, *The Naked Ape: A Zoologist's Study of the Human Animal* (New York, 1967), p. 197.
16. New York, 1934, p. 198.
17. Carson, *Cornflake Crusade*, pp. 15–27.
18. Hesketh Pearson, *G.B.S.: A Full Length Portrait* (New York, 1942), p. 48.
19. Owen S. Parrett, *Why I Don't Eat Meat* (n.p., n.d.).
20. "News From Afar . . . ," *Vegetarian News Digest* . (Summer 1954):15; ibid., "Newsy Notes . . . ," p. 19.
21. "Let Them Have Their Fun," *NYT*, 28 May 1926.
22. "Oscar and a Vegetarian at Odds on Holiday Fare," *NYT*, 29 November 1946; "Nuts, Fruits, Plants Satisfy Vegetarians," *NYT*, 24 November 1950; "Opposition to Exploitation," *NYT*, 28 November 1969.
23. Classified advertisement in *American Vegetarian-Hygienist* 24 (Spring–Summer 1967):19.
24. Carson, *Cornflake Crusade*, pp. 20–22.
25. Efron, "Heydays for the Vegetarians," p. 32.
26. R. J. Cheatham, *Cancer and the Shangri-La* (Bonita Springs, Fla., n.d.); "Health Rejuvenation," Advertisement for the Shangri-La Health Resort, Bonita Springs, Florida, *American Vegetarian-Hygienist* 24 (Spring–Summer 1967):22.
27. "Symon Gould, Ran for President on Vegetarian Ticket in 1960," *NYT*, 25 November 1963.

Part III: No More Room in the Ark?

14. Declining Contact Between Men and Animals

1. Basil Wrighton, "Morals in the Melting Pot" (Address delivered at the Eighth Annual Meeting of the National Catholic Society for Animal Welfare, 28 October 1967), p. 1; Desmond Morris, *The Human Zoo* (New York, 1969), p. 75.
2. "Bluebird is Voted Official State Bird with One Dissenter," *NYT*, 3 March 1970. See also Joseph J. Shomon, "More Wildlife for Urban America," *Conservationist* 24 (February-March 1970): 2–7.
3. Barry Commoner, "Keynote Address: What Good is a Bird," *Proceedings, Sixty-fourth Annual Convention, National Audubon Society* (St. Louis: 1969), p. 10; Jacques Boudet, *Man & Beast: A Visual History*, trans. Anne Carter (London, 1964), p. 292.
4. Richard Lewinsohn, *Animals, Men and Myths* (New York, 1954), p. 275; Hans Mislin, *L'homme parmi les animaux* (Zurich, 1965), p. 191.
5. Jane Rosner, "Urban Ecology in New York City," in a panel discussion, "Environmental Education in Urban America," *Proceedings, Sixty-fourth Annual Convention, National Audubon Society*,, pp. 17–19.

6. John Kieran, A *Natural History of New York City* (Cambridge, Mass., 1959), pp. 322, 342–43, 95, 309–10.

7. "Library Supplies Animals to Young," *NYT*, 1 January 1969.

8. Pamphlets, folders, and leaflets distributed by the RSPCA include *Is This Fun?*, *Performing Animals Cruelty*, *Wild Animals in Circuses*, *Stick and Whip*, *Sad Performers*. For an American view see "To Humanitarians," mimeographed (Washington: Society for Animal Protective Legislation, 17 September 1970).

9. Helen Trevelyan, *Laugh, Clown, Laugh!* (London, 1960), pp. 87–89, 93–94, 100–105; E. Westcott, ed. *Spotlights on Performing Animals* (Ashingdon, England, 1962), p. 7–8.

10. James Fisher, *Zoos of the World: The Story of Animals in Captivity* (Garden City, N. Y., 1967), p. 58; Emily Hahn, *Animal Gardens* (Garden City, N. Y., 1967), pp. 62, 116, 241.

11. Boudet, *Man & Beast*, p. 287; William G. Conway, "The Zoo Story," *Natural History* 77 (December 1968):32–32; idem, "Consumption of Wildlife by Man," *Animal Kingdom* 71 (June 1968):18–23, reprinted in *Defenders* 44 (Spring 1969):70–76; Hahn, *Animal Gardens*, p. 16.

12. Hahn, *Animal Gardens*, p. 15.

13. Fisher, *Zoos of the World*, pp. 146–48.

14. Julia Allen Field, "An Ethic for the Earth," *Defenders* 42 (Summer 1967):133; Robert Reinow and Leona Train Reinow, *Moment in the Sun* (New York, 1967), p. 308.

15. "The Central Park Menagerie," *New York Sun*, 9 December 1877; "Mr. Bergh's Complaint," *NYT*, 20 May 1882.

16. Julia Allen Field, "Reflections on the Death of an Elephant," *Defenders* 42 (Spring 1967):23–24.

17. Brigid Brophy, *Don't Never Forget* (New York, 1966), p. 21.

18. Murray Schumach, "Zoos Trying to be More Liveable," *NYT*, 23 August 1969.

19. [Henry Labouchere], *Diary of the Besieged Resident in Paris* (London, 1871), pp. 217, 224, 247, 268, 308; Frank Schlosser, "Siege Dinners 1870–71," *Living Age* 264, Series 7, vol. 46, pp. 209–15; Herman Dembeck, *Animals and Men* (Garden City, N. Y., 1965), pp. 288–89; L. R. Brightwell, "London Sees it Through," *Animal Kingdom* 47 (January-February 1944: 18–22.

20. "The New Zoos," *Newsweek*, 1 June 1970, p. 58; "Sniper Slays Lions That Killed Youth at Zoo in Portland, Ore.," *NYT*, 7 July 1970; Ambrose Agius, *God's Animals* (n.p., 1970), p. 14; "Sea Lion Poisonings May End 'Open' Zoo," *Baltimore News American*, 20 April 1968; Robin Frames, "Baltimore Zoo Now Facing Major Crisis As Vandals and Thieves Strike," *Baltimore Evening Sun*, 2 July 1968. Similar crimes continued into 1972.

21. Gary K. Clarke, "Museum of Human Stupidity—A Psychological Deterrent to Vandalism in the Zoo," Joseph Lucas, ed., *International Zoo Yearbook* 9 (London, 1969):146–47.

22. "The Roadside Zoo," *Humane Quarterly* 1 (July 1930):4.

23. Roger Caras, "A Lingering of Savages," *Audubon* 71 (July 1969):12, 14; and the following, all from *Defenders*, Alfred G. Etter, "Animal Slums" 40 (Summer 1965):28–29; idem, "Highway Animal Traps" 42 (Fall 1967): 258–59; Jeffrey P. Smith, "Oh, Let Them Out!" 43 (Winter 1968): 398; "Caged Animals" 45 (Spring 1970):24, quoted from Michael Frome, *Vacations, U.S.A.: Getting the Most for Your Travel Dollar* (Washington, 1966).

24. F. H. Davis to Mrs. Ceciel B. O'Marr, 25 November 1969; Cecile B. O'Marr, "Roadside Zoos," *Defenders* 45 (Spring 1970):21–24; idem to author, 21 September 1970.

25. Marston Bates, *Animal Worlds* (New York, 1963), p. 302.

26. J. H. S. Brossard, "The Mental Hygiene of Owning a Dog," *Mental Hygiene* 28:408–13, quoted in Karl A. Menninger, "Totemic Aspects of Contemporary Attitudes Toward Animals," *Psychoanalysis and Culture*, ed. George B. Wilbur and Werner Muensterberger (New York, 1951), p. 56; and ibid., p. 57.

27. Joan Doyle, "Bats in His Ice Box, a Cat's Head in a Can," *Poughkeepsie Journal*, 9 December 1968.

28. Robert A. Wright, "Car Dealer Does it—Gets a Horse," *NYT*, 20 September 1970; "Return of the Horse," *Time*, 17 May 1968, p. 82; "U.S. Involvement Sought With Growing Horse Trade," *Poughkeepsie Jounanl*, 20 July 1969.

29. Carlton E. Buttrick, "President's Annual Message," mimeo-graphed (Delivered at Seventieth Annual Meeting of the Animal Rescue League of Boston, Boston, Massachusetts, 30 April 1969), pp. 7–8; R. D. Reynolds, "Groomers Organize," *National Humane Review* 58 (September–October 1970): 17; Bil Gilbert, *Bears in the Ladies Room and Other Beastly Pursuits* (Garden City, N. Y., 1966), pp. 180–86; Alexander R. Hammer, "Affluence is Fueling Pet Industry Growth," *NYT*, 21 September 1969.

30. Ernest P. Walker, *Studying Our Fellow Mammals* (n.p.: AWI, n.d.), p. 126.

31. Robert Gannon, "Don't Buy That Exotic Pet," *Outdoor World* 2 (September–October 1969):18–21; "Collection Service . . . Lost and Found," *Our Fourfooted Friends* 67 (March 1970):7–9; "Girl Hopes to Find an African Home for Pet Chimp," *Defenders* 44 (Spring 1969):16–17, reprinted from *National Observer*, n.d.

32. (New York, 1969), pp. 112–13. Readers tempted to acquire a chimpanzee would do well first to read Cathy Hayes, *The Ape in Our House* (New York, 1951).

33. "Hearings Held on Whitehurst Bill to Broaden Laboratory Animal Welfare Act," *Information Report AWI* 19 (April–May–June, 1970):1–2; Conway, "Consumption of Wildlife by Man," *Defenders* 44 (Spring 1969): pp. 70–76.

34. Kathleen Szasz, *Petishism: Pets and Their People in the Western World* (New York, 1968), p. 185; Mrs. Patricia O. Blosser, Secretary-Treasurer, National Association of Pet Cemeteries, to author, 14 June 1972. Ralph

Reppert, "Burials for Pets at $18 to $1,000," *Baltimore Sun,* 4 May 1958.

35. " 'Rich' Cat Dies at 20; Keeper to Get $15,000," *NYT,* 14 December 1968; "Tortoise Gets Just Desserts," *NYT,* 27 September 1968; "By the Will of Mrs. Mary J. Bradford . . .," *NYT,* 1 November 1897.

36. Tom Burns Haber, "Canine Terms Applied to Human Beings and Human Events: Part I," *American Speech* 40 (May 1965):83–101; idem, "Canine Terms . . . Part II," ibid., 40 (December 1965):243–71.

37. "Animal Defamation," *Green Bag* 9:135.

38. Kieran, *Natural History of New York,* p. 148.

39. Charlotte Curtis, "Decor for a Gala Rivals Guests' Diamonds," *NYT,* 11 August 1969.

15. The Unwanted Animal

1. Marston Bates, *Animal Worlds* (New York, 1963), pp. 282, 285.

2. *Puppies and Kittens, 10,000 an Hour* (Washington: HSUS, n.d.); " 'Please Help Me!' " *NYT,* 17 January 1970, advertisement of the National Cat Protection Society.

3. "Unwanted," *Our Dumb Animals* 101 (April 1968):3; *Puppies and Kittens . . .*; Interview, John J. Stanton, Service Department, HSUS, 26 November 1969; *Please—Mr. and Mrs. Pet Owner—Have a Heart* (Deerfield, Illinios: Orphans of the Storm, n.d.), p. 2. The Ogden Nash verse is quoted in Mrs. John Warren Beach, "SPCA Can't, Owners Must Cope with Cats," *Patent Trader* (Mount Kisco, N. Y.), 12 July 1969.

4. *Please—Mr. and Mrs. Pet Owner . . .,* p. 1; Robert Terpstra, "Only Birth Control Can End Animal Buchenwalds," *Washington Post,* 8 May 1969; "101st Annual Report: The Pennsylvania Society for the Prevention of Cruelty to Animals," *Animaldom* 39 (March 1969):1.

5. *A Report on Animal "Overpopulation"* (Washington: HSUS, 1970), p. 1; "Roving Dog Packs Endanger Residents of City Ghettos," *National Humane Newsletter* 16 (June 1970):1; Ernest P. Walker, *Studying Our Fellow Mammals* (n.p.: AWI, n.d.), p. 6.

6. Dr. Wolfgang Jöchle to author, 8 July 1970.

7. "Los Angeles to Have First Municipal Spay Clinics," *NCSAW Report,* October 1970, p. 1; *Report on Animal "Overpopulation,"* pp. 1–4; David Hendin, "10,000 Pets Born Every Hour Dogging U.S. Population Crisis," *Pittsburgh Press,* 19 June 1970; *Please—Mr. and Mrs. Pet Owner . . .,* p. 4.

8. "Dogs' Birth-Control Pill Going on British Market," *NYT,* 28 March 1969; Le Docteur Pierre Rousselet, "La 'pilule' pour chiennes et chattes," *La Voix des Bêtes,* New Series, no. 22 (March 1969).

9. Dr. Wolfgang Jöchle to author, 8 July 1970.

10. Manton M. Marble to Henry Bergh, 24 March 1867, ASPCA Archives; Charlotte Baker Montgomery, "Meeting Animal Friends," mimeographed (Nacogdoches, Tex.: Humane Society of Nacogdoches County, 1967), p. 6.

11. Hans Zinsser, *Rats, Lice and History* (New York, 1960), pp. 6, 123–36.

12. C. W. Hume, *The Status of Animals in the Christian Religion* (London, 1957), p. 39; Joan Hunter, "Baby Opossums," *Living Museum* 30 (March 1969: 84–85.

13. C. W. Hume, *The Religious Attitude Toward Animals* (London, n.d.), p. 3.

14. Konrad Lorenz, *On Aggression* (New York, 1963), p. 161; Zinsser, *Rats, Lice*, pp. 143, 145–47; R. S. R. Fitter, *London's Natural History* (London, 1946), pp. 59–60.

15. Fitter, *London's Natural History*, pp. 88–89; Zinsser, *Rats, Lice*, pp. 147–49.

16. Martin Tolchin, "City Officials Say Rats Thrive Here," *NYT*, 1 August 1967; Sandra Blakeslee, "Biological 'Trap' To Eradicate Rats Set," *NYT*, 31 March 1969; Zinsser, *Rats, Lice*, pp. 151–52.

17. Alison Owings, "Why is This Rat Smiling?" *Washingtonian* 4 (July 1969):30–31.

18. "Rats Keep Youths from Cleaning Lot in 109th Street Drive," *NYT*, 1 September 1967; "City Rats Are Called Too Tough for Cats," *NYT*, 8 August 1967.

19. "Park Avenue Rats," *NYT*, January 1969; "Rat Control Money Still Awaits Approval of the Budget Bureau," *NYT*, 28 November 1968.

20. Jacques Boudet, *Man & Beast: A Visual History*, trans. Anne Carter (London, 1964), p. 192.

16. Rodeo: Cruelty Packaged as Americana

1. *Behind the Rodeo Gate!* (Washington: HSUS, n.d.). Humane societies are generally skeptical of the claim of the American Humane Association that it can, and does, effectively "supervise" rodeos.

2. Michael Pousner, "The Yeas and Neighs of Rodeo Cruelty," *New York Daily News*, 30 June 1971; "Banner Year Ends at National Finals," *Rodeo Sports News*, 1 December 1969.

3. *To Protect Rodeo Livestock* (Denver: AHA, n.d.), p. 1; " '69 Rodeo Champs," *Hoofs and Horns* 39 (January 1970):18.

4. Mel Morse, *Ordeal of the Animals* (Englewood Cliffs, N J., 1968), p. 51; Clifford P. Westermeier, *Man, Beast, Dust: The Story of Rodeo* (Denver, 1947), p. 91.

5. Mary S. Robertson, *Rodeo: Standard Guide to the Cowboy Sport* (Berkely, Calif., 1961), p. 74; Gene Lamb, *Rodeo Back of the Chutes* (Denver, 1956), p. 87.

6. "Banner Year Ends at National Finals," *Rodeo Sports News*, 1 December 1969, p. 1; ibid., "Proposed Rule Changes," p. 4.

7. "Cowboy Hall of Fame Preserving a Heritage," *Hoofs and Horns* 39 (November 1969):8; "Barrel Racing Championship on Line at Oklahoma City," *Rodeo Sports News*, 1 December 1969; " '69 Rodeo Champs," *Hoofs and Horns* 39 (January 1970):19.

8. Westermeier, *Man, Beast, Dust*, pp. 353–55.

9. Joe B. Frantz and Julian Ernest Choate, Jr., *The American Cowboy: The Myth and the Reality* (Norman, Okla., 1955), pp. 158–60.

10. David Brion Davis, "Ten-Gallon Hero," in *The American Experience*, Henning Cohen, ed. (Boston, 1968), p. 252.

11. "Rodeo Makes Its First Call in Town, at City Hall," *NYT*, 26 September 1958; "The President Swaps Yarns With Cowboy," *NYT*, 30 September 1959.

12. Frantz and Choate, *American Cowboy*, pp. 8, 12; Charles Wellington Furlong, *Let 'er Buck: A Story of the Passing of the Old West* (New York, 1921), p. xv.

13. Robertson, *Rodeo*, p. 141.

14. Harold Peterson, "Earning a Varsity Letter Out West." *Sports Illustrated*, 1 July 1969, p. 39.

15. Robert D. Hanesworth, *Daddy of 'Em All* (Cheyenne, Wyoming, 1967), no pagination.

16. Clifford P. Westermeier, "Seventy-five Years of Rodeo in Colorado," *Colorado Magazine* 28 (January 1951): 14; Jacques Boudet, *Man & Beast: A Visual History*, trans. Anne Carter (London, 1964), p. 215; Westermeier, *Man, Beast, Dust*, p. 34.

17. Westermeier, *Man, Beast, Dust*, p. 34.

18. Furlong, *Let 'er Buck*, p. xii; Lura Tularski, "Saddle Chatter," *Nevada State Journal*, 25 June 1967; Robertson, *Rodeo*, p. 87; Westermeier, *Man, Beast, Dust*, p. 363.

19. Mody C. Boatright, "The American Rodeo," in *The American Experience*, ed. Hennig Cohen, pp. 272–73.

20. Westermeier, *Man, Beast, Dust*, pp. 36–37, 42.

21. "Cowboys and Wild Horses," *Denver Republican*, 15 October 1887, quoted in Westermeier, "Seventy-five Years . . .," p. 18.

22. "The Cowboy Tournament," *Denver Republican*, 15 October 1887, quoted in Westermeier, "Seventy-five Years . . .," p. 20.

23. Lamb, *Rodeo Back of the Chutes*, p. 59; "Rodeo: The Five Standard Events," *HSUS California Branch News and Previews* (Winter 1970), no pagination; Westermeier, *Man, Beast, Dust*, p. 312.

24. Westermeier, *Man, Beast, Dust*, p. 309.

25. Lamb, *Rodeo Back of the Chutes*, p. 58.

26. Pp. 59–60.

27. For a detailed analysis of steer "busting" see *Is Your Entertainment Worth This?* (Wheatland, Wyo.: Wyoming Humane Society, n.d.).

28. *To Protect Rodeo Livestock*, foreword, no pagination; "Rodeo," *FOA Actionline*, n.d., p. 15; Boatright, "The American Rodeo," p. 276.

29. Westermeier, *Man, Beast, Dust*, pp. 195–96.

30. "Memorandum on Rodeo Cruelties," mimeographed (Washington: HSUS, n.d.), no pagination.

31. Morse, *Ordeal of the Animals*, pp. 49–50.

32. Robertson, *Rodeo*, pp. 35, 37.

33. Morse, *Ordeal of the Animals*, p. 51.

34. Frantz and Choate, *American Cowboy*, p. 21; Westermeier, *Man, Beast, Dust*, pp. 178–79.

35. Lamb, *Rodeo Back of the Chutes*, pp. 149–50.

36. Ibid., pp. 151–53, 159.

37. Hanesworth, *Daddy of 'Em All*, pp. 18–19.

38. Ibid., pp. 23–24; Westermeier, *Man, Beast, Dust*, pp. 383–84.

39. Hanesworth, *Daddy of 'Em All*, pp. 76, 81, 86–87, 115, 125, 175.

40. Ibid., pp. 151, 138.

41. Robertson, *Rodeo*, pp. 114, 135; *Pendleton Round-Up and Colorful Happy Canyon* (Pendleton, Ore., 1969), no pagination.

42. 18 March 1970.

43. Robertson, *Rodeo*, pp. 93–95, passim.

44. Westermeier, *Man, Beast, Dust*, pp. 397–98; Gene Pruett, "And Did I Ever Tell You . . . ," *Hoofs and Horns* 39 (November 1969):6, 34; Fred Hervey, "The Wildest Prison Rodeo," *Western Horseman* 23:16–17 (December 1958).

45. Robertson, *Rodeo*, pp. 119–21, 126, 129–30, 132.

46. Virginia Johnson, "Far East Rodeo," *Western Horseman* 23 (July 1958):10 41–42.

47. Arthur W. Moss, *Valiant Crusade: The History of the R.S.P.C.A.* (London, 1961), pp. 149–51.

48. Robertson, *Rodeo*, pp. 65–66, 128.

49. Christine Stevens, "Fighting and Baiting," in Emily Stewart Leavitt, *Animals and Their Legal Rights* . . . (n.p.: AWI, 1968), p. 127.

50. Ibid., pp. 122–23.

51. Max Lerner, "The Role of Sports in Modern America," in *America as Civilization* (New York, 1957), pp. 812–19, quoted in *The History of Popular Culture Since 1815*, ed. Norman F. Cantor and Michael S. Werthman (New York, 1968), p. 185.

52. Pearl Twyne, "Horses," in Leavitt, *Animals and Their Legal Rights*, pp. 91–92; "Abolish the Sport of Rodeo?" *Denver Record Stockman*, 20 April 1967.

53. "Bill to Ban Bucking Straps Debated at County Meeting," *Baltimore Sun*, 2 November 1967.

17. Hard Noses and Bleeding Hearts

1. *Grit and Steel* 65 (May 1963):5–6.

2. Ibid., 66 (March 1964) :5.

3. John Hunt, *A World Full of Animals* (New York, 1969), p. 215; *TCWP News Bulletin*, February and July, 1968; ibid., February and November, 1969; ibid., September and December, 1970.

4. James Wallace, "Crowd Gathers to Watch 50 Dogs Battle 3 Raccoons Near Andalusia," *Alabama Journal*, 29 September 1969; "HSUS Asks Alabama to Stop Cruelty to Coons," *News of HSUS* 14 (November–

December 1969):3; "Good Clean Fun in Mississippi," *TCWP News Bulletin*, December 1970, p.3.

5. Mrs. Ann Gough Hunter to author, 12 December 1969.

6. William Graham Sumner, *Folkways...* (Boston, 1940), p. 586; "One Must See a Bull-Fight, Even if Only Once" (London: RSPCA, n.d.).

7. Justus George Lawler, "Do Animals Have Rights?" *Jubilee* 12 (November 1965): 36–40; idem, *The Range of Commitment: Essays of a Conservative Liberal* (Milwaukee, 1969), p. 153; Ambrose Agius, *God's Animals* (n.p., 1970), pp. 79–80, 84–85; Basil Wrighton, "Justice and the Animals," *The Ark*, April 1952, reprinted by NCSAW (Washington, n.d.), p.6, footnote 11.

8. *Bull-Fighting* (London: RSPCA, n.d.), p. 3.

9. Desmond Morris, *The Naked Ape* (New York, 1967), p. 191; *Pan Am's Going Great Guide to Europe* (n.p.: Pan American World Airways, Inc., 1969), p. 6; "Scary News for Rich South American Bachelors," Advertisement of Braniff Airways, Inc., *Business Week*, 22 February 1969; *South American Safaris. Hunting and Fishing* (n.p.: Braniff International, 1969), p. 5; "The Civilized Safari or Crocodiles Without Tears," advertisement of Braniff Airways, Inc., *Natural History* 77 (June-July 1968):15; "Panamá is Wild," Advertisement of El Panamá Hotel, *Holiday*, October 1969, p. 34. The word "Coke" is a registered trademark and should be capitalized. It appears here in lowercase only because that was the usage followed by my source.

10. *"Comment se faire bronzer comme une star, manger comme un gourmet, vivre comme un Milord, dans le Sud de la France,"* advertisement of the French Government Tourist Office *NYT*, 8 March 1971; Edith N. Snow, "Ferdinand is Alive and Well in France," *Boston Globe*, 18 January 1970; Cleveland Amory, "The Terrible Truth Behind the Moment of," *Holiday* 46 (October 1969): 79.

11. "Colorado Bullfights," *NCSAW Report*, October 1970, p. 2; "Florida Bullfight Repealed," *NCSAW Report*, undated but *ca.* July 1971, p. 3.

12. Mel Morse, *Ordeal of the Animals* (Englewood Cliffs, N.J., 1968), pp. 152–55; "Humanitarians Defeat Bill to Legalize Dog Racing in California," *News of HSUS* 14 (September–October 1969):3.

13. Morse, *Ordeal*, pp. 112–22; "Anger at Yonkers," *Newsweek, 28 June 1971; Louis Effrat, " 'Tranquilizer' Pills Plague U.S. Tracks,"* International Herald Tribune* (Paris), 6 November 1970; Bob Hebert, "Anita Bans Rider; Battery Use Suspected," *Los Angeles Times*, 22 October 1971.

14. Morse, *Ordeal*, p. 122.

15. Ibid., pp. 155–58.

16. Pearl Twyne, "Horses," in Emily Stewart Leavitt, *Animals and Their Legal Rights: A Survey of American Laws from 1641 to 1968* (n.p.:AWI, 1968), pp. 83, 87–90; Morse, *Ordeal*, pp. 122–26; Wendell Rawls, Jr., *The Shocking Plight of the Tennessee Walking Horse* (Nashville: Nashville Tennessean, 1969); U.S. House of Representatives, Subcommittee on Public Health and Welfare of the Committee on Interstate and Foreign Com-

merce, *Horse Protection Act of 1970:* Hearing on H.R. 14151, H.R. 15261 and S. 2543, 91st Cong., 2nd sess., 21 September 1964, pp. 14–15, 22–23; Paul Twyne to author, 5 January, 1971.

17. Dixon Wecter, *The Saga of American Society: A Record of Social Aspiration 1607–1937* (New York, 1937), pp. 444–45.

18. Jennie Holliman, *American Sports 1785–1835* (Durham, N.C., 1931), pp. 39–40; J. Stanley Reeve, *The Golden Days of Fox Hunting* . . . (Philadelphia, 1958), pp. 19, 21, 47–48, 50.

19. Virginia Lee Warren, "Fox Hunt: It's a Lively Art at School," *NYT,* 10 December 1967; Henry Stephen Salt, *Killing For Sport* (London, 1915), pp. 155–56; Ingeborg Flugel, "Some Psychological Aspects of a Fox-Hunting Rite," *Int. J. Psa.* 12 (1931); 485–87.

20. "After Giving the Traditional Blessing . . . ," Picture caption, *Washington Post,* 20 October 1968; Wecter, *Saga,* p. 445.

21. Glynn Mapes, "Yoicks! Fox-Hunting Territory is Overrun by Suburbia's Sprawl," *Wall Street Journal,* 9 January 1969.

22. Quoted in Wecter, *Saga,* p. 445.

23. H. G. Wells, quoted in William Alan Swallow, *Quality of Mercy: History of the Humane Movement in the United States* (Boston, 1963), p. 179.

24. William G. Conway, "Consumption of Wildlife by Man," *Animal Kingdom* (n.d.), reprinted in *Defenders* 44 (Spring 1969): 70.

25. Fred Myers (Jonathan Fieldston, pseud.), "Lust to Kill" (Washington: HSUS, n.d.); "An Invitation to Join the Vilas-Oneida Wilderness Society," *Defenders* 45 (Fall 1970): 254.

26. Bil Gilbert, "Hunting is a Dirty Business," *Friends of Animals, Inc., Fall 1970 Report* (New York, 1970), pp. 20–21; Frank Graham, *Since Silent Spring* (Boston, 1970), pp. 43–44.

27. Karl A. Menninger, "Totemic Aspects of Contemporary Attitudes Toward Animals," in *Psychoanalysis and Culture,* George B. Wilbur and Werner Muensterberger, eds. (New York, 1951), pp. 55, 45.

28. Devereux Butcher, "Killing for Fun" (Washington: HSUS, n.d.), excerpted from *Exploring our National Wildlife Refuges* (Boston 1963); John Burbey, "Wolves, Wolves and Wolves," *Hunter's Horn* 49 (December 1969):28–29.

29. U.S. House of Representatives, Subcommittee on Fisheries and Wildlife Conservation of the Committee on Merchant Marine and Fisheries, *Hearing on H.R. 15188,* 91st Cong., 2nd sess., 16 March 1970, p. 11.

30. "The Audubon View . . . Goose Mismanagement and Shooting Galleries," *Audubon* 72 (November 1970):140–41; Roger A. Caras, *Death as a Way of Life* (Boston, 1970), p. 79; "35 Named in Raids on Bighorn Sheep," *NYT,* 7 February 1971; "4 Admit Roles in Poaching Bighorns," *Riverside* (Calif.) *Daily Enterprise,* 8 June 1971.

31. Charles D. Niven, *History of the Humane Movement* (New York, 1967), p. 159; Caras, *Death as a Way,* pp. 153–54; *Your Humane Society Reports: Hunting Comes Under Attack as Public Concern for Wildlife Grows* (Washington: HSUS, 1970), p. 2.

32. Hope Sawyer Buyukmihci, *Unexpected Treasure* (New York, 1968), p. 162; Robert Reinow and Leona Train Reinow, *Moment in the Sun* (New York, 1967), p. 98.

33. Pearl Twyne, "Horses," in Leavitt, *Animals and Their Legal Rights*, p. 93; Walter Sullivan, "Alaska Curbs Hunting of Bears, Decimated by Oilmen and Killing from Air," *NYT*, 7 May 1970.

34. Joan McIntyre, "Festival of Wolves," *Not Man Apart* 1 (December 1970):8; "Wolf Killed by Snowmobile Wins Bounty from Canada," *NYT*, 25 May 1970; Stephen Green, "Snowmobiles Roar Through Peace and Quiet," *National Observer*, 18 January 1971.

35. Gil Lazan, "The Thrill Killers," *American Forests* 7 (May 1969): 6–7

36. "Dashing Through Snow Can be Perilous Sport," *NYT*, 29 November 1970; "Minnesota Regulates Snowmobiles . . . ," *News of HSUS* 15 (January–February 1970):8; "Colorado Acts to End Animal Torment by Snow Vehicles," *National Humane Newsletter* 15 (October 1969):1; Elizabeth N. Layne, *"Field Notes: Abominable Snowmen,"AH* 21 (February 1970): 113; Seth S. King, "Snowmobiles Mix Headaches With Thrills," *NYT*, 9 February 1970; " . . . Join the March to Beaver's," advertisement of Eager Beaver Sales, *Register-Star* (Hudson, N.Y.), 30 November 1970.

37. Ferris Weddle, "Snowmobiles and Wildlife," *Defenders* 43 (Fall 1968):312–15; "Colorado Acts to End Animal Torment . . .," p. 1; Randolph E. Kerr, "How to Use Your Snowmobile," *Conversationist* 25 (October–November 1970):48.

38. Dwight A. Davis, "Green Mountain Coon and Cat Club," *Full Cry* 30 (January 1970):41; James A. Harris, "We Got Our Cat," ibid., pp. 45, 50; "Quiet, Please!," *Conservationist* 25 (June–July 1971):40.

39. David Bird, "Controversy Over Snowmobiles Renewed at Legislative Hearing," *NYT*, 15 October 1969.

40. "They Have Been Dispossessed," *TCWP News Bulletin*, May 1970, p.2.

41. U.S. Senate, Committee on Commerce, *Endangered Species: Report to Accompany H.R. 11363*, 91st Cong., 1st sess., 1969, S. Rept. 91–526, p.20.

42. John H. Hess, "French Anthropologist, at Onset of 70's, Deplores the 20th Century," *NYT*, 31 Dec. 1969.

18. Fashion Fads and Fun Furs

1. J. Howard Moore, *The Universal Kinship* (Chicago, 1908), pp. 275, 284; William Graham Sumner, *Folkways* . . . (Boston, 1940), pp. 194, 196, 190; R. v. Krafft-Ebing, *Psychopathia Sexualis* (Brooklyn, N.Y., 1928), pp. 219, 281; Mary Hamman, "Conservation Ruffles Fur in Fashion World," *Smithsonian* 1 (September 1970):54.

2. Thomas Gilbert Pearson, *Adventures in Bird Protection: An Autobiography* (New York, 1937), pp. 258–59, 83, 189, 192–93.

3. Ibid, p. 220.

4. *The Whims of Fashion* (Washington: HSUS, n.d.); Christine Stevens,

"Trapping," in Emily Stewart Leavitt, *Animals and Their Legal Rights: A Survey of American Laws from 1641 to 1968* (n.p.:AWI, 1968), pp. 129–33; *Tortured for Their Furs* (London: RSPCA, n.d.).

5. F. Jean Vinter, *Facts About Furs* (London: UFAW, 1957), p. 1.

6. "Stop, Listen—and Write," *FOA Actionline*, January 1971; Vinter, *Facts About Furs*, p.20.

7. "Campaign Against Furs," *NYT*, 8 January 1970; William G. Conway, "The Consumption of Wildlife by Man," *Defenders* 44 (Spring 1969): 74, reprinted from *Animal Kingdom*, n.d.; "Latest From Paris by Monique," *New York Daily News*, 30 June 1970.

8. Schuyler Van Vechten, Jr., Vice-President, Abercrombie & Fitch Co., 1 June 1970, to David G. De Vries, *Defenders* 45 (Summer 1970):173; *Your Humane Society Reports . . .* (Washington: HSUS 1970), p. 1; "Furs, Fashion, and Conservation," *Vogue*, 1 September 1970, reprinted by *World Wildlife Fund* (Washington, 1970).

9. "If You Respect Life Wait Twenty Years Before You Buy Your Next Leopard Coat From Us," advertisement of Georges Kaplan, *NYT*, 21 September 1968, repeated 22 November 1969.

10. Bernadine Morris, "Spotted Cat Gets an Unexpected Ally—a Furrier," *NYT*, 24 September 1968.

11. William G. Conway, "Biologist's Despair," *NYT*, 2 November 1969.

12. "The War on Fur Coats Grows," *NYT*, 20 November 1969; "War on Fur Industry Grows," *ISPA News* (Western Hemisphere Edition) 2 (Spring 1970):2; "Telephones Against Cruelty," *FAO Actionline*, February 1971, p. 1; "Local Letter Halts Sale of Skins," *Lakeville* (Conn.) *Journal*, 15 January 1970.

13. Angela Taylor, "Fur Coats: Facing Extinction at Conservationists' Hands?" *NYT*, 30 December 1969; Peter Tonge, "Exposing the Public to the Horror of 'Legalized Brutality,' " *Christian Science Monitor* 4 June 1971; Alice Herrington to author, 29 April 1970.

14. Alice Herrington, "Slaughter on St. Paul Island," *Friends of Animals, Inc., Fall 1970 Report* (New York, 1970), pp. 7–14; *News Release from Friends of Animals, Inc.*, August 1970, pp.1–3; ibid., 15 June 1971, p. 3; A.T. Pedersen, "Pickets Active, Cameras Grind at Fouke Auction," *Women's Wear Daily*, 2 April 1971

15. "Facts About Seal Hunting," mimeographed (Washington: HSUS, n.d.), pp. 1–2; Herrington, "Slaughter on St. Paul Island," p. 11; "Protest, Priorities, and the Alaska Fur Seal," *Audubon* 72 (March 1970):114–15; "The Pribilof Island Seal Hunt," *ISPA News* (Western Hemisphere Edition) 2 (Spring 1970):3; "Seal Brutality Won't End Until Demand for Luxury Pelts Stops," *News of HSUS* 14 (March–April 1969):2; "Seal Hunt Brutality Reaches New High; HSUS Asks for Immediate Relief Measures by Government," *News of HSUS* 15 (October 1970):4.

16. "Sealing," *ISPA News* 2 (Summer 1970):2; Brion Davies, "A Lonely Place," *Defenders* 45 (Winter 1970):361.

17. For the historical background of the controversy see Peter Lust,

The Last Seal Pup: The Story of Canada's Seal Hunt (Montreal, 1967), pp. 30–34, passim; a recent eye-witness account is Brion Davies, *Savage Luxury: Slaughter of the Baby Seals* (New York, 1971); "Sealing: Good and Bad News," *HSUS News*, March, 1972.

18. George Laycock, "The Gator Killers," *Audubon* 70 (September–October 1968):77–93.

19. "Is It a Crocodile or Alligator?" *NYT*, 25 February 1970.

20. C. E. Wright, "Is the Alligator Doomed?" *NYT*, 18 January 1970; Cynthia Medley, "One Way to Halt Poaching—Gator Farming," ibid.

21. Roxana Sayre, "Econotes," *Audubon* 73 (January 1970):100; Charlayne Hunter, "U.S. Alligator Skins Sales Ban Unlikely to Curb Fashions Here," *NYT*, 14 December 1969.

22. Havelock Ellis, *Studies in the Psychology of Sex* (Philadelphia, 1928) 5:71–76; Cleveland Amory, *What is the Fund for Animals?* (New York: Fund for Animals, n.d.); "101st Annual Report," Pennsylvania SPCA *Animaldom* 39 (March 1969):2; *1970* (New York: Hunting World, 1969), pp. 39, 41, 44–45, 79.

23. Jean-François Marmontel, "Le philosophe soi-disant," *Contes moraux par Marmontel* . . . (Paris: 1825, 1826, 1833), 5:32–33.

24. Judy Klemesrud, "At Mark Cross, the Era of the Crocodile Handbag Ends," *NYT*, 16 June 1970.

25. Ibid.

19. Animal Experiments: Trying It on the Dog

1. Henry K. Beecher, *Research and the Individual* (Boston, 1970), pp. 3, 5–6, 10–13; Basil Wrighton, *Justice and Animals* (Washington: NCSAW, n.d.), p. 5; "Doctors Debate Moral Aspects of Using People in Experiments," *NYT*, 15 August 1966; *Research and Education, or Education's "Barbarous Inheritance"* (New York: UAA, n.d.), p. 7; *Long Beach* (Calif.) *Independent*, n.d., quoted in "Commentary," *The A-V* 79 (January 1971):7.

2. "Survey Shows Need for Expanded Lab Animal Facilities," *Laboratory Management*, October 1970, quoted in *Emergency!* (New York: UAA, 1970); *Help!* (Washington: HSUS, n.d.).

3. *Bulletin of the Theological Section of UFAW* (London, 1961), p. 5; Willard L. Sperry, *The Ethical Basis of Medical Practice* (New York, 1950), p. 11.

4. Robert W. Stock, "The Mouse Stage of the New Biology," *NYT Magazine*, 21 December 1969, p. 51.

5. Konrad Lorenz, *On Aggression* (New York, 1963), p. 226.

6. C. W. Hume, *Historical Note on the British Act of 1876 Regulating Animal Experiments* (New York: AWI, n.d.), pp. 1–2, reprinted from *The UFAW Handbook on the Care and Management of Laboratory Animals*; idem, *Man and Beast* (London, 1962), pp. 59–64.

7. For a favorable view of the law, as amended in 1970, see Christine Stevens, "Laboratory Animal Welfare," in Emily Stewart Leavitt, *Animals and Their Legal Rights: A Survey of American Laws from 1641 to 1970*

(n.p.:AWI 1970), pp. 46–60; "P.L. 89–544, the Laboratory Animal Welfare Act, the First Year," *AWI Sixteenth Annual Report* (New York, 1967), pp. 2–4; "Animal Welfare Act of 1970 Passed by House and Senate," *AWI Information Report* 19 (October–November–December 1970):1; "Animal Welfare Act Signed by President . . .," *National Humane Newsletter* 16 (February 1971):1. For sharply critical analyses, compare "Animal Procurement Measure Becomes Law," *NCSAW Report*, September 1966, pp. 1–2; "Federal Law on Dealers Amended," *NCSAW Report*, February 1971, p. 4; George Abbe, "For the Tortured—New Hope?" *Social Questions Bulletin* 5 (May 1969):19.

8. Beecher, *Research and the Individual*, p. 36.

9. Israel Shenker, "Caricatures Put Scientists on Pedestal," *NYT*, 13 December 1969.

10. Cleveland Amory, "What You Can Do to Help Animals," *Cosmopolitan*, June 1968, p. 108; "Along the Vivisection Front—Potpourri," *The A-V* 78 (October 1970):130; "Ford to Go On Using Baboons for Tests," *NYT*, 19 December 1967; John D. Morris, "Net Safety 'Belt' Tested in Autos," *NYT*, 4 January 1970.

11. Lawrence K. Altman, "12 Dogs Develop Lung Cancer in Group of 86 Taught to Smoke," *NYT*, 6 February 1970; Walter Sullivan, "The Beagle Smoked; the Beagle Got Lung Cancer," *NYT*, 8 February 1970; Lincoln Pierson Brower, "Smoking and Cancer," *NYT*, 15 February 1970.

12. Amory, "What You Can Do to Help . . . ," p. 107; Thomas O'Toole, "Flying Off to Combat? Birds Alerted for War," *Washington Post*, 8 October 1969; Patrick Parkes to Hon. Melvin Laird, 9 October 1969; John S. Foster, Jr., to Patrick Parkes, 22 October 1969; S. L. Wilhelmi to author, 20 January 1971.

13. Noel Epstein, "All the Liquor You Can Drink on the House—All for Science's Sake," *Wall Street Journal*, 3 January 1968.

14. For this paragraph and the one following it, I have drawn generally upon Clyde R. Bergwin and William T. Coleman, *Animal Astronauts: They Opened the Way to the Stars* (Englewood Cliffs, N.J., 1963).

15. John Noble Wilford, "Apollo Rehearsal for Shot Smooth," *NYT*, 1 July 1969; "NASA Cuts Short Monkey's Flight," *NYT*, 8 July 1969; "Space Monkey Dies: Autopsy is Planned," *NYT*, 9 July 1969; "Bonny Flight is Attacked," *New York Daily News*, 10 July 1969; Paul Harvey, "Inhumanity to Animals," syndicated newspaper column, *ca.* August 1969, reprinted in *NCSAW Report*, November 1969, p. 2.

16. John Hillaby, "Sanctified Torture," *New Scientist*, 9 January 1969, pp. 69–70; Abbe, "For the Tortured—New Hope?" pp. 18–19.

17. "Remarks of F. Barbara Orlans, Ph.D.", *AWI Information Report* 1 (October–November–December 1969):5; Dale McFeatters to Mrs. George E. Nettleton, 11 March 1970.

18. "Amateur Monkey Surgery Continues Unabated," *AWI Information Report* 19 (April–May–June 1970):1; *AWI Nineteenth Annual Report* (New York, 1970), p. 5.

19. Marianne Cole in *New York World Telegram* (Brooklyn edition) 1 February 1956.

20. W. W. Armistead, "Although the Interest of High School Students in Biological Research Certainly Is Commendable . . . ," mimeographed (Washington: AWI, n.d.), p. 1; "Remarks of F. Barbara Orlans . . . ," p. 5.

21. *UFAW Report & Accounts 1st April 1969–31st March 1970* (Potters Bar, Herts., 1970), pp. 17–18; Justus George Lawler, "Do Animals Have Rights?" *Jubilee* 12 (November 1965):38, 40.

20. *The Most Dangerous Animal in the World*

1. Marston Bates, *Expanding Population in a Shrinking World* (New York, 1963), pp. 23–24; Emily Hahn, *Animal Gardens* (Garden City, N.Y., 1967), pp. 265–66.

2. Mark Twain's epigram appears as a headpiece to Chapter 27 in *Following the Equator.*

3. "Release of Brutality Film Ends as Result of Strong Protests," *News of HSUS* 12 (December 1967):8; "Upsurge of Violence Shows Need to Affirm 'Reverence for Life,'" *News of HSUS* 13 (July–August 1968):3; "Supervision of Animal Action in Movies Provokes Serious Concern," *News of HSUS* 14 (March–April 1969):3.

4. Randall M. Evanson, "Merchandising and Manhandling," *Defenders* 43 (Fall 1968): 256–57; Herndon G. Dowling, "Urban Snakes: An Identity Crisis," *Natural History* 78 (April 1969):69–70; "Ann Landers," *Poughkeepsie Journal*, 19 July 1970.

5. Evanson, "Merchandising and Manhandling," p.256.

6. "AVMA,AHA Condemn Easter Chicks," *National Humane Review* 58 (March-April 1970):21; "Avoid Easter 'Pets,'" *Our Dumb Animals* 101 (April 1968):7.

7. Christine Stevens, "Laws Regulating the Sale of Small Animals and Birds," in Emily Stewart Leavitt, *Animals and Their Legal Rights: A Survey of American Laws from 1641 to 1968* (n.p., 1968), pp. 108–109.

8. "A Real Live Pony Given Away Free in Gimbels Win-A-Pony Lucky Draw," advertisement of Gimbel Brothers, *NYT*, 27 August 1970.

9. Martin Weil, "The Elephant in the Window is Dead," *Washington Post*, 13 January 1967; Julia Allen Field, "Reflections on the Death of an Elephant," *Defenders* 42 (Spring 1967):22–23; Weil, "The Elephant in the Window is Dead," p. 24.

10. Advertisements quoted appeared in *Science News*, 16 April 1966; "U.S. Opens Drive on Jeweled Bugs," *NYT*, 21 February 1971.

11. Tom Dammann, "The Travels of an Illegal Bug with No C.I.A. Connections," *NYT*, 21 March 1971.

12. Leonard Lee Rue, "Foxes and Bounties," *Chronicle of the Horse*, 20 June 1969, pp. 18–19; H. Chas. Laun, "A Decade of Bounties 1960–70," *Defenders* 45 (Spring 1970):44.

13. R. E. Chambers, "Highway Mortality of Squirrels," *Conservationist*

23 (June–July 1969):40; "Carnage of Animals on American Highways," *ISPA News* 2 (Autumn 1969):3; Cameron Thatcher, "Highway Grave-yard," *National Wildlife*, 31 October 1968, p. 29; John R. Paul to author, 5 January 1971.

14. Marguerite Evans Isaacs to author, 17 January 1970; Jim Hardie, "Sport! On the Tamiami Trail of the Everglades," *Defenders* 42 (Summer 1967):181.

15. Hardie, "Sport! On the Tamiami Trail . . . ," p. 181; John A. Hunt, *A World of Animals* (New York, 1969), p. 195; Walton B. Sabin, "New Bird Ranges and Environment," *Conservationist* 24 (June-July 1970):26.

16. Desmond Morris, *The Human Zoo* (New York, 1969), pp. 75–76; Phyllis Cobbs, "Two Cases of Cruelty to Animals Reported by Shelter in Briarcliff," *Patent Trader* (Mount Kisco, N.Y.), 17 July 1966; mimeo-graphed agents' reports, Washington, D.C., Humane Society, 1969, vari-ous dates.

17. Donald E. Carr, *The Deadly Feast of Life* (Garden City, N.Y., 1971), p. 216; William A. Shurcliff, *SST and the Sonic Boom* (Cambridge, Mass., 1969), Chapter 21, "Injury to Animals," no pagination; "Aftermath in Britain," *NYT*, 4 September 1970.

18. "Cape Cod Branch," *Our Fourfooted Friends* 67 (March 1970):16–17; ibid., "Another Cruelty of Man's Invention," p. 3.

19. Lawrence Van Gelder, "Seared and Polluted, City Manages to Live," *NYT*, 30 July 1970; Lawrence K. Altman, "Zoo Cat's Death Starts Lead-Poison Study," *NYT*, 15 June 1971; "Death of 1,500 Cats Forecast in Closing of Naval Shipyard," *NYT*, 24 June 1966; "AHA Sends Aid to Riot Torn Detroit," *National Humane Review* 55 (September–October 1967):20.

20. Barry Commoner, "What Good is a Bird?" *Proceedings, Sixty-fourth Annual Convention, National Audubon Society* (Saint Louis, 1969), p. 10; Ethel Thurston, *Please Boycott Cruelly Manufactured Articles* (New York: NCSAW, n.d.), pp. 1–2; Robert Reinow and Leona Train Reinow, *Moment in the Sun* (New York, 1967), p. 55; Ronald Blythe, *Akenfield: Portrait of an English Village* (New York, 1969), pp. 259–64; *Bulletin of the Theological Section of UFAW* (London, 1961), pp. 4–5; Carlton E. Buttrick to author, 6 May 1970. A book-length survey of production-line rearing methods is Ruth Harrison, *Animal Machines: The New Factory Farming Industry* (New York, 1964). The study describes conditions prevailing in Great Britain, but many of the revelations about agricultural intensivism apply equally to the United States.

21. Emily Stewart Leavitt, *Animals and Their Legal Rights*, pp. 33–36; Alice Herrington and Bill Gottlieb, *Fact Sheet on Livestock Slaughter* (New York FOA, n.d.); *Stop!* (Washington: HSUS, n.d.); *Dear Friend . . .* mimeo-graphed (Brooklyn, N.Y.: ICHS, n.d.); Batya Bauman, "How Kosher is Kosher Meat?" *Reconstructionist*, 17 April 1970, pp. 19–23; Arnold H. Lubasch, "Suit Challenges Kosher Slaughtering," *NYT*, 4 January 1972; "Kosher Slaughter Challenged," *NCSAW Report*, February 1972. Slaugh-

tering methods, including the Jewish and Muslim, and new knowledge of animal physiology and pharmacology, were surveyed in England by a UFAW symposium 20 January 1971. The results were published as *Humane Killing and Slaughterhouse Techniques* (Potters Bar, Hertfordshire, 1971).

22. John Hunt, *A World Full of Animals* (New York, 1969), pp. 319–20; Arthur W. Moss and Elizabeth Kirby, *Animals Were There: A Record of the Work of the R.S.P.C.A. During the War of 1939–1945* (London, n.d.), pp. 13–14. Another treatment is Chapter 8 in Arthur W. Moss, *Valiant Crusade: The History of the Royal Society for the Prevention of Cruelty to Animals* (London, 1961).

23. William Zinsser, *The Lunacy Boom* (New York, 1969), pp. 33–34; George Laycock, "Amchitka Revisited," *Audubon* 74 (January 1972): 113–115.

24. "Army Nerve Gas Claim: 17 Years Without a Fatality," *Poughkeepsie Journal*, 1 March 1970; "Trains Loaded for Nerve Gas . . . ," *NYT*, 8 August 1970; Carr, *Deadly Feast*, p. 279; Frank Graham, Jr., *Since Silent Spring* (Boston, 1970), pp. 204–205.

25. "Land Falls Victim to Ravages of War," *Poughkeepsie Journal*, 1 January 1970; Douglas Robinson, "Rhinoceroses and Elephants Are Among the War Victims in South Vietnam," *NYT*, 13 September 1968; "Hanoi Reporter Describes Trail and Tells of 'Tunnels of Fire,' " *NYT*, 11 March 1971; "U.S. Curbs Sales of a Weed Killer," *NYT*, 16 April 1970; Thomas Whiteside, *Defoliation* (New York, 1970), p. xiii; Walter Sullivan, "Zoologist Back from Vietnam . . . ," *NYT*, 4 April 1969.

26. "Land Falls Victim . . . ," *Poughkeepsie Journal*; "Drop Elephants into Vietnam," *National Humane Newsletter* 13 (February 1968):3; "A New Vietnamese Issue: Kindness to Elephants," *NYT*, 19 January 1968.

27. "Purple Geese & Other Fighting Fauna," *Time*, 4 October 1968; "More Dogs to be Used to Hunt Drugs," *Poughkeepsie Journal*, 30 April 1971; "Military Dogs Get One-Way Tickets to Vietnam," *Poughkeepsie Journal*, 5 April 1970; Mrs. J. C. Yarbrough, "U.S. Military Dogs Left in Vietnam," *Atlanta Constitution*, 10 December 1970.

28. John Lilly, *Man and Dolphin* (Garden City, N.Y.), pp. 218–19.

29. "The Environmental Issue," *NYT*, 6 November 1970.

30. Gladwin Hill, "Copter Runs Animal 'Travelers Aid' in Los Angeles," *NYT*, 8 September 1970; "Veterinarian Doctors Free-Roaming Creatures," *Poughkeepsie Journal*, 12 July 1970; "Cruelty at Sea," *NYT*, 1 March 1971.

31. Fernand Méry, "Le Président vous parle: instruire l'opinion c'est bien mais l'union fera la force," *Les Amis des Bêtes*, no. 25 (1969), pp. 3–5.

32. New York, 1967, pp. ix, 25.

Bibliographical Note

Humanitarianism as an expression of conscience and concern for the lower animals has not produced an abundance of historical writing. This note, abstracted from my chapter references, presents a selective list of useful items found to have a broad, general bearing upon the theme, and is offered as a guide to further reading.

The conflicts over theological and philosophic questions are delineated in C. W. Hume, a modern humanist with scientific training, in his *Man and Beast* (1962) and *The Status of Animals in the Christian Religion* (1957). Excellent brief summaries are Professor Crane Brinton's article, "Humanitarianism," in the *Encyclopedia of the Social Sciences* and the pamphlet, *Bulletin of the Theological Section of UFAW* (London: Universities Federation for Animal Welfare, March 1961). An illuminating synthesis is Professor Lynn White, Jr.'s, lecture, "The Historical Roots of Our Ecological Crisis," delivered at the 1966 meeting of the American Association for the Advancement of Science and later printed in *Science*, 10 March 1967.

The social and literary background of the concept of fair play for animals as it arose in England has been explored and interpreted by an American scholar, Dix Harwood, in his *Love for Animals and How it Developed in Great Britain* (1928). The protection of animals as an organized movement with a definite rationale, first appearing in England, is treated in detail in Edward G. Fairholme and Wellesley Pain, *A Century of Work for Animals* ... (1924); Arthur W. Moss, *Valiant Crusade* . . . (1961); and Arthur W. Moss and Elizabeth Kirby, *Animals Were There: A Record of the Work of the R.S.P.C.A. During the War of 1939–1945* (n.d.). An emotional but eloquent essay on British kindness and cruelty is E. S. Turner, *All Heaven in a Rage* (1964). Charles D. Niven, *History of the Humane Movement* (1967), is a brief and readable survey emphasizing the leadership of England in the field of animal protection, also summarizing usefully the humanitarian programs in the countries of continental Europe.

Henry Bergh's pioneering work in New York is fully documented by manuscript diaries, letter and minute books, scrapbooks of memoranda and contemporary newspaper cuttings in the archives of the American Society for the Prevention of Cruelty to Animals in New York City. The best biography, based largely upon the Bergh holdings at the ASPCA, is Zulma Steele, *Angel in Top Hat* (1942). The principal source for George T. Angell of Boston is his *Autobiographical Sketches and Personal Recollections* (n.d.). Some historical background may be found in William Alan Swallow, *Quality of Mercy* (1963) and scattered through annual reports, periodicals, bulletins, anniversary brochures, and press releases of the thousand-odd animal welfare organizations in the United States.

Older but still useful works include Sydney H. Coleman, *Humane Society Leaders in America* (1924), Roswell C. McCrea, *The Humane Movement* (1910), Francis H. Rowley, *The Humane Idea* . . . (1912) and William J. Schultz, "The Humane Movement in the United States, 1910–1922," *Bulletin of Social Legislation* no. 6 (1924).

For present-day problems and issues, as well as the robust flavor of controversy over tactics and strategies, I have examined an extensive file of humanitarian magazines, bulletins, annual reports, and such fugitive materials as leaflets, folders, mimeographed reports issued by conservationist and anticruelty associations; also various newspapers, especially *The New York Times*, which consistently prints news articles and editorial comment on animal-related subjects. The same newspaper, soon to be completely indexed back to 18 September 1851, the date of its first issue, is a rich source of information on nineteenth-century life in America and the early effort to create a new climate of opinion toward animals. Existing as well as earlier anticruelty laws of the various states and the foreign statues are summarized in Emily Stewart Leavitt, *Animals and Their Legal Rights* (1968), revised in 1970. Useful discussions of current topics are also included in Leavitt, such as humane slaughter of food animals, experimental laboratory animals, humane education in the schools, and trapping for furs.

Index

Index prepared by Philip V. Lockwood

257

Ferrets, 140
Fetishism, 190–191
Feudalism, 23
Field, Julia Allen, 142
Fiesta de los Vaqueros, La (rodeo), 166
First Amendment, 209
Fiske, Minnie Maddern, 122–123, 127
Fitzstephen, William, 23
Fletcher, Horace, 133
Florida turtles, 101–102
Folklore, American, 68–71
Fontenelle, Bernard Le Bovier de, 40
Football, 6, 58–59
Ford, Paul Leicester, 84
Ford Motor Company, 197
Foster, Mrs. George O., 82
Fouke Fur Company, 188
Fourteenth Amendment, 209
Fox & Company (G.), 186
Fox hunting, 45, 55, 56, 57–58, 66, 175–177
Foxes, 11, 51, 206
Francis of Assisi, St., 18, 21, 43, 117, 133
Francis I, King of France, 23
Franciscans (religious order), 21
Franco-Prussian War, 143
Frank Leslie's Illustrated Newspaper, 82, 84
Franklin, Benjamin, 69
Frederick II, Emperor, 22, 40
French Academy, 26
French Folklore Society, 117
Friends of Animals, Inc., 119, 125, 187, 188
Froilanus, St., 21
Frontier Days Rodeo, 164
Froude, J. A., 195
Fund for Animals, Inc., 124, 125
Fur and Feather (journal), 121
Fur industry, 59, 64, 117, 130, 183–191
    seal hunt, 187–188
    trapping methods, 184–185
Fürtwängler, Wilhelm, 133

Galen (physician), 192
Galsworthy, John, 142
Gamecock, The (magazine), 170
Gander pulling (sport), 65
Gandhi, Mohandas, 133
Garments, animal, 146
Garrison, William Lloyd, 112
Gas station zoo operators, 72
Gassendi, Abbé Pierre, 40
Gaston, Lucy Page, 133
Gay, John, 46
Geese, 10, 64
    domestication of, 5
    war use of, 211–212
George IV, King, 50
George V, King, 44

Gerstäcker, Friedrich, 67
Gilbert, Bil, 177
Gimbel Brothers (department store), 205
Girl Scout Handbook, 121
Girls' Rodeo Association, 158
Glanvill, Joseph, 26
Goethe, Johann Wolfgang von, 48, 153
Golden Legend, 120
Goldsmith, Oliver, 132
Gould, Symon, 135
Gower, Pauline, 55
Graham, Sylvester, 130
Grammont, Jacques-Phillipe Delmas de, 52
Great Britain, 17–18, 43–52
    caged bird population, 44
    dog population, 44
    kindness to animals legislation, 48–52
    organizations devoted to animals, 44
    sow execution (1386), 30–31
    swan-upping holiday, 43–44
Greece (ancient), 9–10, 29
Greeley, Horace, 97, 133
Greeley, Mrs. Horace, 82–83
Green Mountain Coon and Cat Club, 180
Greyhound (automobile emblem), 6
Grit and Steel (magazine), 170–171

Hackney coaches, 88
Hamsters, 146
Hannibal, 210
Hensen, Dr. Eric H., 114
Hare coursing (sport), 56
Harewell, Bishop, 20
Harp seals, 185, 189
Harris, James A., 180
Harris, Mary Hazell, 125
Harrowby, Earl of, 99
Harsaphes (ram god), 8
Hartfield, T. W., 102
Harun al-Rashid, 22
Harvey, Paul, 200
Hathor (cow god), 8
Hawks, 152
Hayes, Rutherford B., 112
Heart transplants, 201
Hediger, Dr. Heini, 142
Hell's Kitchen (New York City), 83
Hemingway, Ernest, 173
Hempel, Frieda, 122
Henry III, King of England, 22
Henry II, King of France, 23
Henry III, King of France, 22
Henry Bergh Foundation, 105
Herbicide 2-4-5 T, 211
Herodotus, 8
Heron (automobile emblem), 6
Herring gulls, 141